Tomart's Price Guide to
Character & Promotional
GLASSES

including Pepsi, Coke, Fast-Food, Peanut Butter and Jelly Glasses;
plus Dairy Glasses & Milk Bottles

by Carol Markowski

Edited by Tom Tumbusch

Color Photography by Tom Schwartz

Black & White Photography by Tom Schwartz and Contributing Collectors

TOMART PUBLICATIONS
division of Tomart Corporation
Dayton, Ohio

Dedicated to

NICOLAS MICHAEL MARKOWSKI
born November 7, 1991
my first grandchild
"what a joy you are"

Prices listed are based on the author's experience and are presented as a guide for information purposes only. No one is obligated in any way to buy, sell or trade according to these prices. Condition, rarity, demand and the reader's desire to own determine the actual price paid. No offer to buy or sell at the prices listed is intended or made. Buying and selling is conducted at the consumer's risk. Neither the author nor the publisher assumes any liability for any losses suffered for use of, or any typographic errors contained in, this book. The numeric code system used in this book is not consistent with previous collectible guides published by Tomart Publications. All value estimates are presented in U.S. dollars. The dollar sign is omitted to avoid needless repetition.

Revised and updated Second Edition, 1993

© Copyright 1993, Carolyn Markowski

Published by Tomart Publications, Dayton, Ohio, 45439

Library of Congress Catalog Card Number: 89-51636

ISBN: 0-914293-18-4   Manufactured in the United States of America

2 3 4 5 6 7 8 9 0 1   8 7 6 5 4 3 2 1 9 0

TABLE OF CONTENTS

ACKNOWLEDGEMENTS

Tom and Jean Hoder — Thanks for all your help, for letting me photograph some of your glasses and for being my friend.

John La Pare — What would the Coca-Cola prototype section be without your help and photos? Thank you, my dear friend. "See you in Atlantic City."

Larry Schlick — Always there with help, glasses, photos and information. You're a Sweetheart. "From old phonographs to promotional glasses, we're some pair."

Roe Blake — I ask and you come through for me – my sincere thanks.

Tom Tumbusch — Thank you once again for giving me the opportunity. May Tomart Publications grow and prosper with every price guide it publishes. I'm honored to have been a part of the Tomart family and grateful to have had the good fortune to be its first "outside" author.

TO THOSE WHO CONTINUE TO PROMOTE THE HOBBY

Tom Hoder — Thanks for starting "Glass Alley", the annual glass collectors convention held the first Sunday in December at the Lake County Fairgrounds in Grayslake, Illinois. For more info, contact Tom at 444 S. Cherry, Itasca, IL 60143.

Tom Hoder, Pete Kroll, Mark Chase, Mike Kelly — Thanks for holding auctions and giving collectors the opportunity to find what they need.

Mark Chase, Mike Kelly — Thanks for publishing the *Collectors Glass News*. It's a neat newsletter, packed with information about new releases and rarities. "Much luck with your new book."

TO THOSE WHO PUT IT ALL TOGETHER

Schwartz Studios for the photography
Type One Graphics, Printing Preparations, Central Printing, Carpenter Lithographing Company for type imaging, separations, and printing.

FOREWORD

Early glasses, like most items collected today, weren't designed with the collector in mind. Coke glasses were produced before the turn of the century. Since a syrup line was required to maintain the quality of the beverage, it was just as easy to promote the product name on the glass.

Around 1930 glasses featuring comic and radio characters were offered as premiums. Series of Popeye, the Green Hornet and Disney characters and individual glasses featuring Bobby Benson and Charlie McCarthy are some of the earliest issues. Radio Orphan Annie began offering shake-up mugs made of Beetleware, an early plastic material, in 1931, but plastic and aluminium are largely viewed differently by the true glass collector. These products could easily be a subject of their own book some day.

Mickey Mouse appeared on at least two different milk glass designs in 1931.

In 1933, however, Herman "Kay" Kamen devised a plan to merchandise Mickey and other Disney characters on a local or regional basis. Manufacturers of toys, games and watches could sell their products on a national basis, but local dairies, bakers and gas stations could not. Kamen learned about their substantial promotional budgets when he was in the advertising business and formed a Dairy, Bakery and Special Promotions division in early 1934 to capitalize on the opportunity.

The idea was to develop a proven campaign and sell the national quality promotional program to one company in each city. The dairy campaign featured Mickey and his friends on glasses and milk bottles. The initial campaign was so successful there has been a character glass promotion on most major Disney animated films ever since. Many featurettes and main character issues have been the subject of character glass promotions and souvenir glasses sold at Disney theme parks.

Early character glasses were containers for cottage cheese or sour cream. Back then most dairy products were delivered door to door by the milkman who delivered his goods in time for breakfast. Character glass promotions helped him increase his sales silently with advertisements printed on bottle collars. A new glass was featured each week and often customers could purchase missing glasses at the end of the promotion. Owens-Illinois Glass Company of Toledo, Ohio manufactured Disney promotional glasses under a license from Kay Kamen and the Disney Character Merchandise Division up through the *Lady and the Tramp* issues in 1955. They had 26 regional offices to service the nearly 300 dairies which used the various programs.

In 1939, MGM and Sealtest were offering a similar promotion using characters from the *Wizard of Oz*. The premiums were stopped for several years because of war material shortages, but the practices of glass promotions resumed soon after when rationing ended. One of the most successful promotions in the '40s was the Big Top Peanut Butter Favorite Song series. This was followed by a states series.

The early '50s saw the birth of the "suburb" and with it a new way of buying food. Many men returning home from the war were given their G.I. pay in one large sum as they were discharged. Finding themselves with a substantial amount of money, for probably the first time in their lives, they sought to improve their lifestyle by moving to the small communities that were popping up just outside the cities. Having no established dairies, grocery stores or meat markets, these communities were supplied by a new type of store – the supermarket. Here a shopper could find any food item they wanted, pre-packaged and distributed by large national corporations.

In an attempt to lure shoppers into buying their product instead of the competition's sitting on the shelf right next to it, companies began licensing popular film, television and comic strip characters to put on their packages. In 1953 Welch's jelly began packaging their products in a pop-up top glass container bearing images of Howdy Doody. When emptied, it could be used as a drinking glass. With the image of Howdy appealing to children and the practicality of a free glass appealing to mothers, this promotion was a huge success. Big Top Peanut Butter continued to base their marketing on the use of premium glasses. They were joined by Swifts Peanut Butter and Kraft's Cheese Spread issued in reusable character or decorated glasses. Since many types of food processing required glass containers the age of character glass packaging for the grocery industry began to mushroom ... and continues today.

The private automobile became the preferred method of transportation by the mid-'50s and oil companies competed hard for market share. Gas stations began to spring up everywhere. To compete for your business it was not uncommon for a gas station attendant to fill your tank, wipe your windshield and offer you a premium. These premiums were almost always household goods, many of which were glasses. The classic frosted ice tea glass was a favorite. The most popular focal point of each state was featured on these glasses for local distribution. The Oklahoma Indians – a set of eight glasses, a pitcher and wood carrier – was a gas station premium issued and distributed by the Knox gas stations throughout Oklahoma in 1959. The purpose of a large set was to guarantee your return to that gas station. Each state had its own set to offer. Texas had its flags, California had its flowers, Arizona had its cacti, and Ohio had its Indians and Presidents.

Glass premiums evinced very little popularity in the '60s. The few glasses issued were usually mail-in premiums produced by cereal and drink mix manufacturers.

The early '70s, however, saw the rise of what would be the biggest distributor of premium glasses – the "fast-food chain." At this time fast-food restaurants offered every variety of soft drink available (Coke, Pepsi, Dr. Pepper, etc.). In order to persuade a thirsty patron (and often the fast-food chain) to choose their soda over the competition's, the soft drink companies began offering free (or inexpensive) glasses with the purchase of their beverage. Soft drinks are also the most profitable item fast-food restaurants sell so there was plenty of room for promotion. The Pepsi Cola Company launched this practice in 1973, when they issued 18 glasses bearing the images of different Warner Brothers cartoon characters. These glasses were made available to any fast-food restaurant which offered Pepsi Cola as a selection. The

Warner Brothers glasses were such a huge success that Pepsi tried Super Heroes ... and continued to license cartoon character glasses throughout the remainder of the '70s.

Meanwhile Pepsi's main competitor, the Coca-Cola Company, began issuing glass premiums. Coke, however, was gearing its glasses towards a different market. While Pepsi was producing cartoon glasses aimed at children, Coke was producing glasses with more adult themes, such as the upcoming Bicentennial Celebration and local sports figures.

There was a limited number of established characters and the fast-food chains saw other benefits to using their own characters on promotional glasses. If they didn't serve Pepsi, they had to do something to remain competitive.

Eventually the soda companies and the fast-food chains began to co-sponsor glasses in order to lower licensing and production costs. *Star Wars* glasses were issued with both the "Burger King" and the "Coca-Cola" logos. *Indiana Jones* glasses were issued with the "Seven Up" logo along with the logo of any fast-food chain that wished to co-sponsor the set (Wendy's, Taco Time, Brown's Chicken, and In and Out Burger).

Glasses have continued to be issued sporadically throughout the '80s, but their popularity has waned in favor of a cheaper, yet larger plastic cup. Unfortunately, most of the recent popular films to be licensed for drinking containers have been printed on plastic. *Roger Rabbit* cups, *Indiana Jones and the Last Crusade* cups, and *Batman* cups were all made of plastic. (A set of 6 *Batman* movie glasses were distributed in Canada.) Those of us who collect glasses, though, hope it is a short-lived trend. Plastic products aren't as colorful and don't hold up. To us economy is a poor substitute for the quality, displayability and charm of a real glass.

THE MARKET REPORT

Millions of collectible glasses remain to be transferred from kitchen cabinets to the collector's market. The average collectible glass is still under $10, but some are sold for over $1000. There are also many popular sellers in the $30-$50 range.

Some test issues are still being offered in a single city and new issues continue to be released ... but at a much slower rate than the heyday of collectible glasses in the '70s.

The number of collectors is definitely increasing. Many people already have a good start right on their kitchen shelf. When people discover glasses are increasing in value they are usually removed from daily use. Then they are sold, collected or stored in hopes of value appreciation.

Original Coke glasses continue to be the value leaders, but many isolated or test character glass issues, such as the Sneaky Pete Li'l Abner, Popeye's Famous Fried Chicken Popeye character and certain Disney sets, are in strong demand at $30-$50 per glass. Many issues are popular sellers in the $10-$30 per glass range. And you can still collect thousands of glasses for under $10 each.

So glass collecting is still a hobby anyone can afford especially since some very valuable glasses can still be found at yard, garage and barn sales for 25¢-50¢ each.

There are a growing number of eager collectors willing to pay a fair price and many opportunities for dealers to find exceptional bargains to help cover the increased costs of doing the better shows.

Glass collecting is just getting a good start. The potential for demand to drive up the values of better glasses is exceptional.

WHAT COLLECTIBLE GLASSES ARE INCLUDED?

Any glass marked with an advertising logo, character or design is collected by someone. Glasses issued by breweries, railroads, hotels and a wide variety of other sources fall under this broad advertising/promotional category, but are not included. This book deals exclusively with character, sports, fast-food and similar glasses generally associated with milk, soft drinks and food products – both in this country and foreign countries

To some collectors it is the Coke or Pepsi logo which makes the glass collectible. Others collect just the cartoon or sports figures illustrated. Generally the glasses were distributed in connection with the sale of a food or drink product.

Certain similar products were sold as retail glassware, but are collected because of the similarity to promotional glasses.

HOW TO USE THIS BOOK

Character and Promotional Glasses was designed to be an authoritative and easy to use collector's guide. It utilizes an identification and classification system designed to create a standard identification number for each individual collectible glass and associated item.

The format is a classification system – one similar to the yellow pages of a telephone book. If you want to locate a Popeye glass, flip through the book until you find classification numbers beginning with a P and read the alphabetical category heading until you reach "Popeye." Classification headings have been established according to usage by collectors. Li'l Abner glasses, for example, are listed at the classification of "Al Capp", but if you follow the above procedure you will find a cross-reference at the classification of "Li'l Abner" which directed you back to the classification of "Al Capp" where known Li'l Abner character glasses are listed.

The classification format is standardized for the most part. However, if there was a better way to communicate more information in less space, a different approach was used.

Items are listed by year at each classification. Each item is assigned a reference code number consisting of one letter and four numbers. Use of these numbers in dealer and distributor ads and collector's correspondence is encouraged. Permission for such use to conduct buying, selling and the trade of collectible glasses in lists, letters or ads is hereby granted.

The identity code numbers also serve to match the correct listing to a nearby photo. In certain vast classifications, such as song and state glasses, a cross section of available material is used for illustration.

THE VALUES IN THIS PRICE GUIDE

This book is a collector's and dealer's guide to average prices, in a range of conditions. The real value of any collectible is what a buyer is willing to pay. No more. No less. Prices are constantly changing – up and down.

Many factors have a bearing on each transaction. Not the least of these are perceived value, emotional appeal or competitive drive for ownership.

Most dealers want the highest return they can get and continually test collectors with higher prices.

Supply and demand – always factors in measuring value – are a bit more predictable for those knowledgeable in a given area of collectibles. These people have a feel for how often they see a given item become available for sale. Since everyone has different experience, however, there are many different ideas on which items are rare or more valuable.

The availability of the items listed in this book is definitely limited. No one can say how limited, but it is certain no more originals will be manufactured.

The quantities of collectible glasses range anywhere from thousands up into the many millions. Generally, the items which generated the greatest interest originally were the items produced in the largest quantities. And since there were so many of them produced back then, they still turn up on a regular basis on kitchen shelves, in boxes and even warehouses.

The majority of collectible glasses aren't old enough to consider the known quantities a valid basis for establishing values. New edition items fulfill the demand of many new collectors coming into the hobby. Of course, most of these new collectors have an interest in older material too. Often they keep up with the newer material while specializing in selected categories of older items. There are rare and even some common items in high demand – and the value of these items outperforms the market as a whole – at least until the supply catches up with the demand. You never know when large quantities of items this new may turn up.

Collecting should be pursued for the interest and satisfaction involved. There are much better investments at most financial institutions. *Fortune*, *Business Week* and other business publications have done extensive articles on the pitfalls of speculating in what these magazines categorize as "exotic" investments.

What it all boils down to is the two ways collectible glasses are sold ... pre-priced or by auction to the highest bidder.

This book reports market prices based on items sold or traded by dealers and collectors nationwide. It reflects sales on the whole, with the understanding an auction price is the one all other bidders refused to pay.

Collectors who buy at yard sales and flea markets can generally purchase for less. Often they have first choice of items offered for sale; sometimes at exceptional bargain prices. But they also incur substantial time and travel expenses.

Mail and gallery auctions are preferred by collectors who don't have the time or the ability to visit major shows. Money spent and current resale value also tend to be of less concern to the auction buyer. The winning bidder must outlast the others who have an emotional fix on ownership or perhaps need the specific piece to "complete" a collection.

It's difficult to say who actually spends more money in pursuit of their collecting interest ... the aggressive hunter at low cost outlets or the auction buyer. This much is sure, there are substantial costs involved beyond the money spent on collectibles by the original buyer not normally considered in the "price" ... and higher overhead costs are included in auction sales where the "price" includes everything.

RARITY

Some collectible glasses were available for years after they were first offered. Examples of this type of continuous distribution include jam, jelly and peanut butter glasses of the 40s and 50s. On the other hand, fast-food glasses from the late 70s and 80s were generally only available for one week per promotion.

Rarity doesn't always equate to value. In glass collecting the strongest demand is often generated by people wishing to obtain items of special interest. Thus, rarity is only a part of value. Character popularity, cross-overs to other collecting fields (such as Coke or Pepsi) and the type of glass (anything showing a camera, Santa Claus, or telephone, for example) may become stronger factors. Other collectors often specialize in areas which cross the glass collecting line. Those who collect only Star Wars, Norman Rockwell or Disney, for example.

Price also has some regional influences. In Los Angeles and New York, prices are often substantially higher. To some extent this mirrors population density and the availability of disposable income. Realizing these regional price situations exist, and that isolated individuals will always let emotions rule in auction bidding, the values represented in this guide are average estimates taking into account what a given item has sold for over a period of time.

CONDITION

Condition, like beauty, is in the eye of the beholder. When money becomes involved, the eye seems to take on an added dimension of X-ray vision or rose-colored glasses – depending on whether you are buying or selling.

However, let there be no mistake about the price spreads set down on the following pages. The top price refers to items in "Mint", like-new condition – no scratches, never repaired, free of any defects whatsoever selling in a top market. Mint items probably were never used and especially never washed in a dish washer.

The low end price describes items in "Good" condition. That means, first and foremost, the item is complete with absolutely no chips or paint missing. Slightly faded graphics, minor scratches, out-of-register or bad silk screen job, and similar shortcomings are factors that depreciate value and regulate such items to the complete, but "Good" classification. Of course, some complete items with excessive wear, chips, cracks, missing graphics or other mistreatment are less than good; either poor or only a filler until a better glass is found. The value of poor condition items would obviously be less than the lowest price shown.

The range in between Good and Mint is the condition in which most items will be found. Very Good, Fine, or Very Fine are the most common grades used. In general, a "Fine" condition item would be one with only minor wear, scratches, blemishes, etc. The item has been in circulation – used, but given some care. The value would be somewhat less than the average in the price range as true "Mint" items command a premium.

Rarity, condition and the amount of material available in the marketplace all have a direct effect on value. The overriding factor, however, is the number of individuals who wish to acquire any given collectible glass and have the money to satisfy their desire.

All prices shown in this book are U.S. dollar values with the dollar signs removed to avoid repetition.

GLASS COLLECTING INFORMATION

One of the most interesting facets of collecting glasses is the millions of them out there and available at reasonable prices. It is possible to develop a substantial collection in a short period of time. Yet, there are always those choice, hard to find items.

Finding your more difficult wants often leads to sources where higher value items can be found ... collector groups, mail auctions and larger national shows.

There are well established collector groups for Coke and Pepsi items. Glasses are only a small part of their interest, but often a source of that special Coke or Pepsi glass. There is also one group for collectors of all glasses. All have newsletters full of contacts who are interested in buying, selling or trading. Here are their addresses and fees at time of publication:

Coca Cola Collectors News
8414 Tiffany Drive
San Antonio, TX 78230

The official publication of "The Coca Cola Collectors Club International", annual membership dues $25 ... free classified ads with membership only.

Pepsi Cola Collectors Club
P.O. Box 1275
Covina, CA 91722

Newsletter for "The Pepsi Cola Club", annual membership dues $15 ... free classified ads with membership.

Collectors Glass News
P.O. Box 308
Slippery Rock, PA 16057

A quarterly newsletter devoted entirely to promotional glass collecting. Photos of new releases, hard to find and rare glasses are a special feature. Annual subscription rate is $10.

Shows and Events

Often, better glasses are found at antique toy or advertising shows. The larger the event, the better your chances of finding outstanding items. Smaller events often yield good bargains.

The annual Great Lakes Toy and Doll Show consisting of over 200 tables of collectibles, toys and dolls, added a special section devoted to collectors of cartoon and character glasses called "Glass Alley." The show serves as the annual convention for all glass collectors. It is held the first Sunday in December at the Lake County Fairgrounds, Grayslake, Illinois (45 miles N.W. of Chicago). For information contact Tom Hoder, 444 South Cherry, Itasca, IL 60143.

More than one show may be held at a location each year. A growing number of other toy and/or antique advertising shows where glasses are sold are being held regionally. Announcements publicizing these events appear regularly in antique and toy publications.

Auctions

Hake's provided mail/phone auction for a wide variety of collectibles ... a few rare glasses are included in about every auction. The annual subscription rate for six illustrated mail auction lists is $15. The address is:

Hake's Americana and Collectibles
P.O. Box 1444
York, PA 17405

There are also mail auctions devoted strictly to items of interest to the glass collector. These are:

Glasses, Mugs and Steins Mail Auction
P.O. Box 207
Sun Prairie, WI 53590

Over 1000 glasses offered each sale. Much of the sale is devoted to "Breweriana", but at least 300 or more are character glasses. $5 per auction catalog.

Ho-Mar Mail Auctions

An auction devoted entirely to cartoon, sports, historical, fast-food and soft drink glasses. $3.50 per auction catalog. Contact:

Tom Hoder
444 South Cherry
Itasca, IL 60143

PHOTOGRAPHING GLASSES

Depicting the collectible glassware in this book posed a number of problems. In the majority of cases the illustration completely surrounds the glass. So the first problem is to select the half of the glass best protraying the subject matter. Next is to avoid the reverse image from confusing the side selected.

An obvious solution would be to fill the glass with something to prevent the reverse image showing through. Filling, however, can change the complexion of the glasses and, for the most part, the glasses in this book have been photographed exactly the way they will be found at flea markets and antique shows ... empty.

Using special lighting techniques, good definition between front and reverse sides has been achieved ... except in rare cases where filling was required to make the illustration readable. Often the reverse side show through even enhances the photograph ... and provides a clearer (excuse the pun) idea of how the glasses will look when displayed in your collection.

LOCATING THE EXACT GLASS IN THIS BOOK

This book provides three ways to find the exact glass in question – 1) the Table of Contents, 2) the classification system, and 3) the Index.

The Table of Contents provides the page number on which the titled classification begins. All other citations in the book provide a classification number reference rather than a page number.

The classification system is easy to follow once you have a general understanding of how it is constructed. Each identification begins with a letter of the alphabet based on the name of the set or individual glass; i.e., Holly Hobbie will be found at the letter "H".

The four numbers which follow the letter have been assigned at random to accommodate the number of listings at any given letter. Lower numbers coordinated with the generally alphabeti-

cal sequence of the names of individual glasses or sets; i.e., Hershey glasses are H2000 and Holly Hobbie is found at H5000.

The Index provides the classification number for a large cross reference of glasses. To locate the exact glass find the letter in the alphabetical sequence of the text material, then locate the number within the letter group for positive identification.

ADDITIONS AND CORRECTIONS

Hundreds of new glasses have been added to this edition. New issues continue and older glasses keep popping up. so this book will never be complete. However, our goal is to keep it as up to date as possible. Readers are encouraged to help. If you find glass issues which are not included, please send as much information as possible to:

Carol Markowski
3141 W. Platte Avenue
Colorado Springs, CO 80904

| A1000 | A1000 | A1002 |

A&W FAMILY RESTAURANT

A&W Restaurants originally made these glasses to use in their restaurants. When people began taking them as souvenirs, A&W began to sell them. A1000 comes in two variations.

A1000	A&W Bear, "The Great Root Bear"	8 - 10
A1001	A&W Bear, "The Great Root Bear" pitcher	20 - 30
A1002	A&W Bear, w/back to us	2 - 4

| A1006 | A1005 | A1006 |

A1003	A&W Bear, "The Great Root Bear" w/creased bottom	5 - 10
A1004	Mug, A&W Root Beer in circular logo, clear letters, 3 sizes	7 - 15
A1005	Mug, A&W Root Beer in circular logo, filled letters, 3 sizes	7 - 15
A1006	Mug, A&W oval logo, 4 sizes	7 - 15
A1007	Mug, A&W oval logo in map shape, 4 sizes	7 - 15

| A1100 | A1107 | A1105 |

| A1108 | A1106 | A1109 |

ACTORS, Coke

On this medium-size bell shape glass is a circle with photo of actor who won the "Susie" Humanitarian Award.

A1100	Mary Tyler Moore, 1974	20 - 40
A1105	Don Rickles, 1976	20 - 40
A1106	Jack Albertson, 1978	20 - 40
A1107	Monty Hall, 1975	20 - 40
A1108	Jan Murray, 1977	20 - 40
A1109	Teddy Kollack, 1982	20 - 40

A1120   A1121   A1122

ACTORS, Arby's, 1979
Smoke-colored glass

A1120	Charlie Chaplin, Take 1	4 - 8
A1121	Abbott and Costello, Take 2	4 - 8
A1122	Laurel and Hardy, Take 3	4 - 8

A1123   A1124   A1125

A1123	Mae West, Take 4	4 - 8
A1124	Little Rascals, Take 5	4 - 8
A1125	W.C. Fields, Take 6	4 - 8

A1128   A1130   A1131

ACTORS, No Logo
Similar in design to the Arby's set

A1126	Clark Gable	15 - 25
A1127	Humphrey Bogart	15 - 25
A1128	Jean Harlow	15 - 25
A1129	Marilyn Monroe	15 - 25
A1130	Theda Bara	15 - 25
A1131	W.C. Fields	15 - 25

A1135

ACTORS, Single Glasses
A1135 Humphrey Bogart, "Here's lookin' at you, Kid!" 7 - 15

A1200   A1201   A1202   A1203

AL CAPP, No Logo Shmoos Set, 1949
Comes in 3½", 4¾" and 5¼" sizes – 5¼" size is difficult to find. Some color variations exist.

A1200	Daisy Mae, pink	15 - 20
A1201	Li'l Abner, red, black	15 - 20
A1202	Lonesome Polecat, blue	15 - 20
A1203	Mammy Yokum, light green	15 - 20

A1204   A1205   A1206   A1207

A1204	Marryin' Sam/Sadie Hawkins, turquoise	15 - 20
A1205	Pappy Yokum, green	15 - 20
A1206	Shmoos, orange	15 - 20
A1207	Unwashable Jones, dark blue	15 - 20

A1220   A1221   A1222

AL CAPP, No Logo, 1975
A1220	Daisy Mae	45 - 60
A1221	Joe Btsptflk	45 - 60
A1222	Li'l Abner	45 - 60
A1223	Mammy Yokum	45 - 60
A1224	Pappy Yokum	45 - 60
A1225	Sadie Hawkins	45 - 60

AL CAPP, Sneaky Pete's Hot Dogs, Birmingham, AL, 1975
A1230	Daisy Mae	50 - 80
A1231	Joe Btsptflk	50 - 80
A1232	Li'l Abner	50 - 80
A1233	Mammy Yokum	50 - 80

A1230	A1231	A1232	A1234	A1233	A1235	A1250

A1234	Pappy Yokum	50 - 80
A1235	Sadie Hawkins	50 - 80

A1223	A1224	A1225

AL CAPP, Dogpatch, U.S.A.

A1240	Li'l Abner, ruby glass	25 - 30
A1241	Daisy Mae, ruby glass	25 - 30

AL CAPP, Single Glass

A1250	Li'l Abner/Daisy Mae, Kickapoo Joy Juice, Moxie, 1977	10 - 15
A1251	Lil'l Abner, Daisy Mae, child	6 - 15

ALASKA, Historical Series, Wet-Rex Corp., 1977

A1301	Gold Mining, gold pan/shovel	5 - 10
A1302	Alaska Pipeline, Prudhoe Bay	5 - 10
A1303	Totem Pole, Haida Indian/Russian Priest	5 - 10
A1304	Mt. McKinley, mountain sheep	5 - 10
A1305	Eskimo and Husky Pup	5 - 10
A1306	Kodiak Brown Bear, flag	5 - 10

ALICE IN WONDERLAND, Canada, Secma Inc., 1990

A1350	Alice	5 - 10
A1351	March Hare	5 - 10
A1352	Humpty Dumpty	5 - 10
A1353	Queen of Hearts	5 - 10
A1354	Tweedle Dum and Tweedle Dee	5 - 10
A1355	Rabbit	5 - 10
A1356	The Mad Hatter	5 - 10

A1240	A1241	3-1/2"	4-3/4"

A1356	A1360	A1361	A1375

ALICE IN WONDERLAND

Multi color, 4³/₄", no date or logo

A1360	The Dutchess was very ugly	15 - 25
A1361	"Herald read the Accusations," said the King	15 25

A1350	A1351	A1352	A1353	A1354	A1355

ALICE IN WONDERLAND, Apoll Films Wien Merchandisin Munchen KG, Germany, 1984

A1375	Alice w/all characters, Glass #1 to a set	8 - 12

ALPHABET

A variety of glasses featuring an alphabet theme have served as containers for jelly, peanut butter and cheese spreads

A1395	Alphabet theme glasses	5 - 20

AMERICAN GREETINGS CORP. (see HOLLY HOBBIE)

AMERICAN WILDLIFE, Sunoco, 1991

A1401	Bald Eagle	2 - 5
A1402	Humpback Whale	2 - 5
A1403	Bison	2 - 5
A1404	Moose	2 - 5

ANDY PANDA (see WALTER LANTZ)

A1401	A1402	A1403	A1404

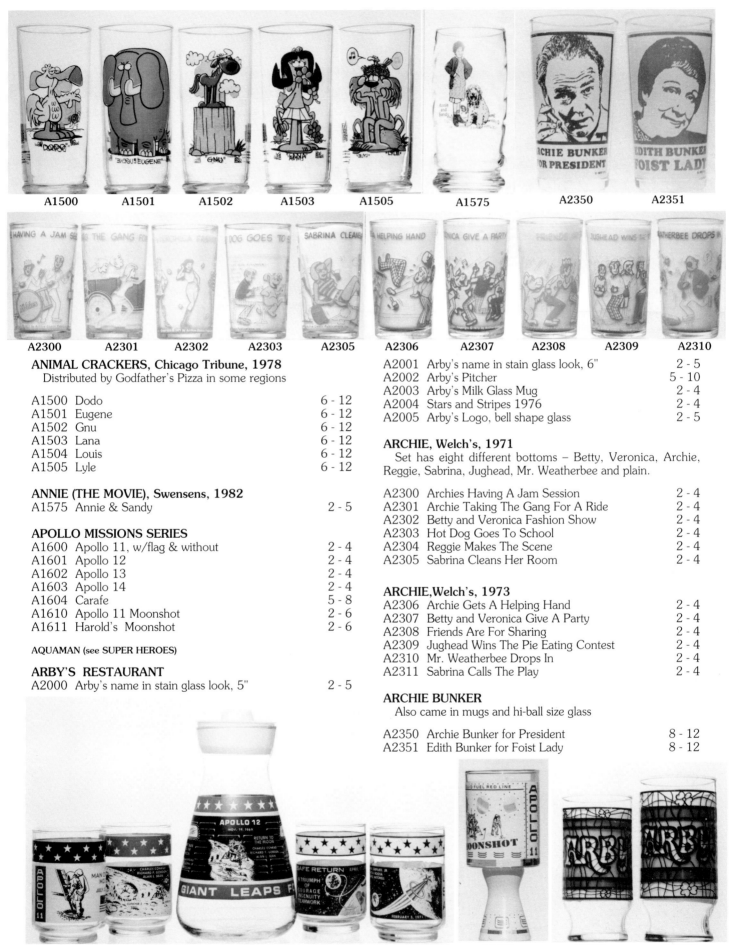

A1500	A1501	A1502	A1503	A1505

A1575

A2350 A2351

A2300	A2301	A2302	A2303	A2305

A2306	A2307	A2308	A2309	A2310

ANIMAL CRACKERS, Chicago Tribune, 1978
Distributed by Godfather's Pizza in some regions

A1500	Dodo	6 - 12
A1501	Eugene	6 - 12
A1502	Gnu	6 - 12
A1503	Lana	6 - 12
A1504	Louis	6 - 12
A1505	Lyle	6 - 12

ANNIE (THE MOVIE), Swensens, 1982
A1575	Annie & Sandy	2 - 5

APOLLO MISSIONS SERIES
A1600	Apollo 11, w/flag & without	2 - 4
A1601	Apollo 12	2 - 4
A1602	Apollo 13	2 - 4
A1603	Apollo 14	2 - 4
A1604	Carafe	5 - 8
A1610	Apollo 11 Moonshot	2 - 6
A1611	Harold's Moonshot	2 - 6

AQUAMAN (see SUPER HEROES)

ARBY'S RESTAURANT
A2000	Arby's name in stain glass look, 5"	2 - 5

A2001	Arby's name in stain glass look, 6"	2 - 5
A2002	Arby's Pitcher	5 - 10
A2003	Arby's Milk Glass Mug	2 - 4
A2004	Stars and Stripes 1976	2 - 4
A2005	Arby's Logo, bell shape glass	2 - 5

ARCHIE, Welch's, 1971
Set has eight different bottoms – Betty, Veronica, Archie, Reggie, Sabrina, Jughead, Mr. Weatherbee and plain.

A2300	Archies Having A Jam Session	2 - 4
A2301	Archie Taking The Gang For A Ride	2 - 4
A2302	Betty and Veronica Fashion Show	2 - 4
A2303	Hot Dog Goes To School	2 - 4
A2304	Reggie Makes The Scene	2 - 4
A2305	Sabrina Cleans Her Room	2 - 4

ARCHIE, Welch's, 1973
A2306	Archie Gets A Helping Hand	2 - 4
A2307	Betty and Veronica Give A Party	2 - 4
A2308	Friends Are For Sharing	2 - 4
A2309	Jughead Wins The Pie Eating Contest	2 - 4
A2310	Mr. Weatherbee Drops In	2 - 4
A2311	Sabrina Calls The Play	2 - 4

ARCHIE BUNKER
Also came in mugs and hi-ball size glass

A2350	Archie Bunker for President	8 - 12
A2351	Edith Bunker for Foist Lady	8 - 12

A1600	A1601	A1604	A1602	A1603	A1610	A2000	A2001

ARIZONA CACTUS, Blakely Gas, 1959

These glasses were a gas station giveaway. They came in a tall frosted cylinder shape or a clear stout round bottom in 2 sizes and had a matching pitcher and a wood carrier.

A2450	Barrel	3 - 5
A2451	Century Plant	3 - 5
A2452	Cholla	3 - 5
A2453	Octillo	3 - 5
A2454	Organ Pipe	3 - 5
A2455	Prickly Pear	3 - 5
A2456	Saguaro	3 - 5
A2457	Yucca	3 - 5
A2458	Pitcher	10 - 20
A2459	Wood Carrier	10 - 20

ASTERIX, Dargaud, S.A. Paris, 1968

A2490	Asterix Challenging Soldier on horseback	5 - 8
A2491	Asterix and Friend carrying Chief Abraracourcix	5 - 8

ASTERIX, Diete Coke, Canada, 1985

From a French comic – also issued in Canada

A2500	Obelix	10 - 15
A2501	Asterix	10 - 15
A2502	Idifix	10 - 15
A2503	Chief Abraracourcix	10 - 15
A2504	Fabula of Obelix	10 - 15
A2505	Romain	10 - 15

A2490   A2491

ASTERIX, Dijon Mustard, Canada, 1986

A2530	Obelix kissing young girl	10 - 15
A2531	Obelix and Idifix in water	10 - 15
A2532	Asterix w/Chief Abraracourcix	10 - 15
A2533	Asterix boxing Romain	10 - 15
A2534	Asterix w/two young girls	10 - 15

AUNT FANNY'S CABINS

A2600	Tall Slender Mint Julep Glass	10 - 20

AVON PEDRSTAL GLASSES

A2610	1890 Gibson Girl	5 - 10
A2611	1920 Flapper	5 - 10
A2612	1940's "man-tailored suit"	5 - 10
A2613	1950's "crinoline era"	5 - 10
A2614	Mini Skirts	5 - 10
A2615	Naturale Hair`	5 - 10

B.C. ICE AGE COLLECTOR SERIES, Arby's, 1981

B1101	Anteater	3 - 5
B1102	B.C.	3 - 5
B1103	Fat Broad	3 - 5
B1104	Grog	3 - 5
B1105	Thor	3 - 5
B1106	Wiley	3 - 5

B.C. CHARACTERS, Johnny Hart

Marathon Oil Company of Findlay, Ohio offered these glassware premiums in gas stations throughout Ohio, Indiana and Kentucky. Circa 1979.

B1111	Anteater	2 - 5
B1112	Thor, 2 sizes	2 - 5
B1113	B.C.	2 - 5
B1114	Grog, mug	2 - 5
B1115	Pitcher, frosted, different images	8 - 12
B1116	Pitcher, clear, different images	8 - 12
B1117	Cookie Jar, white flashing, different images	10 - 15
B1118	Cereal Bowl	3 - 4
B1119	Large bowl	4 - 6

BALLON FESTIVALS

B1120	Battle Creek International, 1988	5 - 8

BARNEY (see MGM)

BART SIMPSON, England, circa 1990

B1125	Don't Have a Cow, Lady	12 - 20
B1126	No Way, Man	12 - 20
B1127	Cool Man	12 - 20

BASEBALL (see SPORTS)

BASKETBALL (see SPORTS)

B1125 - B1127

BATGIRL, BATMAN (see SUPER HEROES)

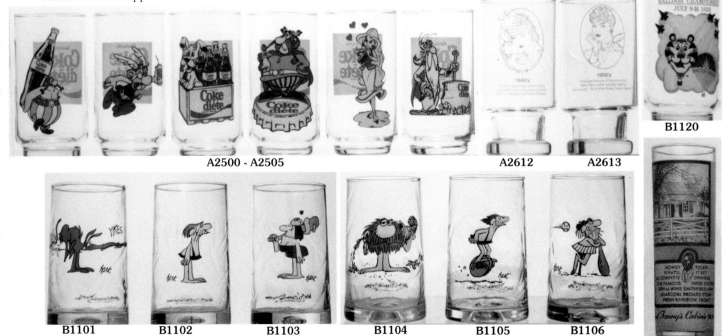

A2500 - A2505   **A2612   A2613**   **B1120**

B1101   B1102   B1103   B1104   B1105   B1106   A2600

14

B1150	B1151	B1152	B1153	B1154	B1340	B1341	B1375

BATTLESTAR GALACTICA, Universal Studios Inc., 1979
B1150	Apollo	5 - 8
B1151	Commander Adama	5 - 8
B1152	Cylon	5 - 8
B1153	Starbuck	5 - 8
B1154	Battlestar Galactica, all characters	10 - 15

BEATLES
There were many licensed and unlicensed glasses made in the United States and England. There were also many Beatles - type glasses, using characters that resembled the Beatles in appearance.

B1300	John	150 - 200
B1301	George	150 - 200
B1302	Paul	150 - 200
B1303	Ringo	150 - 200

BEATLES, Single Glasses
B1340	Mop Heads, not the Beatles	25 - 45
B1341	Yellow Submarine, the lithography on this glass is not the same design as the movie version. It is either an unofficial version or from the record album cover.	100 - 150
B1342	Group, all four	50 - 100
B1343	Beetles, not Beatles	10 - 25

BEEKIST HONEY
B1375	Circus Parade	5 - 8

BETTY BOOP, King Features Syndicate, 1988
These glasses created by Bright Ideas Unlimited come in both clear & frosted glass in 5" and 6" (4 total) in black, pink & red.

B1400	Betty Boop Glasses	5 - 8

BICENTENNIAL Celebration Glasses (also see FLAGS)
The 200th birthday of our country brought about a patriotic surge throughout the United States. Many historical themes were used on promotional glasses.

B2000	1776, green and blue, distributed by Herfy's	3 - 6

BICENTENNIAL Collector Series, Arby's, 1976
Using characters from Leonardo TTV, Jay Ward and Harvey Cartoons. This set comes in both 16 oz and 12 oz. The 12 oz comes with and without the Arby's logo.

B2010	Bullwinkle To The Defense	12 - 25
B2011	Bullwinkle Crosses The Delaware	12 - 25
B2012	Casper And Nightmare's Midnight Ride	12 - 25
B2013	Dudley Takes Tea At Sea	12 - 25
B2014	George By Woody	12 - 25
B2015	Hot Stuff Makes It Hot For The Red Coats	12 - 25
B2016	Never Fear, Underdog Is Here	12 - 25
B2017	Woody Has Spirit	12 - 25
B2018	Rocky In The Dawn's Early Light	12 - 25
B2019	Underdog Saves The Bell	12 - 25

PRESIDENTS AND PATRIOTS BICENTENNIAL SERIES, Burger Chef, 1976
B2050	Abraham Lincoln	5 - 8
B2051	Benjamin Franklin	5 - 8
B2052	George Washington	5 - 8
B2053	John F. Kennedy	5 - 8
B2054	Paul Revere	5 - 8
B2055	Thomas Jefferson	5 - 8

The Coca-Cola Company called all of their bicentennial series "Heritage Collector Series From The Coca-Cola Company." Nicknames have been given to the various sets by collectors.

"SPIRIT OF 76", Coca-Cola, 1976
B2070	Betsy Ross/George Washington	3 - 6
B2071	Paul Revere/Declaration of Independence	3 - 6
B2072	The Minutemen/Valley Forge	3 - 6
B2073	Nathan Hale/John Paul Jones	3 - 6

"PATRIOTS OF THE AMERICAN REVOLUTION", Coca-Cola, 1976
B2185	Patrick Henry	3 - 6
B2186	Paul Revere	3 - 6
B2187	George Washington	3 - 6
B2188	John Paul Jones	3 - 6

B2000

B2050 - B2055

B1400

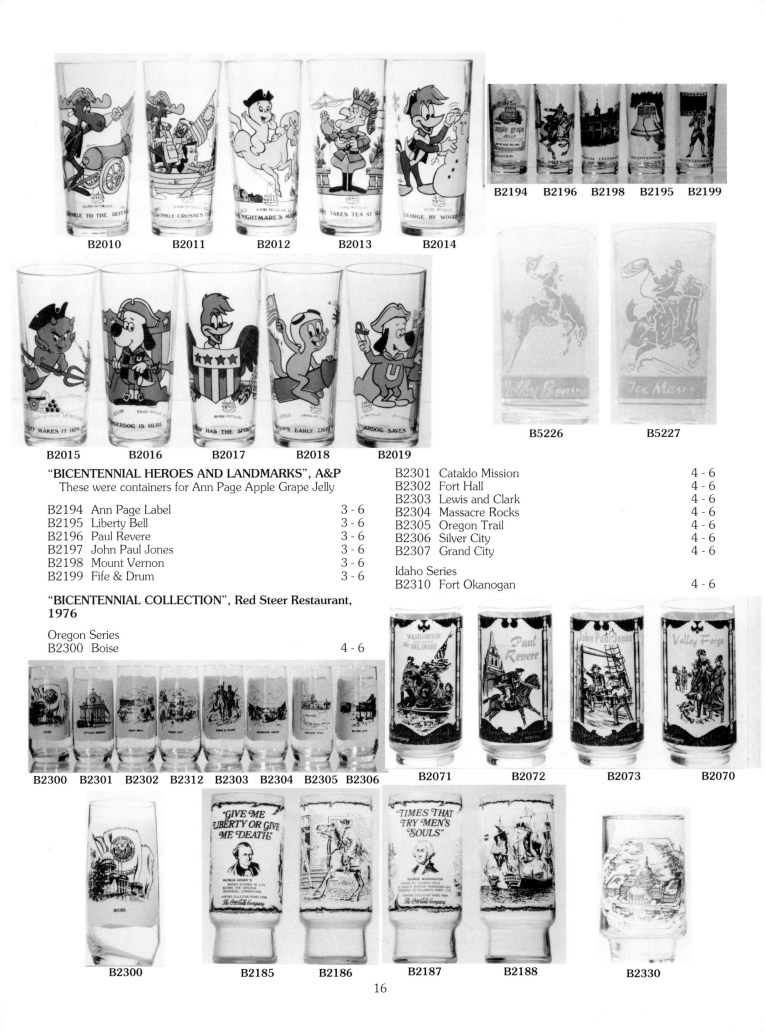

B2010 B2011 B2012 B2013 B2014

B2194 B2196 B2198 B2195 B2199

B2015 B2016 B2017 B2018 B2019

B5226 B5227

"BICENTENNIAL HEROES AND LANDMARKS", A&P

These were containers for Ann Page Apple Grape Jelly

B2194	Ann Page Label	3 - 6
B2195	Liberty Bell	3 - 6
B2196	Paul Revere	3 - 6
B2197	John Paul Jones	3 - 6
B2198	Mount Vernon	3 - 6
B2199	Fife & Drum	3 - 6

"BICENTENNIAL COLLECTION", Red Steer Restaurant, 1976

Oregon Series
B2300	Boise	4 - 6

B2301	Cataldo Mission	4 - 6
B2302	Fort Hall	4 - 6
B2303	Lewis and Clark	4 - 6
B2304	Massacre Rocks	4 - 6
B2305	Oregon Trail	4 - 6
B2306	Silver City	4 - 6
B2307	Grand City	4 - 6

Idaho Series
B2310	Fort Okanogan	4 - 6

B2300 B2301 B2302 B2312 B2303 B2304 B2305 B2306

B2071 B2072 B2073 B2070

B2300 B2185 B2186 B2187 B2188 B2330

16

B2500 - B2504

B6010   B6012   B6013

B5900   B5901   B5902   B5903

B2403   B6000   B6001

B2311	Fort Simcoe	4 - 6
B2312	Idaho City	4 - 6
B2313	Olympia	4 - 6
B2314	Whitman Mission	4 - 6

FAMOUS BUILDINGS, Coca-Cola, 1976

B2325	Mt. Vernon	5 - 8
B2326	Betsy Ross House	5 - 8
B2327	Jefferson Memorial	5 - 8
B2328	Monticello	5 - 8
B2329	Washington Monument	5 - 8
B2330	U.S. Capitol	5 - 8
B2331	Independence Hall	5 - 8
B2332	Statue of Liberty	5 - 8

BIG BABY HUEY (see HARVEY CARTOONS)

BIG BIRD (see Appendix A)

BIG BOY RESTAURANT

B2400	Big Boy, 12 oz	2 - 4
B2401	Big Boy, mug, clear	2 - 4
B2402	Big Boy, Shoney's	2 - 4
B2403	Big Boy 50th Anniversary	2 - 4

BIG TOP PEANUT BUTTER CIRCUS SET

B2500	Juggling Clown	5 - 10
B2501	Lion on Ball	5 - 10
B2502	Ringmaster	5 - 10
B2503	Dancing Elephant	5 - 10
B2504	Seal Balancing Ball	5 - 10
B2510	Big Top Parade	5 - 10

BOBBY BENSON

Early '30s radio premium issue, came in at least three colors – yellow, green, or red. The program was sponsored by the H-O Oats Company.

B5226	Bobby Benson	25 - 50
B5227	Tex Mason	25 - 50
B5228	Polly and Aunt Lil	25 - 50

BOND

Only the Roger Moore character is represented on these glasses.

B5900	A View To A Kill	10 - 15
B5901	For Your Eyes Only	10 - 15
B5902	Moonraker	10 - 15
B5903	The Spy Who Loved Me	10 - 15

BORDON'S

B6000	Elsie and Gang, bicentennial theme	8 - 12
B6001	Elsie in Dutch costume	8 - 12

The following have yellow bands around the top and feature the character head only.

B6002	Elsie	15 - 20
B6003	Elmer	15 - 20
B6004	Beulah	15 - 20
B6005	Beauregard	15 - 20

The following show the head with stars around it – come in $5^7/_8$" and $4^5/_8$".

B6010	Elsie	10 - 15
B6011	Elmer	10 - 15

B2510

AUNT ELSIE B6050   BABY BEULAH B6051   CELESTINE B6052   LITTLE LOLA B6053

B6030   B6046

B6040   **B6044**   **B6002**   **B6041**   **B6012**   **B6010**   **B6199**

B6002   **B6005**   **B7800**

B6012	Beulah	10 - 15
B6013	Beauregard	10 - 15

The following have standing full figure line drawings of the character.

B6020	Beulah	8 - 15
B6021	Beauregard	8 - 15
B6022	Elsie	8 - 15
B6023	Elmer	8 - 15

Single Glasses

B6030	Measuring glass	10 - 15

These were cottage cheese glasses.

B6040	Beulah and Elmer in sports car	10 - 15
B6041	Elsie and Elmer in action scene	10 - 15
B6042	Beulah and Elsie on roller skates	10 - 15
B6043	Elsie and Beauregard tugging on rope	10 - 15
B6044	Elmer and Beauregard shooting arrows	10 - 15
B6045	Elmer firing a gun	10 - 15
B6046	Elmer chased by a bee, round bottom	10 - 15

The following have red bands around the top.

B6050	Aunt Elsie	8 - 12
B6051	Baby Beulah	8 - 12
B6052	Celestine	8 - 12
B6053	Little Lola	8 - 12

BORIS (see WARD)

BOSCO BEAR, 1950s
The 3³/₈" glasses contained Bosco brand chocolate syrup.

B6100	Bosco Bear picking flowers	10 - 15
B6101	Bosco Bear being chased by bees	10 - 15
B6102	Bosco Bear being attacked by crabs	10 - 15
B6103	Bosco Bear skating & whistling	10 - 15

BOZO THE CLOWN, Capital Records, Inc., 1965
Features Bozo the Clown at the top of the glass and one of his buddies in full figure at the bottom.

B6199	Bozo (2 sides only)	8-15
B6200	Belinda	8 - 15
B6201	Buthcy	8 - 15
B6202	Elvis and Circus Boss	8 - 15
B6203	Mr. Lion and Whacko	8 - 15
B6204	Prof. Tweedyfoofer	8 - 15
B6205	Tico and Taco	8 - 15
B6206	Whacko Wolf	8 - 15

BUBBLE UP

B7000	Pedestal	3 - 6
B7001	100% Natural Flavor	3 - 6
B7002	Reach for Bubble Up	3 - 6

BUCK ROGERS (see Appendix A)

BUDDY & GINGER

B7800	Stillicious Syrup	5 - 8

BUGS BUNNY (see WARNER BROTHERS)

BULLWINKLE (see WARD, BICENTENNIAL, CB LINGO)

BURGER CHEF RESTAURANTS, 1976

B8001	Burgerinis Rabbit Hops Away	40 - 60
B8002	Burger Chef & Jeff Go Trail Riding	40 - 60
B8003	Burgorilla Falling Head Over Heels	40 - 60

B6100 - B6102

B6200   **B6202**   **B6203**   **B6204**   **B6205**   **B6206**   **B7001**   **B7002**

B8050   B8051   B8052   B8053   B8060   B8061   B8062   B8063

B8001   B8002   B8004   B8005   B8006   B8064   C1056

B8004	Fangburger Gets A Scare	40 - 60
B8005	Frankenburger Scores	40 - 60
B8006	Werewolf Goes Skateboarding	40 - 60

BURGER CHEF, Single Glass
B8010	Burger Chef & Jeff	10 - 20

BURGER KING, THE MARVELOUS MAGICAL, 1978
This set features only the Burger King himself.

B8050	See These Burgers, burgers/gold	15 - 25
B8051	I'll Turn Onions Into Rings, onion rings/green	15 - 25
B8052	I've Got The Magic That It Takes, shakes/red	15 - 25
B8053	It Isn't Luck , It Isn't Chance, fries/blue	15 - 25

BURGER KING, Single Glass
B8056	Burger King Pedestal "Where Kids are King"	4 - 6
B8057	Put a Smile in Your Tummy	5 - 10

BURGER KING CHARACTERS, 1979
B8060	Burger Thing	4 - 6
B8061	Duke of Doubt	4 - 6
B8062	Marvelous Magical Burger King	4 - 6
B8063	Sir Shake A Lot	4 - 6

B8064	Wizard of Fries	4 - 6

C.B. LANGUAGE SERIES (Called "CB Lingo"), Pizza Hut
In the C.B. Lingo set, Jay Ward and Leonardo TTV characters are used to express the CB language of truckers.

C1000	Bullwinkle - blue express truck	40 - 60
C1001	Bullwinkle - police car	40 - 60
C1002	Bullwinkle - green truck	40 - 60
C1003	Bullwinkle - fishing pole	40 - 60
C1004	Underdog - w/CB mike	40 - 60
C1005	Dudley Do-Right - helicopter	40 - 60

CABBAGE PATCH KIDS, 1984
C1050	Juice Set w/Carafe, sold in toy stores & department stores in conjunction w/the Cabbage Patch dolls	10 - 15
C1056	12 oz, boy & girl	3 - 5
C1057	Pitcher, matches above	7 - 10

CALIFORNIA RAISINS, Applause, 1989
C1070	Juice	4 - 6
C1071	12 oz	4 - 6
C1072	16 oz	4 - 6

B8006   B8056   C1000   C1001   C1002   C1003   C1004   C1005

C1071	C1072	C1070	C2300	

CALLAHAN'S, Pepsi

C1090	The Blues Burgers	10 - 15
C1091	The Fried Pipers	10 - 15
C1092	The Pop Stars	10 - 15
C1093	Hot Diggity	10 - 15

CAPTAIN AMERICA (see SUPER HEROES)

CARE BEARS, Pizza Hut, 1983

Good Luck Bear and Friends Bear were distributed in St. Louis, MO and its surrounding areas. The promotion went nationwide the following year minus Good Luck Bear and Friends Bear.

C2000	Cheer Bear	1 - 2
C2001	Friends Bear	7 - 15
C2002	Funshine Bear	1 - 2
C2003	Good Luck Bear	7 - 15
C2004	Grumpy Bear	1 - 2
C2005	Tenderheart Bear	1 - 2

CARE BEARS "THOSE CHARACTERS FROM CLEVELAND", 1986

C2010	Bedtime Bear	1 - 3
C2011	Cheer Bear	1 - 3
C2012	Good Luck Bear	1 - 3
C2013	Share Bear	1 - 3

CARE BEARS GLASS MUGS, American Greetings, 1984
Days of the Week Series

C2040	Monday	1 - 3
C2041	Tuesday	1 - 3
C2042	Wednesday	1 - 3
C2043	Thursday	1 - 3
C2044	Friday	1 - 3
C2045	Saturday	1 - 3
C2046	Sunday	1 - 3

CARE BEARS "LES CALENOURS", American Greetings, Canada, 1984

C2060	Bedtime (Dodonours)	5 - 12
C2061	Cheer (Godourson)	5 - 12
C2062	Friends (Capenours)	5 - 12
C2063	Funshine (Solours)	5 - 12
C2064	Grumpy (Grognours)	5 - 12
C2065	Tenderheart (Dounours)	5 - 12

CASPER (see HARVEY CARTOONS)

CHARLIE BROWN (see PEANUTS)

CHARLIE McCARTHY, 1930s

C2300	Charlie McCarthy/Edgar Bergen	20 - 40
	This was a radio premium mail away.	

CHARMERS, Hallmark Corp., 1975-76

C2350	When there's love in the home, there's joy in the heart.	2 - 3
C2351	Try your best to see the best in others.	2 - 3
C2352	Thankfulness grows where thoughtfulness shows.	2 - 3
C2353	It's good to take some time to do whatever makes a happy you.	2 - 3

CHILLY WILLY (see WALTER LANTZ)

CHIPMUNKS, Bagdesarian Production, 1985

Although there is no sponsor's name on the glass, these were distributed by Hardee's.

C2000	C2001	C2002	C2400	C2401	C2402	C2403

C2003	C2004	C2005	C2010	C2011	C2012	C2013

C3000 C3001 C3002 C3003 C3030 C3031 C3032 C3033

C3013 C3016 C3011 C3014 C3150 C3151 C3152 C3153

C3100 C3101 C3102 C3103 C3104 C3105 C3010 C3012

C3016	Toy Shop, 1988	2 - 4

C2400	Alvin	2 - 4
C2401	Chipettes	2 - 4
C2402	Simon	2 - 4
C2403	Theodore	2 - 4

CHRISTMAS (also see COKE, DISNEY, HOLLY HOBBIE, McDONALD'S, PEPSI, APPENDIX A)

CHRISTMAS CAROL, Subway Limited

C3000	Bob Cratchit	8 - 12
C3001	Bob Cratchit and Tiny Tim	8 - 12
C3002	Ghost of Christmas Past and Present	8 - 12
C3003	Ebenezer Scrooge	8 - 12

(also see DICKENS, DISNEY)

CHRISTMAS GLASSES, McCrory's, Coca-Cola

These were issued annually and are not a set.

C3010	100th Anniversary, 1982	2 - 4
C3011	Santa Reindeer, sleigh, 1983	2 - 4
C3012	Family room set for Christmas, Santa waving w/toy bag, 1984	2 - 4
C3013	Santa putting star on tree, reindeer w/sled of presents, 1985	2 - 4
C3014	Santa flying away, 1986	2 - 4
C3015	North Pole scene, 1987	2 - 4

CHRISTMAS POEM SERIES, Pepsi, 1982 and 1983

The glass style was changed from a crimped base to the round bottom shape in 1983.

C3030	Stockings on Fireplace	3 - 5
C3031	Mouse in Bed	3 - 5
C3032	Reindeers Over Roof	3 - 5
C3033	Santa Claus	3 - 5

CHRISTMAS SANTAS BY NORMAN ROCKWELL (see NORMAN ROCKWELL)

SANTA SERIES 1, Sundblom, Coca-Cola

C3100	1 of 3, 1961	2 - 4
C3101	2 of 3, 1960	2 - 4
C3102	3 of 3, 1947	2 - 4

SANTA SERIES 2

C3103	1 of 3, 1943	2 - 4
C3104	2 of 3, 1946	2 - 4
C3105	3 of 3, 1948	2 - 4

CHRISTMAS SONG SERIES, Pepsi, 1983 and 1984

The exact same design and glass style was used in both years.

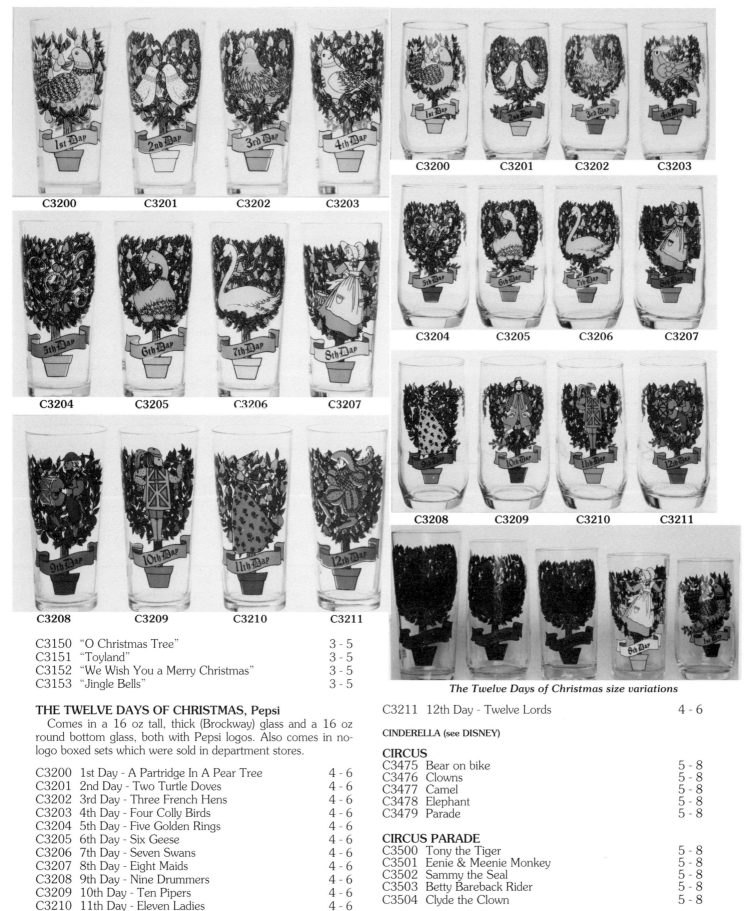

C3200   C3201   C3202   C3203

C3204   C3205   C3206   C3207

C3208   C3209   C3210   C3211

C3200   C3201   C3202   C3203

C3204   C3205   C3206   C3207

C3208   C3209   C3210   C3211

The Twelve Days of Christmas size variations

C3150 "O Christmas Tree"	3 - 5
C3151 "Toyland"	3 - 5
C3152 "We Wish You a Merry Christmas"	3 - 5
C3153 "Jingle Bells"	3 - 5

THE TWELVE DAYS OF CHRISTMAS, Pepsi

Comes in a 16 oz tall, thick (Brockway) glass and a 16 oz round bottom glass, both with Pepsi logos. Also comes in no-logo boxed sets which were sold in department stores.

C3200	1st Day - A Partridge In A Pear Tree	4 - 6
C3201	2nd Day - Two Turtle Doves	4 - 6
C3202	3rd Day - Three French Hens	4 - 6
C3203	4th Day - Four Colly Birds	4 - 6
C3204	5th Day - Five Golden Rings	4 - 6
C3205	6th Day - Six Geese	4 - 6
C3206	7th Day - Seven Swans	4 - 6
C3207	8th Day - Eight Maids	4 - 6
C3208	9th Day - Nine Drummers	4 - 6
C3209	10th Day - Ten Pipers	4 - 6
C3210	11th Day - Eleven Ladies	4 - 6
C3211	12th Day - Twelve Lords	4 - 6

CINDERELLA (see DISNEY)

CIRCUS

C3475	Bear on bike	5 - 8
C3476	Clowns	5 - 8
C3477	Camel	5 - 8
C3478	Elephant	5 - 8
C3479	Parade	5 - 8

CIRCUS PARADE

C3500	Tony the Tiger	5 - 8
C3501	Eenie & Meenie Monkey	5 - 8
C3502	Sammy the Seal	5 - 8
C3503	Betty Bareback Rider	5 - 8
C3504	Clyde the Clown	5 - 8

C3500　　C3501　　C3502　　C3503　　C3504

C4081　　C4090　　C4095　　　　　　C3476

C3475　　　　C3476　　　　C3477

C4041　　　　C4070　　　　C4091

COCA-COLA (also see BURGER KING, CHRISTMAS, COLLEGES, DAIRY QUEEN , McDONALD'S, MOTHER'S PIZZA, NEW KIDS ON THE BLOCK and OLYMPICS)

In 1886 John Pemberton, a druggist and pharmaceutical chemist in Atlanta, GA, developed a syrup he thought would serve as a headache remedy. Since two of the major ingredients were coca bean and extract of cola, the mixture became known as "Coca-Cola." Pemberton died in 1888 and the company was taken over by Asa Chandler. In 1900, when the Coca-Cola Company conceived the idea of manufacturing a special glass, advertising was not their primary purpose. Coca-Cola syrup was manufactured to be used in the combination of 1 ounce of syrup to 5 ounces of carbonated water. This combination was important to the continuity of the taste of Coca-Cola. If the proportions were not exact, the drink became too weak or too strong. If an ounce of syrup was dispensed into a larger glass and it was filled to the top with soda water, the drink was too weak. The fountain clerk would then have to add more syrup to get the proper taste. Since the syrup was the expensive ingredient, this cut into the fountain's profits (because the Coca-Cola Company advertised that the drink sold everywhere for 5 cents). To avoid this profit loss for the fountain operators, Coke commissioned a 7 fluid ounce glass with a syrup line and the words "Drink Coca-Cola" etched on it, which they sold to the fountain operators for exactly what it cost — 3¹/₂ cents.

C4000	1900-1904 straight sided, Coca-Cola script logo w/a syrup line. This is the very first glass.	50 - 200
C4001	1901 silver plated holder for the above glass This holder was created so women would look more dainty when drinking Coke.	50 - 100

Flare style glasses and all have syrup lines

C4005	1904 flare	50 - 150
C4010	1905-11, word "trademark" in tail	50 - 150
C4015	1912, large "5 cents" and "DRINK"	50 - 100
C4020	1912-13, small "5 cents" and "DRINK"	50 - 100
C4025	1914-18, "DRINK"	50 - 100
C4030	1916, word "BOTTLE", no syrup line	50 - 100
C4035	1927, modified flare, "trademark" in tail	25 - 50

Bell style glasses

C4040	1929-40, word "trademark" in tail	20 - 30
C4041	1941-46, word "trademark" under logo	10 - 20
C4045	1946-69, word "DRINK" above logo	5 - 10
C4046	1970, "ENJOY COKE"	2 - 4
C4070	1976, reproduction glass, 6 oz flare w/syrup line	5 - 8
C4071	1976, reproduction gift pack of 4 flare glasses & a pewter holder	20 - 40

Foreign country glasses

C4080	Canada, "DRINK Coca-Cola trademark reg"	5 - 8
C4081	Canada, "Savourez Coke diete"	5 - 8
C4082	Mexico, "TOME Coca-Cola Morca Reg"	5 - 8
C4085	Mexico, "Disfrute Coca Cola"	5 - 8
C4086	Mexico, "Guadalajara Des Rute Coca-Cola"	5 - 8
C4090	Germany, "TRINK Coca Cola"	6 - 10
C4091	Germany, "TRINK Coca Cola Schutzmarke/ Koffeinhaltig"	6 - 10
C4095	Germany, "TRINK Coca Cola Limonade Koffeinholtig"	6 - 10
C4100	Korea, "Enjoy Coke" in Korean letters	5 - 8
C4125	Coca Cola, hour glass shape, musical notes, Japan	10 - 20
C4126	"100" Centennial Celebration, Japan	12 - 25
C4127	Drink Carbonated Coca Cola "100", Japan	12 - 25
C4149	Tour de France, Coke	15 - 25

C4071

C4125 C4126 C4127 C4149 C4154 C4155 C4157 C4160

C4151 C4152 C4158

C4150 France, "Enjoy Coca Cola Savourez Coca Cola" 5 - 8
C4151 China 5 - 10
C4152 Japan 5 - 10
C4153 Ghostbuster II, Belgium 8 - 12
C4154 Coke "Ajoute a nos plaisirs" 8 - 12
C4155 Pique 1986 Volleyball, Mexico 8 - 12
C4156 Coke/McDonald's "Naranjata
       Espana '82", Mexico 8 - 12
C4157 Vollyball '78, Argentina "Gauchito" 8 - 12
C4158 Coke Oriental writing, Japan 8 - 12
C4159 Australia's defense, map of Australia 12 - 20
C4160 Flying Goose, "Enjoy Coke", not tiffany,
       Canada, 1950s 25 - 40

75th Anniversary

Many Coca-Cola bottling companies celebrated their 75th anniversaries by issuing a glass. Most used the traditional bell shaped glass, but some chose more contemporary designs and shapes.

C4170 Athens 4 - 8
C4171 Atlanta, mug 4 - 8
C4172 Augusta, ME, white letters 4 - 8
C4173 Austin, TX, white letters 4 - 8
C4174 Bristol, white letters 4 - 8
C4175 Buffalo, NY, white letters 4 - 8
C4176 Campbellsville, gold letters 4 - 8
C4177 Chicago, white letters 4 - 8

C4178 Cincinnati, white or gold letters 4 - 8
C4179 Columbia, white letters 4 - 8
C4180 Columbia, gold letters 8 - 12
C4181 Columbus, white or gold letters 4 - 8
C4182 Consolidated, white letters 8 - 12
C4183 Dallas, white or gold letters 4 - 8
C4184 Dayton, OH, white letters 4 - 8
C4185 Denver, red letters, in conjunction w/the 50th
       anniversary of the Southland Corp. 5 - 10
C4186 Detroit, gold letters 8 - 12
C4187 Elizabethtown, white or gold letters 4 - 8
C4188 Fayetteville, NC, white letters 6 - 8
C4189 Florida, white or gold letters 4 - 8
C4190 Harrisburg, white or gold letters 4 - 8
C4191 Houston, white and gold 4 - 8
C4192 Huntsville, white letters 4 - 8
C4193 Huntsville, filigree 5 - 10
C4194 Hygeia, white letters 12 - 18
C4195 Kansas City, gold letters 4 - 8
C4196 Jackson, flare tiffany 5 - 10
C4197 Louisiana, white letters 4 - 8
C4198 Louisville, white or gold letters 4 - 8
C4199 Meridan, white or gold letters 4 - 8
C4200 Mobile, AL, white or gold letters 4 - 8
C4201 Nashville, TN, white or gold letters 4 - 8
C4202 Norfolk, white or gold letters 4 - 8
C4203 Philadelphia, gold letters 8 - 12
C4204 Richmond, VA, gold letters 4 - 8
C4205 Roanoke, white letters 4 - 8
C4206 Rockwood, TN, gold letters 8 - 12
C4207 Rome, NY, white letters 4 - 8
C4208 Savannah, GA, white letters 4 - 8
C4209 Selma, white letters 4 - 8
C4210 Shawnee, white or gold letters 4 - 8
C4211 Shelbyville, white letters 4 - 8
C4212 Shelbyville, gold letters 6 - 10
C4213 Spartanburg, white letters 4 - 8
C4214 West Point–La Grange, white letters 6 - 10
C4215 Wometco–Beckly, white letters 6 - 10

C4230

C4185 C4175 C4196 C4193

C4232   C4233   C4234

C4238

C4241

C4257 Jean Batten Wings Across the World
Expo   20 - 30
C4258 Jacksonville, FL, grand opening, 1968
40 - 50
C4259 Tenth Anniversary of the Cola Clan
5 - 10

C4259

C4260

C4260 Springtime in Atlanta   3 - 5
C4261 Mundial, 1982   10 - 20
C4262 Robert C. Porter 50th Anniversary Dinner   75 - 150
C4263 10th Anniversary, Akron Bottling Co.   25 - 50
C4264 25th Anniversary of Bottlers, 1963   50 - 75
C4265 Atlanta Collector's Weekend, 1979   10 - 15
C4266 Cola Clan 11th Anniversary   5 - 10
C4267 Cola Clan 11th Anniversary, different   5 - 10
C4268 Cocon, FL, grand opening,1965   40 - 50
C4269 Orlando, FL, grand opening, 1969   40 - 50
C4270 1982 National Sports Festival   4 - 6
C4271 Plant Opening Greenwood, MS, 1970   40 - 50
C4272 Plant Opening Monroe, LA, 1968   40 - 50
C4273 Plant Opening Kansas City, KS   40 - 50
C4274 Plant Opening San Antonio, TX   40 - 50
C4275 Big Ten Champions   5 - 7

Special Anniversary/Commemorative Occasions

The Coca-Cola Company issued glasses to commemorate 25th and 50th anniversaries, grand openings of new plants, new contracts and officer presentations.

C4230 Employee retirement glass (signatures on
          bottom)   20 - 40
C4231 President Jamisen retirement   40 - 50
C4232 Three-year Safe Driving Chicago Bottlers   20 - 30
C4233 25th Anniversary Convention New England
          States   25 - 40
C4234 "It's the real thing", 1970 Bottlers Meeting   25 - 50
C4235 10th Anniversary Akron Bottling Co,
          "Soap Box Derby"   20 - 40
C4236 50th Anniversary, Atlanta, GA, Robert C.
          Porter   100 - 200
C4237 Australia's Defence, America's Cup, 1987   50 - 100
C4238 750th Anniversary of the City of
          Hannover/Berlin, Germany, set of 3   75 - 150
C4239 1970 Bottlers Meeting, pedestal   15 - 25
C4241 Boy Scouts Diamond Jubilee, "Enjoy Coca Cola" 20 - 30
C4249 San Antonio CCBC Opening,1965   8 - 12
C4250 50th Anniversary, bell shape, gold dipped   250 - 400
C4251 Pewter, bell shape, only 1000 made   250 - 400
C4252 Nashville, first bottler's contract   5 - 15
C4253 San Diego, new plant dedication   5 - 10
C4254 SMU Mustang '83 Cotton Bowl   5 - 10
C4255 The Portsmouth area is for everyone   8 - 12
C4256 World Wide Arts   5 - 10

C4261

C4262

C4263

C4274   C4253

C4251

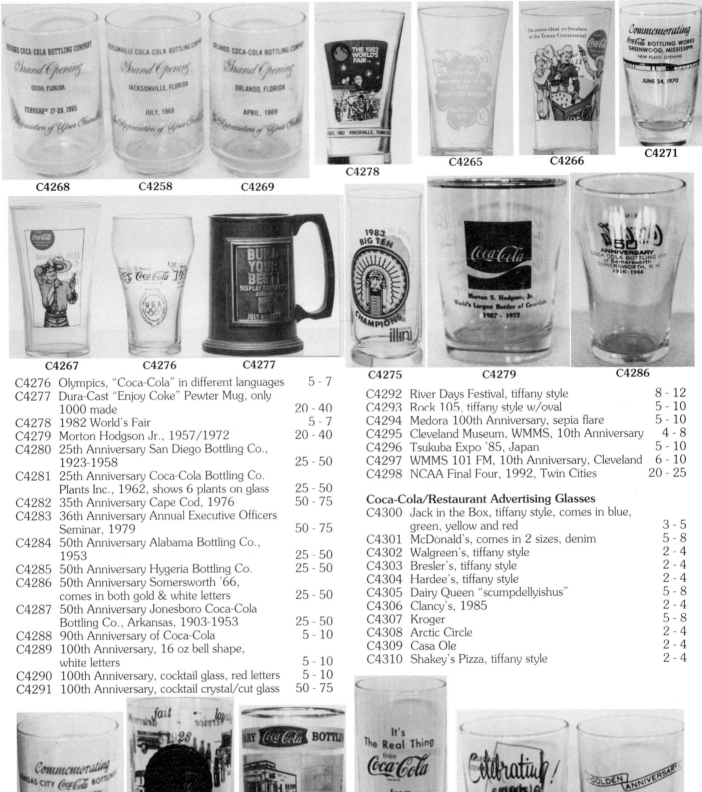

C4268   C4258   C4269   C4278   C4265   C4266   C4271

C4267   C4276   C4277   C4275   C4279   C4286

C4276	Olympics, "Coca-Cola" in different languages	5 - 7
C4277	Dura-Cast "Enjoy Coke" Pewter Mug, only 1000 made	20 - 40
C4278	1982 World's Fair	5 - 7
C4279	Morton Hodgson Jr., 1957/1972	20 - 40
C4280	25th Anniversary San Diego Bottling Co., 1923-1958	25 - 50
C4281	25th Anniversary Coca-Cola Bottling Co. Plants Inc., 1962, shows 6 plants on glass	25 - 50
C4282	35th Anniversary Cape Cod, 1976	50 - 75
C4283	36th Anniversary Annual Executive Officers Seminar, 1979	50 - 75
C4284	50th Anniversary Alabama Bottling Co., 1953	25 - 50
C4285	50th Anniversary Hygeria Bottling Co.	25 - 50
C4286	50th Anniversary Somersworth '66, comes in both gold & white letters	25 - 50
C4287	50th Anniversary Jonesboro Coca-Cola Bottling Co., Arkansas, 1903-1953	25 - 50
C4288	90th Anniversary of Coca-Cola	5 - 10
C4289	100th Anniversary, 16 oz bell shape, white letters	5 - 10
C4290	100th Anniversary, cocktail glass, red letters	5 - 10
C4291	100th Anniversary, cocktail crystal/cut glass	50 - 75
C4292	River Days Festival, tiffany style	8 - 12
C4293	Rock 105, tiffany style w/oval	5 - 10
C4294	Medora 100th Anniversary, sepia flare	5 - 10
C4295	Cleveland Museum, WMMS, 10th Anniversary	4 - 8
C4296	Tsukuba Expo '85, Japan	5 - 10
C4297	WMMS 101 FM, 10th Anniversary, Cleveland	6 - 10
C4298	NCAA Final Four, 1992, Twin Cities	20 - 25

Coca-Cola/Restaurant Advertising Glasses

C4300	Jack in the Box, tiffany style, comes in blue, green, yellow and red	3 - 5
C4301	McDonald's, comes in 2 sizes, denim	5 - 8
C4302	Walgreen's, tiffany style	2 - 4
C4303	Bresler's, tiffany style	2 - 4
C4304	Hardee's, tiffany style	2 - 4
C4305	Dairy Queen "scumpdellyishus"	5 - 8
C4306	Clancy's, 1985	2 - 4
C4307	Kroger	5 - 8
C4308	Arctic Circle	2 - 4
C4309	Casa Ole	2 - 4
C4310	Shakey's Pizza, tiffany style	2 - 4

C4273   C4280   C4281   C4283   C4284   C4287

C4297 C4300 C4301 C4302 C4303 C4304

C4298

C4306 C4305 C4307 C4310 C4311 C4312

C4320

C4313 C4314 C4316 C4317 C4318

C4329 C4330

Canadian C4381 C4318 C4320 C4307 C4333 C4352

C4311	Dags 30th, w/handle	2 - 4	C4320	Krystal 50th Anniversary	3 - 5
C4312	Whataburger, poinsettia	2 - 4	C4324	Whataburger, poinsettia, decanter	4 - 6
C4313	Happy Chef, brown, tiffany style	2 - 4	C4325	Godfather's Pizza, carafe	4 - 6
C4314	Steak and Shake, black & white check	2 - 4	C4326	Whataburger, yellow rose, pitcher	8 - 12
C4315	Bacardi Rum and Coke, glass mug	2 - 4	C4327	Bacardi Rum and Coke, pitcher	15 - 20
C4316	Jim Dandy, tiffany style	2 - 4	C4328	Clancy's, 1976	3 - 5
C4317	Valentino's "Classic Coke"	3 - 5	C4329	Sups, tiffany style	3 - 5
C4318	Seessel's 125th Anniversary	3 - 5	C4330	Bill Thomas Heavenly Halo Burgers	4 - 6
C4319	Whataburger "Classic Coke", yellow rose	3 - 5	C4331	Penguin Point	6 - 8

27

C4319   C4326   C4414   C4415   C4327

C4332	McDonald's, tiffany style	6 - 8
C4333	Carl's	5 - 10
C4334	Hardee's Charbroil Burgers, brown tiffany	5 - 10
C4335	Dairy Queen "Felez Navidad/Season Greetings"	5 - 10
C4336	Dairy Queen Brazier, bell shape mug	6 - 8
C4337	Dalt's	6 - 8
C4338	Duff's Smorgasbord, tiffany style	6 - 8
C4339	Ervin Houchens, building	5 - 10
C4340	Frank Veteres' Pizzeria, tiffany style	5 - 10
C4341	Veteres' "When you think pizza – think deep"	5 - 10
C4342	Friendly's, tiffany flair	6 - 8
C4343	Hecht, bell shape mug	6 - 8

C4344	Henredon Classic/Willow Creek Golf Club	6 - 8
C4345	H.J.C., tiffany style, 2 different sizes	6 - 8
C4346	Howard Johnson's International Conference, 1981, large bell	5 - 10
C4347	Belden, straight glass	8 - 10
C4348	Blimpie's	8 - 10
C4349	Brunswick Bowling Center, tiffany style	8 - 10
C4350	Burger Chef 150 years Marion County	8 - 10
C4351	Calamity Jane's Ice Cream House Coca-Cola Museum	6 - 8
C4352	Calvert and Coke, cupped	6 - 8
C4353	Calvert and Coke, flair	6 - 8
C4354	Chippory Fish and Chips Shops, tiffany style	6 - 8
C4355	Jack's Minit Market	6 - 8
C4356	Jolly Roger's, orange w/3 ships	6 - 8
C4357	Jolly Roger's, tiffany style	8 - 10
C4358	Ken's Pizza Franchise Convention, 1982	6 - 8
C4359	Keystone Pizza, tiffany style	8 - 10
C4360	Kroger's Deli-Bakery, bell shape mug	6 - 10
C4361	Mac's Family Restaurants, tiffany style	8 - 10
C4362	McDonald's Logo in gold, all in French	6 - 10
C4363	Mr. Angus Steak Haus, tiffany style	6 - 10
C4364	Mufso 81	5 - 8
C4365	Nato Nac 1974 Convention, tiffany style	5 - 8
C4366	Nathan's, photo of	40 - 50

C4331   C4333   C4363   C4361

C4324   C4405   C4325   C4406   C4407

C4381

C4374

C4366   C4383   C4408   C4403

C4382   C4403   C4410

C4400   C4411   C4412   C4413   C4414

C4416   C4417

C4401   C4402   C4404

C4367 Penguin Point, tiffany pedestal .... 5 - 8
C4368 Pudgie's, tiffany pedestal .... 5 - 8
C4369 Chicago Pizza Pie Factory .... 5 - 8
C4371 Royal Palm "It's the real thing, Associated

Coca-Cola Bottling Co. Inc", wine glass   10 - 15
C4372 Sonic, tiffany style   8 - 12
C4373 Sonic, same as McDonald's denim
       w/hankerchief out of pocket   6 - 10
C4374 Sonny's Real Pit Bar BQ, tiffany style   6 - 10
C4375 Stuffy's, tiffany style   5 - 8
C4376 Sutton's General Store, bell shape   4 - 8
C4377 Sevensen's   4 - 8
C4378 Taco Time, Holly Hobbie   6 - 10
C4379 Tougas & Nicholson BUVEZ, w/duck   4 - 8
C4380 Wendy's, tiffany style, 2 different sizes   4 - 8
C4381 Historic Medora, 100 Dakota Years   10 - 15
C4382 Pope's Cafeteras 50th   8 - 12
C4383 Swensen's   40 - 50

Tiffany Style Glasses (stained glass)

ENJOY COKE – tiffany style with "Enjoy Coke"
C4400 Diamond pattern   2 - 4
C4401 Stained glass & filigree   2 - 4
C4402 Stained glass & filigree pitcher   5 - 10
C4403 Stained glass & filigree w/sports figure -
       Terry Bradshaw or George Brett   20 - 30
C4404 Stained glass & filigree straw holder, 32 oz,
       matches all of the above   5 - 7
C4405 Stained glass & black lace filigree, same design
       used on Godfather's Pizza carafe, cupped   2 - 4
C4406 Stained glass & black lace filigree pitcher   5 - 10
C4407 Stained glass & black lace filigree, flare   3 - 6
C4408 Stained glass yellow rose, flare   2 - 4
C4409 Stained glass yellow rose pitcher, same as
       C4326 w/o "Whataburger" on back   8 - 12
C4410 Stained glass tulip, flare   3 - 5
C4411 Stained glass holly & berry   2 - 4
C4412 Stained glass poinsettia   2 - 4
C4413 Stained glass kites flying   2 - 4
C4414 Stained glass gold & green flowers   2 - 4

C4418   C4419   C4425   C4427   C4428   C4425   C4429   C4432   C4431

C4426   C4455   C4463   C4464   C4465   C4467   C4468   C4469

C4415	Stained glass straw holder, 32 oz, matches above design	5 - 8
C4416	Stained glass "Coke Adds Life to Everything Nice", green & red w/white daisy, bell shape, 1 of 6	5 - 8
C4417	Stained glass "Coke Adds Life to Everything Nice", red & white w/red peony, bell shape, 2 of 6	5 - 8
C4418	White roses	5 - 8
C4419	Red roses	5 - 8

COKE ADDS LIFE

C4425	Hamburger, bell shape	10 - 15
C4426	Smile face, bell shape	10 - 15
C4427	Tiffany style, bell shape	10 - 15
C4428	Everything Nice, sun w/tongue out	10 - 15
C4429	Everything Nice, sailboat	10 - 15
C4430	Corn on the cob	10 - 15
C4431	Everything Nice, sun winking	10 - 15
C4432	Sandwich, wrap-around graphic	10 - 15

DRINK COCA-COLA – tiffany style with "Drink Coca-Cola"

C4450	Stained glass, design on top only, straight glass	2 - 4
C4451	Stained glass, frosted panels, straight glass	2 - 4
C4452	Stained glass, frosted panels, cupped glass	2 - 4
C4453	Stained glass, frosted panels, flare glass	3 - 5

C4454	Flowers over oval	5 - 8
C4455	Circles	10 - 15
C4456	Daisy	10 - 15

ENJOY COKE – not tiffany style

C4460	Poinsettia, frosted panel of toys	2 - 4
C4461	Hurricane lamp shape	2 - 4
C4462	All over floral design, brown & orange	2 - 4
C4463	Small squares w/mistletoe	3 - 7
C4464	Snow, street lamp, people walking	3 - 7
C4465	Flowers	5 - 8

Coca-Cola Ladies

Delicious and Refreshing, Japan

C4467	Two ladies	15 - 25
C4468	Lady in fur	15 - 25
C4469	Lady in wide brim hat	15 - 25

Magnificent Ladies of Coke Set, flare shape

C4470	#1 - 1912 tray girl	5 - 8
C4471	#2 - 1920 garden girl	5 - 8
C4472	#3 - 1922 autumn girl	5 - 8
C4473	#4 - 1914 Betty	5 - 8

C4451   C4452   C4453   C4460   C4461   C4462   C4454   C4456

C4470   C4471   C4472

C4473   C4474   C4475

C4476 - C4479

C4480 - C4482

C4486   C4488   C4485   C4487

C4483   C4484

C4485	Girl on beach	8 - 10
C4486	Elaine	8 - 10
C4487	Winter girl	8 - 10
C4488	Girl w/hand on heart	8 - 10

| C4474 | #5 - 1917 Elaine | 5 - 8 |
| C4475 | #6 - 1919 Marion Davies | 5 - 8 |

Calendar Girls, bell shape, etched image in oval

C4476	1909	3 - 5
C4477	1927	3 - 5
C4478	1944	3 - 5
C4479	1954	3 - 5

Single Glasses of Ladies

C4480	Lady sipping from straw, sepia color, flare	2 - 4
C4481	Lady w/glass to lips, sepia color, flare, plain back	2 - 4
C4482	Lady in black hat, 1913 calendar girl, flare	3 - 5
C4483	1901 Calendar girl etched with feather hat	12 - 25
C4484	1909 Calendar girl, Japan	12 - 25

Sepia Ladies, Canada

Large flair, bi-linqual "Une recreation du verre evase original de 16 oz Buvez Coca-Cola Marque Deposee Delicieuxet Rafrachissant"

Coca-Cola Centennial Collection

This etched crystal set comes in 2 different sizes. The front of the glass has a different Coca-Cola girl etched on it; the back has "Centennial Collection" and the date.

C4490	1911	5 - 8
C4491	1924	5 - 8
C4492	1925	5 - 8
C4493	1927	5 - 8
C4494	1944	5 - 8
C4495	1948	5 - 8
C4496	1957	5 - 8

Slogans

C4498	"Enjoy Coca Cola", Dodgers, bell shape	20 - 30
C4499	"Enjoy Coke", food names, bell shape (also comes in straight sided glass)	10 - 15
C4500	"Coke adds life"	1 - 3
C4501	"Have a Coke and a Smile"	1 - 3
C4502	"Coke is it"	1 - 3
C4503	"Things go better with Coke"	1 - 3
C4504	"The Real Thing"	1 - 3

C4498   C4521   C4537   C4522   C4526   C4523

C4499   C4500   C4501   C4502   C4506   C4507   C4508   C4509

"Things Go Better with Coke", Sports Activity Set, 1960s
Lime green and pale red colors on clear glass. Very '50s style, but distributed in the '60s.

C4506	Party, dinner, dancing	3 - 6
C4507	Beach, camping, cookout	3 - 6
C4508	Deep sea fishing, water skiing	3 - 6
C4509	Downhill skiing, diving, golf	3 - 6

Modern

C4510	"Coca-Cola" in script colorful writing all over	2 - 4
C4511	Same as C4500 as covered storage jar	3 - 7
C4512	"Original Formula", red w/white letters	5 - 8
C4513	Bottle	8 - 15
C4514	Sunset	8 - 15

C4534   C4510   C4511   C4527   C4513   C4514   C4515

C4536   C4535   C4530   C4531   C4564

32

C4542

C4542

C4543

C4544

Fountain Glasses, clear bell style

C4540	"Enjoy Coke/Coca-Cola", 20 oz, white letters	2 - 4
C4541	"Enjoy Coke/Coca-Cola", 12 oz, frosted red letters	2 - 4
C4542	"Enjoy Coke/Coca-Cola", 32 oz, white letters	2 - 4
C4543	"Enjoy Coke/Coca-Cola", 12 oz, white letters	2 - 4
C4544	"Enjoy Coke/Coca-Cola", 8 oz, white letters	2 - 4
C4545	"Genuine Coca-Cola Drinkware", frosted red letters	3 - 5
C4546	"Drink Coca-Cola/Enjoy Coke", 12 oz, white letters	2 - 5
C4550	"Drink Coca-Cola/Enjoy Coke", 8 oz, white letters	2 - 4
C4551	"Drink Coca-Cola", 6 oz, white letters	2 - 4
C4552	"Enjoy Coke/Enjoy Coca-Cola", 8 & 12 oz, white letters. An ad in a fast-food restaurant read, "Get your old fashioned Coke glass. 39 cents with the purchase of a medium or large Coke."	1 - 2

C4538

C4566

C4581

C4552

C4546

C4551

C4555	"Coke/Coca-Cola", 6, 8, & 12 oz, red letters Came in a boxed set of 18 – 6 of each size	25 - 30
C4556	Statue of Liberty Centennial Celebration "100 years"	4 - 8
C4560	Statue of Liberty Centennial Celebration "Grand Union"	4 - 8
C4561	Statue of Liberty Centennial Celebration "Founding Sponsors"	4 - 8
C4564	Bell shape pitcher, "Coca-Cola/Coke", red letters	10 - 15
C4565	Bell shape pitcher, "Coca-Cola/Coke", white letter	10 - 15
C4566	Bell shape pitcher, "Enjoy Coke Septemberfest Cola Clan/Midsouth, Elizabethtown, Kentucky"	10 - 15

Christmas Modern

C4580	Coke Classic Santa Express	5 - 8
C4581	Enjoy the Magic of Christmas	5 - 8

C4556   C4560   C4561

C4515	Baseball Player	8 - 15
C4520	"Coca-Cola" in colorful script writing in band	2 - 4
C4521	"Enjoy Coke", red w/white letters	2 - 4
C4522	"Diet Coke", white w/red ribbon	2 - 4
C4523	"Enjoy Coke/Coca-Cola", thick flare w/handle	2 - 4
C4526	"Enjoy Coke/Coca-Cola", thick bell w/handle	2 - 4
C4527	"Enjoy Tab", hour glass shape	2 - 4
C4530	"Enjoy Coca-Cola", stemmed goblet	2 - 4
C4531	"Coke", bowl shape	3 - 5
C4534	"Coke", 32 oz	6 - 10
C4535	"Coke Light", slim	3 - 5
C4536	"Diet Coke", rippled	3 - 5
C4537	"Coke/Coca-Cola", red w/white ribbon	2 - 4
C4538	"North Texas", set of 2 different	2 - 4

Travel Set

Sold as a set in a molded foam box in the late '50s. Matte finish lithography.

C4600	England	10 - 15
C4601	France	10 - 15
C4602	Germany	10 - 15
C4603	Hawaii	10 - 15
C4604	Italy	10 - 15
C4605	Japan	10 - 15
C4606	Mexico	10 - 15
C4607	Spain	10 - 15

Coca-Cola Party Star Promotion

Come in hi-ball, cooler, pedestal, mug and pilster styles.

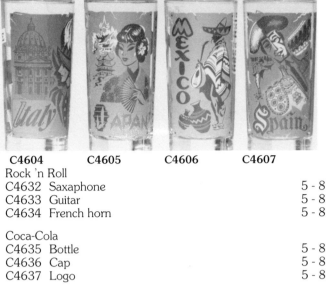

| C4600 | C4601 | C4602 | C4603 | | C4604 | C4605 | C4606 | C4607 |

Holiday
C4620	Lips	5 - 8
C4621	Headphones	5 - 8
C4622	Hand/logo tilted	5 - 8

Freetime
C4623	Hang-glider	5 - 8
C4624	Skateboard	5 - 8
C4625	Surf Sailing	5 - 8

'50s
C4626	Motorcycle	5 - 8
C4627	Jukebox	5 - 8
C4628	'57 Chevy	5 - 8

Broadway
C4629	Male/microphone	5 - 8
C4630	Female/sun glasses	5 - 8
C4631	Female/wind-blown hair	5 - 8

Rock 'n Roll
C4632	Saxaphone	5 - 8
C4633	Guitar	5 - 8
C4634	French horn	5 - 8

Coca-Cola
C4635	Bottle	5 - 8
C4636	Cap	5 - 8
C4637	Logo	5 - 8

Western Series by Tom Ryan
   Art from the archives of Brown and Bigelow. Number in set unknown.

| C4700 | Traildriver's Despair | 20 - 40 |
| C4701 | The Noon Break | 20 - 40 |

Collector's Convention Set, Louisville, KY, 1990 (frosted)
| C4710 | Riverboat | 5 - 10 |

| C4628 | C4624 | C4623 | | C4628 | C4627 | C4626 |

| C4629 | C4630 | C4631 | | C4634 | C4633 | C4632 |

C4700   C4701   C4800 - C4802   C4803 - C4805

C4710   C4713   C4711   C4712   C4900   C4902   C4901   C5000   C5001

C4711	Thoroughbred	5 - 10
C4712	Coke Bottle	5 - 10
C4713	Bottling Plant	5 - 10

AC Restaurants, 1983, Holland, Coke

C4800	Man w/long beard	8 - 15
C4801	Man w/wings on his head	8 - 15
C4802	Man carrying rock	8 - 15
C4803	Man, fat	8 - 15
C4804	Man, harp	8 - 15
C4805	Man, apron	8 - 15

Mugs, Coke, Germany

C4900	Car w/Coke license	12 - 25
C4901	Car w/Coca-Cola license	12 - 25
C4902	Bike	12 - 25
C4903	Canadian Goose	12 - 25

Coke Singles

C5000	1990 Coca Cola/Sprite	5 - 8
C5001	Coca-Cola, metal emblem embedded in glass	15 - 25
C5002	Hubert H. Humphrey, The Final Four, 1992	5 - 8

COLLEGES

College sports, campus buildings, fight slogans and team mascots are well represented in the glass collecting world. A book can be written on these glasses alone. The most sought after college glasses, by collectors, are the Coke Collegiate Crest series and the Pepsi Wisconsin Badgers series.

Collegiate Crest, Coke

These glasses were issued by individual bottling companies throughout the United States and Canada.

C6000	Albright College	8 - 12
C6001	Arizona State University	8 - 12
C6002	Arizona University	8 - 12
C6003	Arkansas University	8 - 12
C6004	Athens, Georgia	8 - 12
C6005	Baker University	8 - 12
C6006	Bakersfield, California	8 - 12
C6007	Ball State University	8 - 12
C6008	B.S.U., Noyer Halls	8 - 12
C6009	Cal Poly	8 - 12
C6010	Cal Poly Mustang	8 - 12
C6011	California State at Fresno	8 - 12
C6012	California State at Fullerton	8 - 12
C6013	California State at L.A.	8 - 12
C6014	California State at Long Beach	8 - 12
C6015	Central Missouri State	8 - 12
C6016	Clemson College	8 - 12
C6017	College of San Mateo	8 - 12
C6018	Concordia College	8 - 12
C6019	Cornell at Mt. Vernon, IA	8 - 12
C6020	Dartmouth	8 - 12
C6021	Dickenson College	8 - 12
C6022	East Carolina University	8 - 12
C6023	Eastern Oregon	8 - 12
C6024	Elizabethtown State College	8 - 12
C6025	Georgia State	8 - 12
C6026	Indiana University	8 - 12
C6027	Loyola College	8 - 12
C6028	Memphis State University	8 - 12
C6029	Miami University	8 - 12
C6030	Michigan State	8 - 12
C6031	Michigan State University (MSU)	8 - 12
C6032	Middle Tennessee State University	8 - 12
C6033	Middletown State	8 - 12
C6034	Millerville College	8 - 12
C6035	Mississippi State	8 - 12
C6036	Murray State	8 - 12
C6037	North Carolina University	8 - 12

C6052   C6035   C6047   C6208 - C6212

C6200 - C6203   C6206   C6207   C6204   C6205

C6038	North Texas State	8 - 12
C6039	Ohio State University	8 - 12
C6040	Pennsylvania State University	8 - 12
C6041	Pittsburgh State University	8 - 12
C6042	Texas A&M	8 - 12
C6043	Texas State	8 - 12
C6044	Texas Tech	8 - 12
C6045	Towson State	8 - 12
C6046	Trinity College	8 - 12
C6047	Troy State University	8 - 12
C6048	U.C.L.A	8 - 12
C6049	University of Alabama at Florence	8 - 12
C6050	University of California at L.A.	8 - 12
C6051	University of Delaware	8 - 12
C6052	University of Georgia	8 - 12
C6053	University of Indiana	8 - 12
C6054	University of Nebraska	8 - 12
C6055	University of New Mexico	8 - 12
C6056	University of New York at Canton	8 - 12
C6057	University of Notre Dame	8 - 12
C6058	University of Pittsburgh	8 - 12
C6059	University of Southern California	8 - 12
C6060	University of Texas at Arlington	8 - 12
C6061	University of Wisconsin at Milwaukee	8 - 12
C6062	University of Wisconsin at Oshkosh	8 - 12
C6063	Valaparaiso College	8 - 12
C6064	Vanderbilt College	8 - 12
C6065	Wake Forrest University	8 - 12
C6066	Washington College	8 - 12
C6067	Widener College	8 - 12
C6058	Wisconsin University	8 - 12
C6069	Witchita State	8 - 12
C6070	Abilene Christian University	5 - 15
C6071	Ball State, Studebaker Hall, 1979-80	5 - 15
C6072	Ball State, Residence Halls, 1980	5 - 15
C6073	Ball State, Elliott Hall, 1982-83	5 - 15
C6074	Bradley University	5 - 15
C6075	East Michigan University	5 - 15
C6076	Louisiana State	5 - 15

C6077	Middleton State	5 - 15
C6078	Ohio Institute of Technology	5 - 15
C6079	Schools of Mines, NM	5 - 15
C6080	State University, Canton, NM	5 - 15
C6081	University of Colorado, Boulder	5 - 15
C6082	University of Hawaii, Honolulu	5 - 15
C6083	University of Illinois, Chicago Circle Center	5 - 15
C6084	University of Nebraska	5 - 15
C6085	University of New Hampshire	5 - 15
C6086	University of New Haven, CT	5 - 15
C6087	University of South Florida	5 - 15
C6088	Washington University, St. Louis, 1853	5 - 15
C6089	William Paterson College, NJ	5 - 15

The Nebraska Cornhuskers, Sam's, 1976

This is a Cornhuskers series. The first glass depicts the helmet of the Cornhuskers. The others depict the helmets of opposing teams with their statistics against Nebraska printed on the back.

C6200	Go Big Red/Nebraska Cornhuskers	5 - 7
C6201	TCU Frogs	5 - 7
C6202	OU Sooner	5 - 7
C6203	University of Colorado Buffaloes	5 - 7
C6204	Iowa State Cyclones	5 - 7
C6205	Oklahoma State Cowboys	5 - 7
C6206	Indiana Hoosiers	5 - 7
C6207	Miami Hurricanes	5 - 7
C6208	Kansas Jayhawks	5 - 7
C6209	Hawaii Rainbows	5 - 7
C6210	Louisiana State Tigers	5 - 7
C6211	Missouri Tigers	5 - 7
C6212	Kansas State Wildcats	5 - 7

Wisconsin "Badgers", Pepsi & Mountain Dew

These varsity sports glasses came in both the large (Brockway) thick glass as well as the round bottom glass with the Pepsi logo, the Mountain Dew logo or with no logo at all. To make things even more difficult, from the years 1971 thru 1981 team statistics were on the back of some of the glasses.

| C6850 | C6851 | C6852 | C6853 | C6854 | C6855 |

Round bottom version with stats on back

Prior to 1971, glass mugs with "Bucky Badger" were issued.

C6850	Baseball	10 - 20
C6851	Basketball	10 - 20
C6852	Football	10 - 20
C6853	Hockey	10 - 20
C6854	Track	10 - 20
C6855	Wrestling	10 - 20

COLORADO CENTENNIAL, Carter Oil Co., 1959

These are tall frosted ice tea glasses, common to the late '50s and early '60s. The scenes on the glasses depict events that took place in 1859.

C6915	"Discovery of Gold at Little Dry Creek"	6 - 10
C6916	"The Battle of La Glorieta Pass"	6 - 10
C6917	"Cattle Drive up Texas Trail"	6 - 10
C6918	"Opera House at Central City"	6 - 10
C6919	"Kit Carson discussing Treaty with Ute Indian"	6 - 10
C6920	"Arrival of the First Passenger Train in Denver"	6 - 10

CONEHEADS

These are characters created by Dan Aykroyd, Tom Davis and Lorne Michael for the "Saturday Nite Live" TV show in 1983.

C6922	Old George hasn't lost any of his bartender's touch	8 - 12
C6923	Now, if I were running things	8 - 12
C6924	Marvin, I never said you were too short	8 - 12
C6925	Olive, anyone	8 - 12
C6926	Tomorrow Marv, let's try 6:1	8 - 12
C6927	Of course, it's all confidential, but ...	8 - 12

COON'S CHICKEN INN

This Portland, Oregon restaurant existed in the 1940s and used a black face character as its logo. The entrance doors to the three restaurants that existed were the mouth of the black face bellhop. This glass was made in the 1980s.

| C6929 | Coon's Chicken Inn | 6 - 12 |

COUNTRY KITCHEN, Pepsi, (also see NORMAN ROCKWELL)
| C6930 | Boy and Girl (the Country Kitchen logo) | 8 - 12 |

COUNTRY TIME LEMONADE
| C6940 | Frosted glass | 5 - 8 |

CREATURE FROM THE BLACK LAGOON (see UNIVERSAL MONSTERS)

CUDDLES (see WALTER LANTZ)

CURRIER AND IVES COLLECTOR SERIES, Arby's, 1978
C9001	1 of 4, The Road in Winter	2 - 4
C9002	2 of 4, Winter Pastime	2 - 4
C9003	3 of 4, American Farm in Winter	2 - 4

| C6922 - C6924 | | C6929 |

| C6925 - C6927 | C6917 | C6916 | C6915 | C6919 | C6920 | C6918 |

C9001　　C9002　　C9003　　C9004

D1000　　D1001　　D1002　　D1003

C9010　　C9011　　C9012　　C9013

D1010　　D1015　　D1021　　D0500

C9020　　C9021　　C9022　　C9023

D1030　　C6940　　C6930　　D1020

C9004	4 of 4, Frozen Up	2 - 4

CURRIER AND IVES COLLECTOR SERIES, Arby's, no date

The title appears on the front of the glass in this series.

C9010	The Sleigh Race	2 - 4
C9011	American Homestead Winter	2 - 4
C9012	Christmas Snow	2 - 4
C9013	Winter in the Country	2 - 4

CURRIER AND IVES COLLECTOR SERIES, Arby's, 1981

C9020	The Road in Winter	2 - 4
C9021	Winter Pastime	2 - 4
C9022	American Farm in Winter	2 - 4
C9023	Frozen Up	2 - 4

DAD'S ROOT BEER

D0500	Don't say Root Beer, say have a...	

DAVY CROCKETT (also see DISNEY)

DAFFY DUCK (see WARNER BROTHERS)

DAIRY QUEEN COLLECTOR SERIES, 1976

D1000	Girl & boy w/ice cream cones	8 - 12
D1001	Girl & boy on horse	8 - 12
D1002	Girl & boy on rail car	8 - 12
D1003	Girl & boy on swing	8 - 12

DAIRY QUEEN Single Glasses

D1010	Dairy Queen logo, short	4 - 6
D1015	Dairy Queen girl	4 - 6
D1020	Dairy Queen winter scene, w/Dr. Pepper	6 - 10
D1021	Banana Split, stained glass look	4 - 6

DANIEL BOONE

D1030	Daniel Boone fighting Indian	10 - 15

DAVY CROCKETT (also see DISNEY)

DAVY CROCKETT, Welch's, no date (mid '50s)

These glasses come in white, blue, orange, red, yellow and green.

D1050	"Ole Grumpy Bear Made His Mistake"	10 - 20
D1051	"Davy Fought This War You See"	10 - 20
D1052	"Steady Nerves and Trigger Squeeze"	10 - 20
D1053	"Davy Had A Creed"	10 - 20
D1054	"When Davy Met An Indian Foe"	10 - 20
D1055	"Davy Was A Happy Boy"	10 - 20

DAVY CROCKETT "Stretched-hide sign glasses"

Variations in color, size, style of glass, scene and wording on the stretched-hide sign make these glasses extremely difficult to describe. They were used as containers for peanut butter, cheese spread, and jelly.

Wording of sign variations:
　"Davy Crockett/1786 - 1836"

D1050 - D1055

D1279 **D1386**

D1277

Davey Crockett "Stretched Hide" - variation of scenes and sizes

D1085 **D1276** **D1385**

D1381 **D1384** *size variation* **D1280**

D1275

"Davy Crockett/Indian Fighter/1786 - 1836"
"Davy Crockett/Hero of The Alamo/1786 - 1836"
"Davy Crockett/Indian Fighter/Statesmen/Hero of the Alamo"
"Davy Crockett/Indian Fighter/Hero of the Alamo"

Size Variations:
   $3^3/_4$", $4^5/_8$", $4^3/_4$", $5^5/_8$", $5^1/_4$" & 6"

Color Variations:
   Opaque sign – green, red, blue, yellow, orange & white. All scenes with opaque signs are brown & yellow.
   See through sign – red, black, white, yellow & blue. Scenes with see through signs are single color drawings in white, yellow, green, brown or red.

Scene Variations:

D1060	Indians by Campfire, Davy on a Horse	8 - 25
D1065	Davy & Friend in a Canoe, Davy on a Horse	8 - 25
D1070	Davy & Friend in a Canoe, Indians in a Canoe	8 - 25
D1075	Indian on a Rock, Davy Fighting an Indian	8 - 25
D1080	Indian on a Rock, Davy Fighting a Bear	8 - 25
D1085	Davy Fighting Mexican Soldier, Alamo	8 - 25
D1090	Davy Making Peace, Indians by Campfire	8 - 25
D1095	Davy Fighting Indian on Horse	8 - 25
D1100	Davy Shooting at Mexicans, Mexican Soldier Falling	8 - 25
D1105	Davy & Friend in Canoe, Indian on Horse	8 - 25

DAVY CROCKETT (comes in 4 sizes, various colors)

D1150	"Coonskin Congressman, Went to Washington 1822"	6 - 12
D1151	"American Pioneer, Grew up in the Forest"	6 - 12
D1152	"Great American, Defender of the Alamo"	6 - 12
D1153	"Backwoods Boy, Born 1786 Limestone, TN"	6 - 12

DAVY CROCKETT Single Glasses

D1275	Davy Crockett, black & brown line drawings, part of a pitcher & tumbler set	
	Pitcher	15 - 25
	Tumbler	8 - 15
D1276	Davy Crockett, green w/white line drawings, part of a pitcher & tumbler set	
	Pitcher	15 - 25
	Tumbler	8 - 15
D1277	Davy Crockett, "Holiday Freeze", tall frosted	12 - 20
D1278	Davy Crockett, 1955, tri panel	12 - 20
D1279	Davy Crockett, "Drink Oatman's Good Milk"	12 - 20
D1280	Davy Crockett, tall yellow & white jar style	8 - 12
D1381	Davy Crockett, standing w/rifle	8 - 15
D1382	Davy Crockett, riding a horse, yellow	8 - 15
D1383	Davy Crockett, same as D1382, juice glass	8 - 12
D1384	Davy Crockett, ribbed base, wrap around scene	8 - 12
	All show Davy in canoe, Indian on a horse. Three different sizes, at least four different colors.	
D1385	Davy Crockett, "Merion Sport Shop" ad	12 - 20
D1386	Davy Crockett "Searles Dairy" ad	40 - 60

DENNIS THE MENACE

D1390	That settles it – You're going to be an only child	15 - 30
D1391	This is my mother	15 - 30
D1392	Would you mind telling my little boy?	15 - 20
D1393	You didn't say "Open the darn door"	15 - 30
D1394	Notice how steady my hand is	15 - 30
D1395	I don't think you're funny	15 - 30

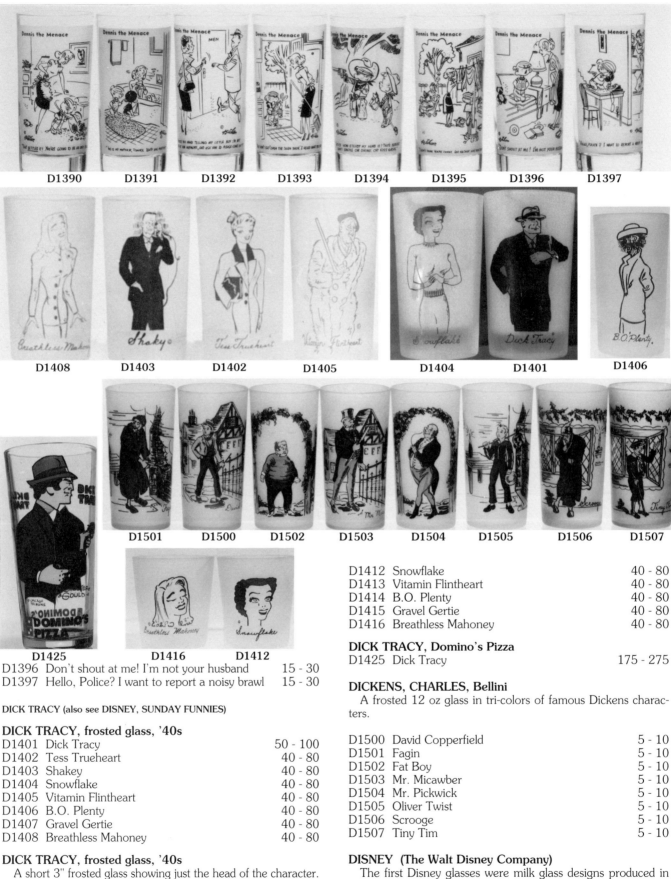

| D1390 | D1391 | D1392 | D1393 | D1394 | D1395 | D1396 | D1397 |

| D1408 | D1403 | D1402 | D1405 | D1404 | D1401 | D1406 |

| D1501 | D1500 | D1502 | D1503 | D1504 | D1505 | D1506 | D1507 |

| D1425 | D1416 | D1412 |

D1396 Don't shout at me! I'm not your husband   15 - 30
D1397 Hello, Police? I want to report a noisy brawl   15 - 30

DICK TRACY (also see DISNEY, SUNDAY FUNNIES)

DICK TRACY, frosted glass, '40s
D1401	Dick Tracy	50 - 100
D1402	Tess Trueheart	40 - 80
D1403	Shakey	40 - 80
D1404	Snowflake	40 - 80
D1405	Vitamin Flintheart	40 - 80
D1406	B.O. Plenty	40 - 80
D1407	Gravel Gertie	40 - 80
D1408	Breathless Mahoney	40 - 80

DICK TRACY, frosted glass, '40s
A short 3" frosted glass showing just the head of the character.

D1409	Dick Tracy	40 - 80
D1410	Tess Trueheart	40 - 80
D1411	Shakey	40 - 80
D1412	Snowflake	40 - 80
D1413	Vitamin Flintheart	40 - 80
D1414	B.O. Plenty	40 - 80
D1415	Gravel Gertie	40 - 80
D1416	Breathless Mahoney	40 - 80

DICK TRACY, Domino's Pizza
D1425	Dick Tracy	175 - 275

DICKENS, CHARLES, Bellini
A frosted 12 oz glass in tri-colors of famous Dickens characters.

D1500	David Copperfield	5 - 10
D1501	Fagin	5 - 10
D1502	Fat Boy	5 - 10
D1503	Mr. Micawber	5 - 10
D1504	Mr. Pickwick	5 - 10
D1505	Oliver Twist	5 - 10
D1506	Scrooge	5 - 10
D1507	Tiny Tim	5 - 10

DISNEY (The Walt Disney Company)
The first Disney glasses were milk glass designs produced in 1931. Two different are known, but others in the set are likely to exist.
The Owens-Illinois Glass Co. of Toledo, Ohio became a Disney licensee in 1936. They produced promotional glasses

D2001	D2000	D2010	D2013	D2019	D2022	D2025	D2028

D2010	D1016	D2019	D2022	D2025	D2028			D2016

size variations

and milk bottles featuring the Disney characters. The company made Disney glasses until the *Lady and the Tramp* series in 1955.

Peter Pan Peanut Butter acquired the rights to Disney's *Peter Pan* in 1953, but used character images only on the lids.

Disneyland was featured on glass issues in 1955 and has been the subject of promotional and souvenir glasses ever since.

Sleeping Beauty was the subject of Big Top Peanut Butter glasses in 1959.

The '60s saw relatively few glasses, but when Walt Disney World opened in 1971 the number of theme park souvenir glasses accelerated.

The *Jungle Book* series and ones from *The Rescuers* were some of the earliest and most colorful of the many fast-food sets. In all, nearly 100 different Disney issues are listed ... many just single glasses. Some issued in 1989 were clear plastic perhaps signaling a trend for the future.

This is the largest section in the book. The organization chosen is basically chronological. Single and two-color glasses are earlier ones.

MICKEY MOUSE, Milk Glass, Borgfeldt, 1931

D2000	Waving arms	50 - 150
D2001	Walking away	50 - 150

CARTOON CHARACTER, First Dairy Series, 1936

The Disney dairy promotion was one of the most successful character glass promotions ever done. Characters also appeared on glass milk bottles.

All glasses in the first series come in two sizes – 4 1/2" and 4 3/4" – and also came in pedestal shape. Values fall in the same range.

Horace has been found in a juice size 3 1/2" and in a different design. Colors are the same for each glass in this series.

The same images also appear on a short stout Bosco glass and are valued at 50% more.

D2010	Mickey	30 - 50
D2013	Minnie	30 - 50
D2016	Donald Duck	30 - 50
D2019	Pluto	30 - 50
D2022	Clarabelle	30 - 50
D2025	Horace	30 - 50
D2028	Funny Bunny	30 - 50

CARTOON CHARACTER, Second Dairy Series, 1936-37

Glasses found from the second series have been the same 4 3/4" size, but the chance of the smaller size exists because these glasses are rarer than the first series. One example of a smaller image has been found and is shown for comparison.

D2030	Elmer	30 - 50
D2031	1st Pig	30 - 50
D2032	2nd Pig	30 - 50
D2033	3rd Pig	30 - 50
D2034	Big Bad Wolf	30 - 50

CARTOON CHARACTER, 1936

Different poses than first dairy series. The Durkee Famous Foods organization of Berkeley, CA packaged mayonnaise in these drinking glasses. The new designs were developed by the Owens-Illinois Pacific Coast Co. and Walt Disney as reported in *Milk Plant Monthly*, August 1936.

D2040	Clarabelle Cow, standing facing left	100 - 200
D2041	Donald Duck, standing, facing left & waving right hand	100 - 200
D2042	The Goof, standing facing right	100 - 200
D2043	Horace Horsecollar, facing left	100 - 200
D2044	Mickey Mouse, standing, facing right	100 - 200
D2045	Minnie Mouse, standing, facing right, looks as if she's thumbing a ride	100 - 200
D2046	Pluto, running, facing left	100 - 200

CARTOON CHARACTER, 1936

Different poses than first dairy series.

D2050	Donald, blue, facing right, raising left hand	40 - 80
D2051	The Goof, green, on knee	40 - 80
D2052	Mickey, black, facing right	40 - 80
D2053	Minnie, black, w/umbrella	40 - 80
D2054	Pluto, brown, on hind feet	40 - 80

41

D2050   D2051   D2052   D2053   D2054

D2030   D2031   D2032   D2033

D2060   D2062   D2064   D2066   D2067

D2075

D2075   D2034

D2090   D2091   D2092   D2094   D2095   D2096

D2090

D2095   D2065

D2055 Horace, brown, sitting on a crate   40 - 80

CARTOON CHARACTER, Musical Notes Series, 1936-37

This series is said to come in bi-color and multi-color and in several different sizes – 4¼" and 4¾". Some are dated and some are not.

D2060	Donald, playing drums	60 - 100
D2061	The Goof	60 - 100
D2062	Horace Horsecollar, playing trumpet	60 - 100
D2063	Mickey	60 - 100
D2064	Minnie, playing violin	60 - 100
D2065	Pluto, busting through drums	60 - 100

Another variety of the above glasses featured different images and bold letters under the image.

| D2066 | Horace Horsecollar, playing flute | 60 - 100 |
| D2067 | The Goof, playing saxophone | 60 - 100 |

GLOBETROTTER SERIES, 1937

This rare series was issued by Prevly Dairy and Mitchell Milk, two of a handful of dairies to use this promotion designed primarily for regional bakeries. Three different glasses are known; however, there were 24 different Globetrotter locations featured on the map used in the promotion.

| D2075 | Globetrotter glasses, each | 75 - 125 |

ATHLETIC SERIES, 1937

Comes in a bi-color modified pedestal and a 4¾" plain glass in a single color. Some came with ads on them.

D2090	Donald, kicking football	40 - 80
D2091	Horace, skiing	40 - 80
D2092	Minnie, tennis	40 - 80
D2094	Mickey, playing baseball	40 - 80
D2095	The Goof, golfing	40 - 80
D2096	Pluto, hunting	40 - 80

SNOW WHITE AND THE SEVEN DWARFS, First Dairy Series, 1938

Glasses in this series from Walt Disney's first animated feature came in a wide variety of sizes – (3½", 4⅜", 4½", 4⅝", 4¾" & 6") – and colors – red, light blue, dark blue, green, black, orange, light orange, red brown, yellow and white have been seen.

D2100	Snow White	15 - 30
D2101	Sleepy	15 - 30
D2102	Dopey	15 - 30
D2103	Doc	15 - 30
D2104	Sneezy	15 - 30
D2105	Happy	15 - 30
D2106	Bashful	15 - 30
D2107	Grumpy	15 - 30
D2108	Tray for set	100 - 150

SNOW WHITE AND THE SEVEN DWARFS, Second Dairy Series – Musical Notes Series, 1938

Glasses in this series depict the characters as they appeared in the "Silly Song" sequence from Walt Disney's first animated feature. Each glass is a single color with eight different colors in

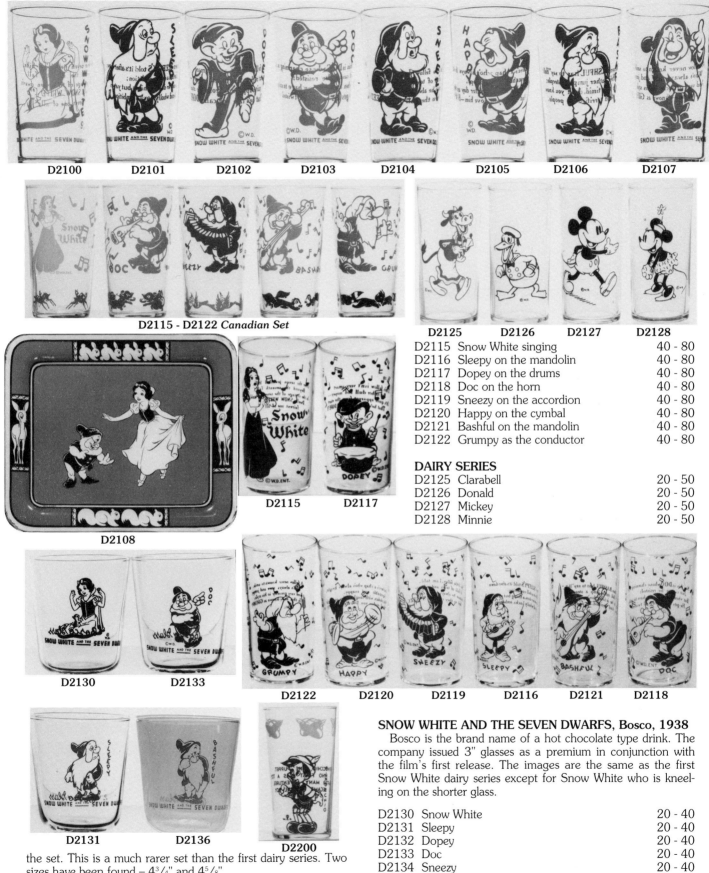

| | D2100 | D2101 | D2102 | D2103 | D2104 | D2105 | D2106 | D2107 |

D2115 - D2122 *Canadian Set*

| D2125 | D2126 | D2127 | D2128 |

D2115	Snow White singing	40 - 80
D2116	Sleepy on the mandolin	40 - 80
D2117	Dopey on the drums	40 - 80
D2118	Doc on the horn	40 - 80
D2119	Sneezy on the accordion	40 - 80
D2120	Happy on the cymbal	40 - 80
D2121	Bashful on the mandolin	40 - 80
D2122	Grumpy as the conductor	40 - 80

DAIRY SERIES

D2125	Clarabell	20 - 50
D2126	Donald	20 - 50
D2127	Mickey	20 - 50
D2128	Minnie	20 - 50

D2108

| D2115 | D2117 |

| D2130 | D2133 |

| D2122 | D2120 | D2119 | D2116 | D2121 | D2118 |

SNOW WHITE AND THE SEVEN DWARFS, Bosco, 1938

Bosco is the brand name of a hot chocolate type drink. The company issued 3" glasses as a premium in conjunction with the film's first release. The images are the same as the first Snow White dairy series except for Snow White who is kneeling on the shorter glass.

D2130	Snow White	20 - 40
D2131	Sleepy	20 - 40
D2132	Dopey	20 - 40
D2133	Doc	20 - 40
D2134	Sneezy	20 - 40
D2135	Happy	20 - 40
D2136	Bashful	20 - 40
D2137	Grumpy	20 - 40

| D2131 | D2136 | D2200 |

the set. This is a much rarer set than the first dairy series. Two sizes have been found – 4³/₄" and 4⁵/₈".

There is also a Canadian set, same as the U.S. set only there are different animal impressions on the bottom of the glass. Values for these glasses are 40 - 60.

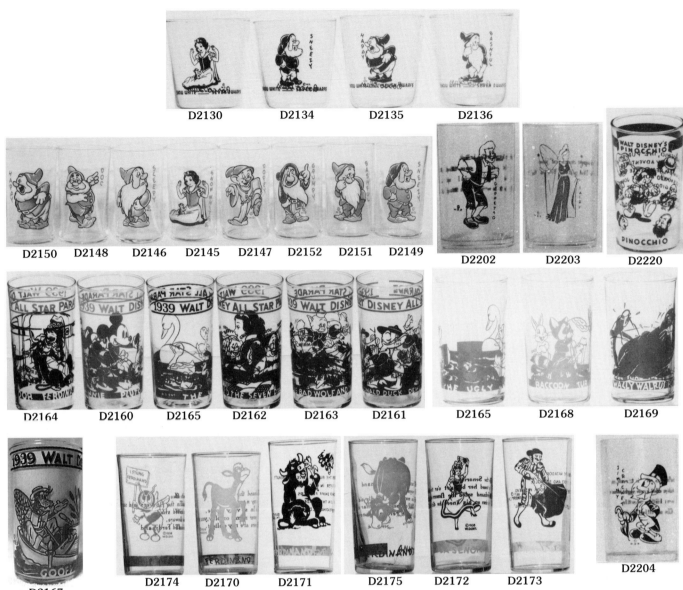

D2130   D2134   D2135   D2136

D2150 D2148 D2146 D2145 D2147 D2152 D2151 D2149

D2202   D2203   D2220

D2164   D2160   D2165   D2162   D2163   D2161

D2165   D2168   D2169

D2167

D2174   D2170   D2171   D2175   D2172   D2173

D2204

SNOW WHITE AND THE SEVEN DWARFS, 1938

There is a set of eight Snow White and the Seven Dwarfs tumblers with full color decals. This set was probably sold in department stores.

D2145	Snow White	40 - 80
D2146	Sleepy	40 - 80
D2147	Dopey	40 - 80
D2148	Doc	40 - 80
D2149	Sneezy	40 - 80
D2150	Happy	40 - 80
D2151	Bashful	40 - 80
D2152	Grumpy	40 - 80

WALT DISNEY ALL STAR PARADE, 1939

The main cartoon characters returned in this 1939 series of 10 glasses which were used as dairy premiums. The first six glasses were also sold as a boxed set in stores and are more common. Some dairies may have used the short set too. Each glass has two colors.

There is a variety that has the same images, but no banner on top.

D2160	Mickey, Minnie, Pluto	20 - 50
D2161	Donald, Donna (Daisy), Huey, Louie, Dewey	20 - 50

D2162	Snow White and the Seven Dwarfs	20 - 50
D2163	The Big Bad Wolf and the Three Pigs	20 - 50
D2164	Ferdinand the Bull	20 - 50
D2165	The Ugly Duckling	20 - 50
D2166	The Greedy Pig and Colt	50 - 75
D2167	Goofy and Wilbur	50 - 75
D2168	Raccoon, Turtle, Fawn, Rabbit	50 - 75
D2169	Wally Walrus and Penguins	50 - 75

FERDINAND THE BULL, 1939

This was a dairy premium series and came in three sizes – $4^3/_8$", $4^1/_2$", and $4^3/_4$".

D2170	Young Ferdinand	30 - 60
D2171	Ferdinand the Bull	30 - 60
D2172	La Senorita	30 - 60
D2173	Matador	30 - 60
D2174	The Bee	30 - 60
D2175	Ferdinand and his Mother	30 - 60

PINOCCHIO, 1940

This is the largest U.S. set of Disney glasses ever issued ... a 12-week dairy promotion with a new glass each week. Each glass is a single color and the color is consistent for each char-

44

D2210   D2202   D2208   D2203   D2209   D2207   D2201   D2204   D2200

D2221   D2222   D2206   D2211   D2205   D2230   D2232   D2233   D2234

D2230-D2235 as the Dumbo series appeared on promotional material without lines at top.

Kay Kamen Art Director, Lou Lispi, shown with the Owens-Illinois representative, holding the Thumper glass.

acter. Comes in at least four different sizes – 4", 4$\frac{1}{2}$", 4$\frac{5}{8}$" and 4$\frac{3}{4}$".

There is a Canadian set which is the same as the U.S. one only there are hats over the top of the glass (similar to musical notes all over the glass). These are valued at 40 - 60 each.

D2200	Pinocchio	15 - 25
D2201	Coachman	15 - 25
D2202	Geppetto	15 - 25
D2203	Blue Fairy	15 - 25
D2204	Jiminy Cricket	15 - 25
D2205	Cleo the Goldfish	15 - 25
D2206	Stromboli	15 - 25
D2207	Monstro the Whale	15 - 25
D2208	Gideon	15 - 25
D2209	Lampwick	15 - 25
D2210	Figaro	15 - 25
D2211	J. Worthington Foulfellow	15 - 25

DISNEY CLASSICS, 1940-41

This rare series is similar to the Walt Disney All Star Parade series, but each glass is only one color. Total number of glasses in series is unknown.

D2220	Pinocchio	30 - 50
D2221	Snow White	30 - 50
D2222	The Ugly Duckling Happy Easter	30 - 50

DUMBO, 1941

A rare six glass dairy promotion depicted characters from the September 1941 film. These are exceptional two-color glasses.

D2230	Dumbo, flying	50 - 100
D2231	Dumbo and the Stork	50 - 100

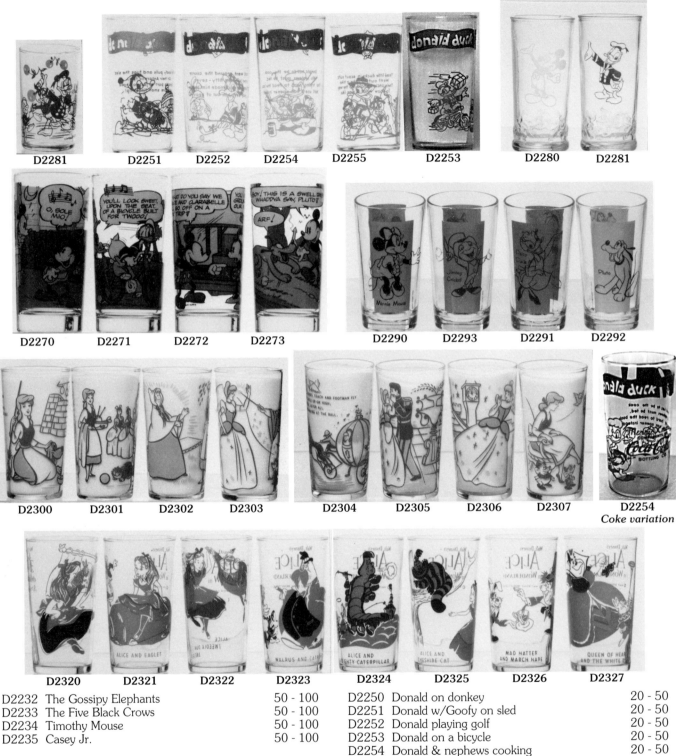

| D2281 | D2251 | D2252 | D2254 | D2255 | D2253 | D2280 | D2281 |

| D2270 | D2271 | D2272 | D2273 |

| D2290 | D2293 | D2291 | D2292 |

| D2300 | D2301 | D2302 | D2303 |

| D2304 | D2305 | D2306 | D2307 |

D2254
Coke variation

| D2320 | D2321 | D2322 | D2323 | D2324 | D2325 | D2326 | D2327 |

D2232	The Gossipy Elephants	50 - 100
D2233	The Five Black Crows	50 - 100
D2234	Timothy Mouse	50 - 100
D2235	Casey Jr.	50 - 100

BAMBI

A Bambi series was designed and at least some prototype glasses made. Character merchandise art director, Lou Lispi, remembers doing the glasses and the unknown representative from Owens-Illinois is pictured holding a Thumper glass. It is unknown if the glasses were produced or if the promotion was canceled due to war material shortages.

DONALD DUCK, 1942

This set also came with "Merry Christmas compliments of the Coca Cola Bottling Company" printed on the glasses. These are rare and are valued at 100 - 200 each.

D2250	Donald on donkey	20 - 50
D2251	Donald w/Goofy on sled	20 - 50
D2252	Donald playing golf	20 - 50
D2253	Donald on a bicycle	20 - 50
D2254	Donald & nephews cooking	20 - 50
D2255	Donald & nephews as Boy Scouts	20 - 50

MICKEY MOUSE COLLECTION

This set was sold in a carton of four.

D2270	Mickey & Minnie, "O Sole Mio"	10 - 20
D2271	Donald & Daisy, "A Bicycle Built For Two"	10 - 20
D2272	Minnie, "What do you say we get Horace and Clarabelle to go off on a campin' trip?"	10 - 20
D2273	"Boy! This is a swell day! Whaddya say, Pluto?" "Arf!"	10 - 20

| D2332 | D2337 | D2331 | D2336 | D2333 | D2330 |

Front *Back*

The Lady and the Tramp series has a standard design on all glasses, with a character featured on the back.

| D2350 | D2354 | D2355 | D2356 | D2357 |

CARTOON CHARACTERS
Base with characters molded in glass. Probably a '40s food container of some sort. Line drawing in different colors.

| D2280 | Mickey | 20 - 25 |
| D2281 | Donald | 20 - 25 |

DOUBLE CHARACTERS,
in color background
These are thick glasses of the type used by food packagers. The images are late '40s or early '50s. Comes in 5" & 6".

D2290	Mickey & Minnie, pink	15 - 20
D2291	Donald & Daisy, orange	15 - 20
D2292	Goofy & Pluto, yellow	15 - 20
D2293	Pinocchio & Jiminy Cricket, blue	15 - 20

CINDERELLA, 1950
Comes in $4^1/4$", $4^5/8$" and $5^1/4$". The $5^1/4$" glass is valued at 25% more. There is also a Canadian set in a different color combination.

D2300	#1	Cinderella w/dog & cat	8 - 15
D2301	#2	Cinderella attending stepsisters	8 - 15
D2302	#3	Godmother appearing	8 - 15
D2303	#4	Godmother creating dress	8 - 15
D2304	#5	Coach & horses	8 - 15
D2305	#6	Cinderella dancing w/Prince	8 - 15
D2306	#7	Clock strikes twelve	8 - 15
D2307	#8	The slipper fits	8 - 15

ALICE IN WONDERLAND
D2320	#1	Alice	15 - 40
D2321	#2	Alice & Eaglet	15 - 40
D2322	#3	Alice & Tweedle Dee & Tweedle Dum	15 - 40
D2323	#4	Alice & Walrus and Carpenter	15 - 40

D2324	#5	Alice & Caterpillar	15 - 40
D2325	#6	Alice & Cheshire Cat	15 - 40
D2326	#7	Mad Hatter & March Hare	15 - 40
D2327	#8	Queen of Hearts & Rabbit	15 - 40

PETER PAN, Canada, 1965
Some glasses in this series came in both 12 oz and 16 oz sizes; while others were issued in one size only.

D2330	Peter Pan, 12 & 16 oz	40 - 60
D2331	Captain Hook, 12 & 16 oz	40 - 60
D2332	Mr. Smee, 12 & 16 oz	40 - 60
D2333	Wendy and Michael, 12 & 16 oz	40 - 60
D2334	Tinkerbell, 12 oz only	40 - 60
D2335	Le Crocodile, 12 oz only	40 - 60
D2336	Big Chief, 16 oz only	40 - 60
D2337	John, 16 oz only	40 - 60

DISNEYLAND JUICE SET, 1955
Has logos for each land on the reverse.

D2345	Mickey Frontierland	10 - 20
D2346	Tinker Bell Fantasyland	10 - 20
D2347	Donald Adventureland	10 - 20
D2348	Goofy Tomorrowland	10 - 20

LADY & THE TRAMP SERIES
Lady and Tramp's images appear on the front of all of the glasses in this set with the supporting characters in silhouette or

| D2404 | D2405 | D2401 | D2402 | D2403 | D2400 | | D2470 | C2474 |

| D2406 | D2407 | D2408 | D2409 | D2410 | | D2411 | D2413 | D2414 |

| D2445 | D2446 | D2447 | D2448 | | D2451 | D2453 | D2455 |

two color drawings on the reverse. There are two sizes, 5¼" & 6¼".

D2350	Jock, the Scotty	30 - 80
D2351	Trusty, the Hound	30 - 80
D2352	Bull, the Bulldog	30 - 80
D2353	Pedro, the Chihuahua	30 - 80
D2354	Peg, the Pomeranian	30 - 80
D2355	Si & Am, the Cats	30 - 80
D2356	Toughy, the Mutt	30 - 80
D2357	Dachsie, the Dachshund	30 - 80

SLEEPING BEAUTY, U.S., 1958

D2400	Sleeping Beauty	12 - 20
D2401	Briar Rose	12 - 20
D2402	Prince	12 - 20
D2403	Samson (horse)	12 - 20
D2404	Fairies – Flora, Fauna & Merryweather	12 - 20
D2405	Maleficent	12 - 20

SLEEPING BEAUTY, Canada, 1959

D2406	#1 Briar Rose & forest friends	20 - 30
D2407	#2 Briar Rose dancing w/Prince	20 - 30
D2408	#3 Fairies making dress	20 - 30
D2409	#4 Princess finds spinning wheel	20 - 30
D2410	#5 Everyone falls asleep	20 - 30
D2411	#6 Prince comes to the castle	20 - 30
D2412	#7 Prince finds Sleeping Beauty	20 - 30
D2413	#8 Prince kisses Sleeping Beauty	20 - 30
D2414	#9 Sleeping Beauty begins to awake	20 - 30

D2415	#10	20 - 30
D2416	#11 Prince & Sleeping Beauty dancing	20 - 30
D2417	#12	20 - 30

WINNIE THE POOH, Sears

D2445	Winnie the Pooh for President	5 - 10
D2446	Pooh & Friends, planting a tree	5 - 10
D2447	Winnie the Pooh & Friends, honey pot	5 - 10
D2448	Pooh & Friends, looking at butterfly	5 - 10

WINNIE THE POOH, Canada, 1965
These glasses featured a line drawing in a single color.

D2450	# 1 Winnie the Pooh	10 - 20
D2451	# 2 Rabbit	10 - 20
D2452	# 3 Tigger	10 - 20
D2453	# 4 Kanga & Roo	10 - 20
D2454	# 5 Piglet	10 - 20
D2455	# 6 Owl	10 - 20
D2465	Happy Birthday Winnie, Canadian	8 - 12

WINNIE THE POOH, Canada, 1965
This numbered set of six 4⅞" glasses were bi-color.

D2470	#1 Pooh as cloud	15 - 25
D2471	#2	15 - 25
D2472	#3	15 - 25
D2473	#4	15 - 25
D2474	#5 Eeyore has a Birthday, yellow & red	15 - 25
D2475	#6 Kanga-Roo	15 - 25

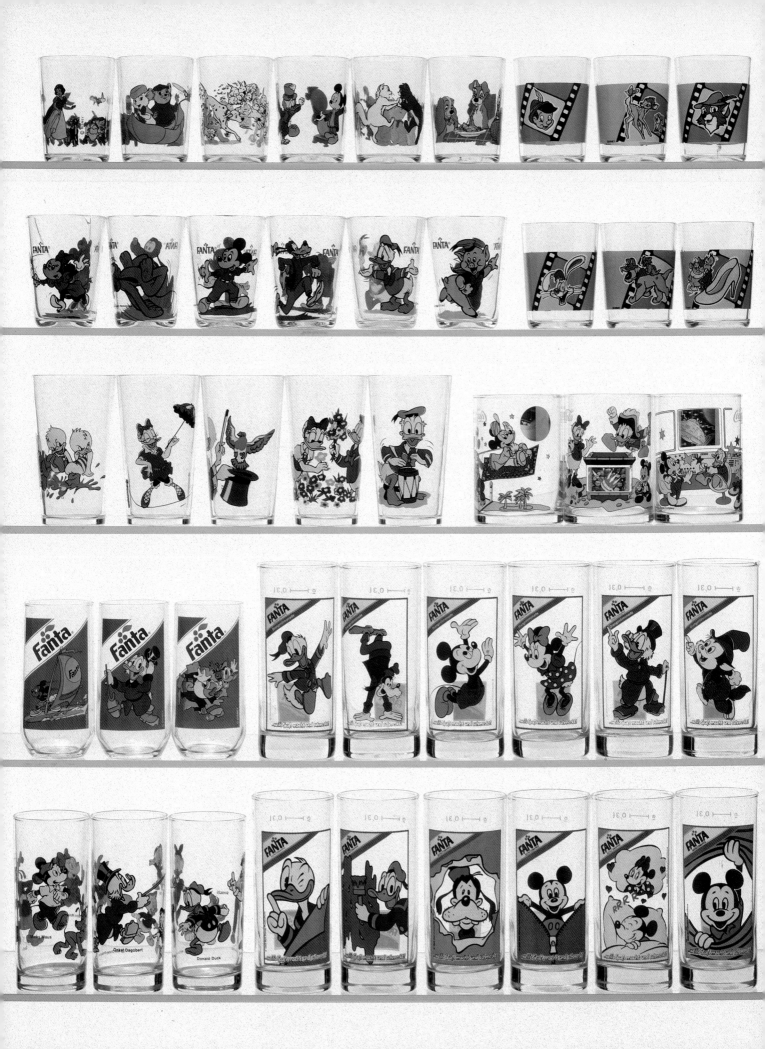

D2500   D2501   D2502   D2503   D2504   D2505

D2506   D2507   D2508

D2520   D2521   D2522   D2523   D2524   D2525

D2511   D2510   D2509

DISNEYLAND LIMITED EDITION, Coke

This fast-food series was issued in western states by Coke. The Disneyland set features the Sleeping Beauty Castle.

D2500	Mickey	10 - 20
D2501	Minnie	10 - 20
D2502	Donald	10 - 20
D2503	Pluto	10 - 20
D2504	Goofy	10 - 20
D2505	Dumbo	10 - 20

WALT DISNEY WORLD LIMITED EDITION, Coke

Same exact image as the Disneyland set except for the castle. The Walt Disney World set features the Cinderella Castle.

D2506	Mickey	20 - 30
D2507	Minnie	20 - 30
D2508	Donald	20 - 30
D2509	Pluto	20 - 30
D2510	Goofy	20 - 30
D2511	Dumbo	20 - 30

WALT DISNEY WORLD SOUVENIR SET

Images for the first five glasses are the same as the Disneyland Limited Edition series.

Four glasses were available as souvenirs when Walt Disney World opened in October 1971. Goofy and Winnie the Pooh

D2521   D2533

were added in 1972. Sears had an exclusive license for Pooh at the time. When Disney's Character Merchandise Division reminded the park of this fact the glass was withdrawn.

D2520	Mickey	8 - 12
D2521	Minnie	8 - 12
D2522	Donald	8 - 12
D2523	Pluto	8 - 12
D2524	Goofy	15 - 20
D2525	Winnie the Pooh	20 - 30

The same images, plus Big Al and Mickey as a Pirate were available on glass mugs. The Pirate mugs were available with Disneyland and Walt Disney World imprints.

D2526   D2527   D2530   D2532   D2534

D2551   D2550   D2552   D2553

D2562   D2563   D2558

D2554   D2556   D2557   D2555

D2561   D2560   D2558   D2559

D2526 Mickey	10 - 15
D2527 Minnie	10 - 15
D2528 Donald	10 - 15
D2529 Pluto	10 - 15
D2530 Goofy	15 - 20
D2531 Winnie the Pooh	15 - 20
D2532 Big Al	10 - 15
D2533 Pirates of the Caribbean	10 - 15
D2534 Same as D2533, but amber	10 - 15

JUNGLE BOOK, Pepsi

Nowhere on these glasses does the name "Jungle Book" appear, nor is there a date on the glass. You would have to be familiar with the characters of this Disney version of the Rudyard Kipling story.

D2550 Bagheera, the panther	40 - 90
D2551 Baloo, the bear	40 - 90
D2552 Colonel Hathi, the elephant	40 - 90
D2553 Kaa, the snake	40 - 90
D2554 King Louie, the monkey	40 - 90

D2594   D2595   D2597 - 1977

D2580   D2581   D2582   D2583

D2596 - 1977   D2596 - 1978   D2597 - 1978

D2584   D2585   D2586   D2587

D2590	D2591	D2592	D2593
D2608	D2657	D2659
D2610	D2611	D2612
D2616	D2617	D2618	D2619
D2613	D2614	D2615

D2555	Mowgli, the boy	40 - 90
D2556	Rama, the wolf	40 - 90
D2557	Shere Khan, the tiger	40 - 90

JUNGLE BOOK, Pepsi, Canada

The glasses do have the name "Jungle Book" on the glass.

D2558	Mowgli, #1	50 - 100
D2559	Shere Khan, #2	50 - 100
D2560	Baloo, #3	50 - 100
D2561	Bagheera, #4	50 - 100
D2562	Flunkey, #5	50 - 100
D2563	King Louie, #6	50 - 100

THE RESCUERS, Pepsi, 1977

D2580	Bernard	12 - 20
D2581	Bianca	12 - 20
D2582	Brutus & Nero	12 - 20
D2583	Evinrude	12 - 20
D2584	Madame Medusa	20 - 50
D2585	Orville	12 - 20
D2586	Penny	12 - 20
D2587	Rufus	30 - 50

HAPPY BIRTHDAY MICKEY 50 YEARS OF MAGIC, Pepsi, 1977-1978

This set was first released in the Midwest in 1977. The design was slightly changed and reissued nationwide in 1978. The 1977 version has more of a "squash & stretch" animation look whereas the 1978 set carries an illustration look. The exclusion of Daisy & Donald and Horace & Clarabelle from certain distribution areas makes them more difficult to find. The 1977 glasses are 50% more valuable.

D2590	Mickey	12 - 20
D2591	Minnie	12 - 20
D2592	Donald & Daisy	20 - 30
D2593	Donald	12 - 20
D2594	Pluto	12 - 20
D2595	Goofy	12 - 20
D2596	Scrooge	12 - 20
D2597	Horace & Clarabelle	20 - 30

MICKEY'S 50TH BIRTHDAY

This single glass was sold at theme parks and in 4-pack sets in stores.

D2608	Mickey lighting candles	7 - 10

WONDERFUL WORLD OF DISNEY SERIES, Pepsi

D2610	Alice in Wonderland	15 - 30
D2611	Bambi	15 - 30
D2612	Lady & Tramp	15 - 30
D2613	101 Dalmatians	15 - 30
D2614	Snow White & the Seven Dwarfs	15 - 30
D2615	Pinocchio	15 - 30

DISNEY ANIMATED CLASSICS, McDonald's and Coke, Canada

D2616	Peter Pan	15 - 30
D2617	Cinderella	15 - 30
D2618	Fantasia	15 - 30
D2619	Snow White & the Seven Dwarfs	15 - 30

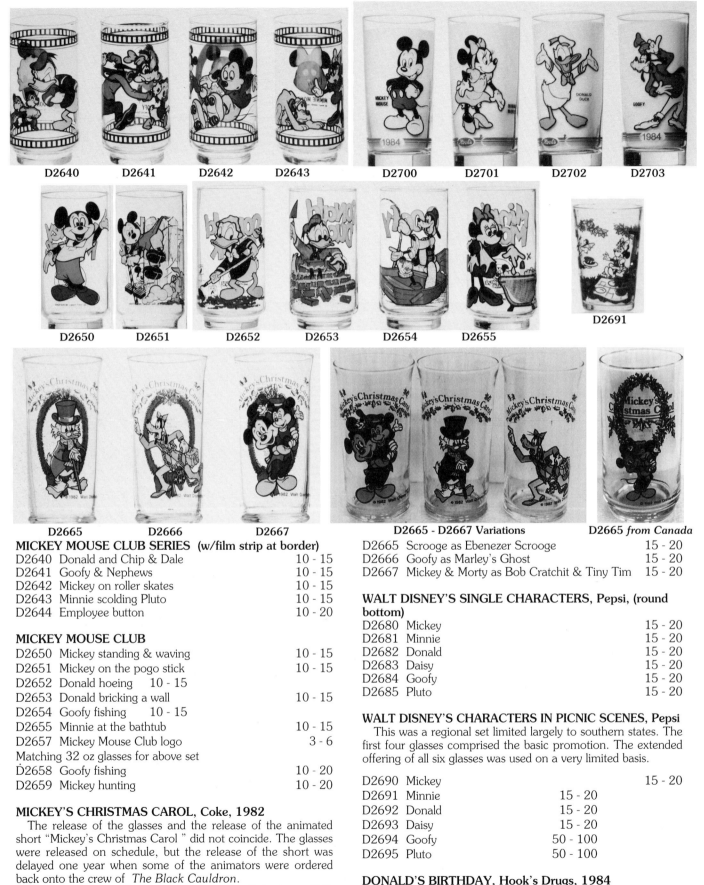

D2640	D2641	D2642	D2643

D2700	D2701	D2702	D2703		

D2650	D2651	D2652	D2653	D2654	D2655

D2691

D2665	D2666	D2667

D2665 - D2667 Variations   D2665 *from Canada*

MICKEY MOUSE CLUB SERIES (w/film strip at border)

D2640	Donald and Chip & Dale	10 - 15
D2641	Goofy & Nephews	10 - 15
D2642	Mickey on roller skates	10 - 15
D2643	Minnie scolding Pluto	10 - 15
D2644	Employee button	10 - 20

MICKEY MOUSE CLUB

D2650	Mickey standing & waving	10 - 15
D2651	Mickey on the pogo stick	10 - 15
D2652	Donald hoeing	10 - 15
D2653	Donald bricking a wall	10 - 15
D2654	Goofy fishing	10 - 15
D2655	Minnie at the bathtub	10 - 15
D2657	Mickey Mouse Club logo	3 - 6
Matching 32 oz glasses for above set		
D2658	Goofy fishing	10 - 20
D2659	Mickey hunting	10 - 20

MICKEY'S CHRISTMAS CAROL, Coke, 1982

The release of the glasses and the release of the animated short "Mickey's Christmas Carol" did not coincide. The glasses were released on schedule, but the release of the short was delayed one year when some of the animators were ordered back onto the crew of *The Black Cauldron*.

Glasses were issued with and without the Coke logo. U.S. issues featured a flair lip; glasses issued in Canada were a different shape and size with French writing on the back

D2665	Scrooge as Ebenezer Scrooge	15 - 20
D2666	Goofy as Marley's Ghost	15 - 20
D2667	Mickey & Morty as Bob Cratchit & Tiny Tim	15 - 20

WALT DISNEY'S SINGLE CHARACTERS, Pepsi, (round bottom)

D2680	Mickey	15 - 20
D2681	Minnie	15 - 20
D2682	Donald	15 - 20
D2683	Daisy	15 - 20
D2684	Goofy	15 - 20
D2685	Pluto	15 - 20

WALT DISNEY'S CHARACTERS IN PICNIC SCENES, Pepsi

This was a regional set limited largely to southern states. The first four glasses comprised the basic promotion. The extended offering of all six glasses was used on a very limited basis.

D2690	Mickey	15 - 20
D2691	Minnie	15 - 20
D2692	Donald	15 - 20
D2693	Daisy	15 - 20
D2694	Goofy	50 - 100
D2695	Pluto	50 - 100

DONALD'S BIRTHDAY, Hook's Drugs, 1984

The Hook's Drugs chain of Indiana issued this set to commemorate Donald's 50th birthday; however, nowhere on the glasses does it say anything about Donald's birthday.

D2680   D2681   D2682   D2683   D2684   D2685   D2705

D2690   D2691   D2692   D2693   D2694   D2695

D2720   D2721   D2722   D2723   D2738   D2736   D2737

D2700	Mickey	25 - 40	
D2701	Minnie	25 - 40	
D2702	Donald	25 - 40	
D2703	Goofy	25 - 40	

D2725	Red car	6 - 10
D2726	Yellow car	6 - 10
D2727	Green car	6 - 10
D2728	Blue car	6 - 10

MICKEY MOUSE JUICE SETS, 1987-89

A set of four juice glasses showing Minnie as a cheerleader & Mickey playing ball. A musical version is also available. These Anchor Hocking sets come with a carafe.

D2705	Athletic juice set, complete	10 - 15
D2706	Musical juice set, complete	10 - 15

THEME PARK JUICE SET

D2710	Mickey	5 - 8
D2711	Minnie	5 - 8
D2712	Goofy	5 - 8
D2713	Winnie the Pooh	5 - 8

MICKEY THROUGH THE YEARS, clear mugs, K-Mart

D2720	1928 Steamboat Willie	3 - 5
D2721	1937 Brave Little Tailor	3 - 5
D2722	1940 Fantasia	3 - 5
D2723	1955 Mickey Mouse Club	3 - 5

MICKEY & MINNIE IN CONVERTIBLE, Theme Park Set, 1988

The image on all four glasses is the same. Only the color of the car is different.

MICKEY THROUGH THE YEARS, Canada, 1988

This set was distributed by Sunoco in Canada.

D2730	1928 Steamboat Willie	5 - 8
D2731	1938 Magician Mickey	5 - 8
D2732	1940 Fantasia	5 - 8
D2733	1953 Mickey Mouse Club	5 - 8
D2734	1983 Christmas Carol	5 - 8
D2735	1988 Modern Mickey	5 - 8

EPCOT PROMOTIONAL SET

D2736	Mickey's Latin Carnival	25 - 40
D2737	Mickey's Safari Tours	25 - 40
D2738	Mickey's South Sea Sail Away	25 - 40

DISNEYLAND, McDonald's, 1989

This set was test marketed in the Joplin, MO area. There was no indication of a national release at time of publication.

D2740	Mickey at Tomorrowland	6 - 10
D2741	Minnie at Fantasyland	6 - 10
D2742	Donald at Critter Country	6 - 10
D2743	Goofy at Adventureland	6 - 10
D2746	Disenyland Souvenir, white background	6 - 10

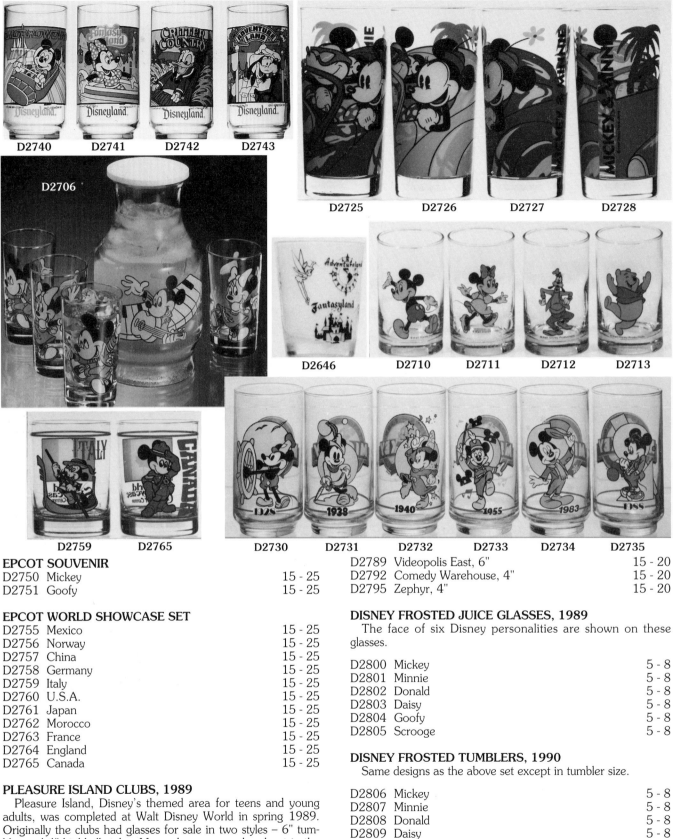

D2740 D2741 D2742 D2743

D2706

D2725 D2726 D2727 D2728

D2646 D2710 D2711 D2712 D2713

D2759 D2765

D2730 D2731 D2732 D2733 D2734 D2735

EPCOT SOUVENIR
D2750	Mickey	15 - 25
D2751	Goofy	15 - 25

EPCOT WORLD SHOWCASE SET
D2755	Mexico	15 - 25
D2756	Norway	15 - 25
D2757	China	15 - 25
D2758	Germany	15 - 25
D2759	Italy	15 - 25
D2760	U.S.A.	15 - 25
D2761	Japan	15 - 25
D2762	Morocco	15 - 25
D2763	France	15 - 25
D2764	England	15 - 25
D2765	Canada	15 - 25

PLEASURE ISLAND CLUBS, 1989
Pleasure Island, Disney's themed area for teens and young adults, was completed at Walt Disney World in spring 1989. Originally the clubs had glasses for sale in two styles – 6" tumbler and 4" highball styles. Many glasses were closed out in the fall of 1989.

D2770	Pleasure Island, 4"	15 - 20
D2771	Pleasure Island, 6"	15 - 20
D2772	Pleasure Island, 6"	15 - 20
D2785	Mannequins, 6"	15 - 20

D2789	Videopolis East, 6"	15 - 20
D2792	Comedy Warehouse, 4"	15 - 20
D2795	Zephyr, 4"	15 - 20

DISNEY FROSTED JUICE GLASSES, 1989
The face of six Disney personalities are shown on these glasses.

D2800	Mickey	5 - 8
D2801	Minnie	5 - 8
D2802	Donald	5 - 8
D2803	Daisy	5 - 8
D2804	Goofy	5 - 8
D2805	Scrooge	5 - 8

DISNEY FROSTED TUMBLERS, 1990
Same designs as the above set except in tumbler size.

D2806	Mickey	5 - 8
D2807	Minnie	5 - 8
D2808	Donald	5 - 8
D2809	Daisy	5 - 8
D2810	Scrooge	5 - 8
D2811	Goofy	5 - 8

MOVIE ACTION SET, Coke (no logo)
Exactly where these glasses were distributed is unknown.

D3000	Bambi	15 - 30
D3001	Baloo	15 - 30
D3002	Winnie the Pooh	15 - 30
D3003	Oliver & Co.	15 - 30
D3004	Dumbo	15 - 30
D3005	Three Little Pigs	15 - 30

DAVY CROCKETT MOVIE SERIES, Canada, 1955

A numbered set of six $4^{5}/_{8}$" glasses.

D3050	#1 Davy fights a bear	6 - 15
D3055	#6 Davy carrying deer	6 - 15

NIKKI, Canada, 1961

This numbered set of six $4^{1}/_{4}$" glasses was based on the Disney movie.

D3065	#5 Emile Genest	?

BIG RED, Canada, 1962

Based on the Disney movie of the same name, six $4^{3}/_{4}$" glasses were issued in a numbered set.

D3071	#2 Rene ordered to stay away from Big Red	?
D3075	#6 Hikers	?

WALT DISNEY, Single Glasses

D4950	Donald Duck Cola	15 - 20
D4951	U.S. Cola Bottle	15 - 20
D4952	Canadian Cola Bottle	15 - 20
D4955	Davy Crockett, Canadian, part of a set	15 - 30
D4960	Mickey/Minnie, tiffany style Coke	12 - 20
D4970	Winnie the Pooh Birthday, Canadian	6 - 12
D4971	Florida Orange Bird	5 - 10
D4972	Chip & Dale	5 - 10
D4973	Winnie the Pooh dancing	8 - 15
D4974	Winnie the Pooh eating honey	8 - 15
D4975	Disneyland, gold leaf souvenir	15 - 20
D4976	Disneyland (cased in white), Fantasyland, Adventureland, Frontierland	8 - 15
D4978	Donald eating a sandwich	25 - 40

D2771   D2772   D2785   D2789   D2792   D2795   D2770

D2800   D2801   D2802   D2803   D2804   D2805

D2751   D2750   D3055

D3065   D3000   D3001   D3002   D3003   D3004   D3005

D4950   D3071   D3075   D4955   D4960   D4970   D4971   D4972

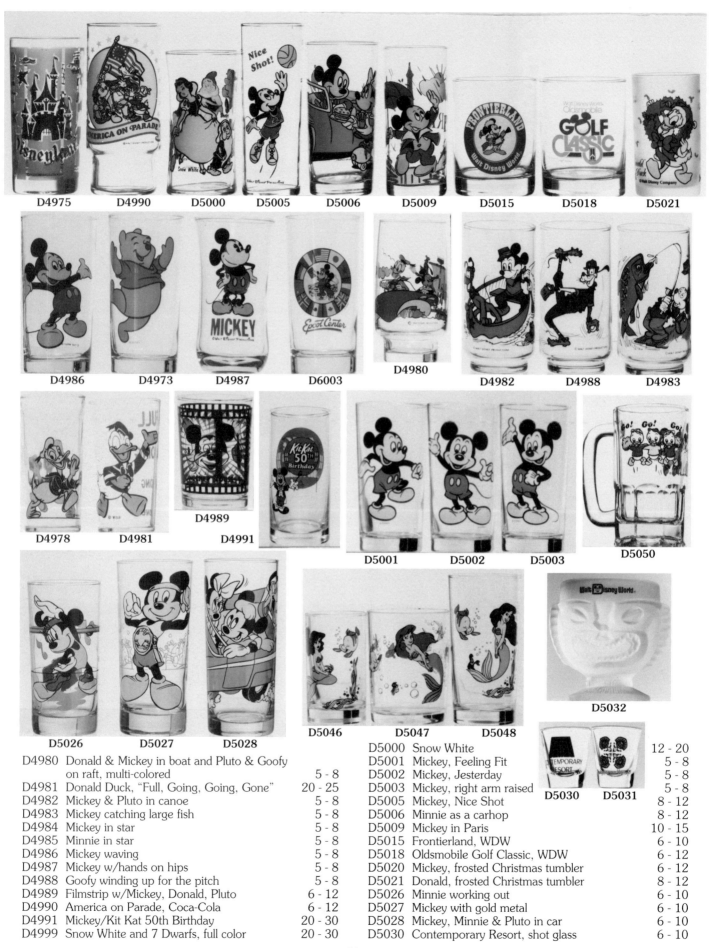

| D4975 | D4990 | D5000 | D5005 | D5006 | D5009 | D5015 | D5018 | D5021 |

| D4986 | D4973 | D4987 | D6003 | D4980 | D4982 | D4988 | D4983 |

| D4978 | D4981 | D4989 | D4991 | D5001 | D5002 | D5003 | D5050 |

D5032

| D5026 | D5027 | D5028 | D5046 | D5047 | D5048 |

D5030   D5031

D4980	Donald & Mickey in boat and Pluto & Goofy on raft, multi-colored	5 - 8
D4981	Donald Duck, "Full, Going, Going, Gone"	20 - 25
D4982	Mickey & Pluto in canoe	5 - 8
D4983	Mickey catching large fish	5 - 8
D4984	Mickey in star	5 - 8
D4985	Minnie in star	5 - 8
D4986	Mickey waving	5 - 8
D4987	Mickey w/hands on hips	5 - 8
D4988	Goofy winding up for the pitch	5 - 8
D4989	Filmstrip w/Mickey, Donald, Pluto	6 - 12
D4990	America on Parade, Coca-Cola	6 - 12
D4991	Mickey/Kit Kat 50th Birthday	20 - 30
D4999	Snow White and 7 Dwarfs, full color	20 - 30

D5000	Snow White	12 - 20
D5001	Mickey, Feeling Fit	5 - 8
D5002	Mickey, Jesterday	5 - 8
D5003	Mickey, right arm raised	5 - 8
D5005	Mickey, Nice Shot	8 - 12
D5006	Minnie as a carhop	8 - 12
D5009	Mickey in Paris	10 - 15
D5015	Frontierland, WDW	6 - 10
D5018	Oldsmobile Golf Classic, WDW	6 - 12
D5020	Mickey, frosted Christmas tumbler	6 - 12
D5021	Donald, frosted Christmas tumbler	8 - 12
D5026	Minnie working out	6 - 10
D5027	Mickey with gold metal	6 - 10
D5028	Mickey, Minnie & Pluto in car	6 - 10
D5030	Contemporary Resort, shot glass	6 - 10

D5031	Polynesian Village Resort, shot glass	12 - 12
D5032	Polynesian Village Resort, luau, frosted	10 - 15
D5035	Caribbean Beach Resort	10 - 15
D5040	Swan Resort, stem glass	6 - 10
D5041	Swan Resort, square	6 - 10
D5045	Captain Jack's, WDW Village, glass mug	3 - 8
D5046	Little Mermaid, juice	8 - 10
D5047	Little Mermaid, short water glass	8 - 10
D5048	Little Mermaid, tumbler	5 - 8
D5050	Mickey, Minnie, Donald's nephews, glass mug	15 - 20
D5055	Baby Mickey/Minnie, full face	6 - 10
D5060	Goofy on Island, glass mug	8 - 12
D5061	Mickey as Captain, glass mug	8 - 12
D5062	Donald & Mickey on the *Geneva*, glass mug	8 - 12
D5063	Donald Waving, glass mug	8 - 12
D5064	Donald, glass mug	8 - 12
D5065	The Resucers, glass mug	8 - 12
D5067	Minnie, glass mug	8 - 12
D5070	Mickey head silhouette	6 - 10
D5075	MGM Studio, Mickey as Director, 12 oz, frosted	7 - 12
D5076	MGM Studio, Mickey w/megaphone, 8 oz, frosted	7 - 12

D5077	MGM Studio, Mickey w/megaphone, tankard, frosted	10 - 15
D5081	Beach Club Resort, WDW	5 - 10
D5082	Yacht Club Resort, WDW	5 - 10
D5088	Dick Tracy, Theme Park	8 - 12

Sam the Olympic Eagle was designed by Disney artist Bob Moore and donated to the Los Angeles Olympic Organizing Committee. Sam was patterned after Sam the Eagle from former Disneyland attraction, "America Sings." These glassware items were sold at Disney theme parks. All glasses depicting Sam are listed at Olympics (see O4000).

D5090	Mickey as Davy Crocket	12 - 15
D6000	EPCOT Center, gold leaf	5 - 10
D6003	EPCOT World Showcase logo, 2 versions	5 - 10
D6030	Steamboat Willie	5 - 10
D6034	Oliver	10 - 15
D6035	Oliver mug	10 - 15
D6036	Walt Disney Studio	10 - 15
D6050	YesterEars, glass	6 - 10
D6051	YesterEars, glass mug	6 - 10
D6053	Mickey, glass coffee break mug	3 - 8
D6054	Easter Parade, mug	6 - 10
D6055	Golf bag shaped tankard w/Mickey golfing	10 - 12
D6060	Snow White, full color	20 - 40
D6061	Snow White, line drawing, single color, heads of dwarfs	20 - 40

D6051

D5035   D5040   D5041   D5045   D5055   D5090   D5067

D5060   D5061   D5062   D5063   D5064   D5065

D5070   D5076   D5075   D6000   D6003   D5081   D5082   D5088

D6030	D6034	D6035	D6036	D7001	D7002	D7000

D7012   D7011   D7010

D7030   D7031   D7032

D7040   D7041   D7042

D7020   D7021   D7022

D7066   D7065   D7067   D7068   D7069   D7070

D7080   D7081   D7082   D7083   D7084   D7085

D7100   D7101   D7102

FOREIGN DISNEY

Disney Babies, with blocks, France

D7000	Donald	6 - 12
D7001	Goofy	6 - 12
D7002	Mickey	6 - 12

Disney Babies, red band, VMC France

D7010	Donald & Mickey	6 - 12
D7011	Goofy	6 - 12
D7012	Minnie & Pluto	6 - 12

Disney Head Shots, HEMA, Holland

D7020	Donald	6 - 12
D7021	Mickey	6 - 12
D7022	Minnie	6 - 12

Totally Minnie, France

D7030	Minnie singing in front of camera	12 - 18
D7031	Minnie dancing to tape recorder	12 - 18
D7032	Minnie putting on make-up	12 - 18

Mickey Through the Years, France

D7040	Mickey in original outfit	12 - 18
D7041	Mickey in tuxedo w/gym shoes	12 - 18
D7042	Mickey as a magician	12 - 18

Disney Filmstrip Series, VMC France

D7050	Bambi	15 - 20
D7051	Cinderella	15 - 20
D7052	Oliver	15 - 20
D7053	Pinocchio	15 - 20
D7054	Robin Hood	15 - 20
D7055	Roger Rabbit	15 - 20

Disney Movies, France

D7065	Aristocats	15 - 20
D7066	Lady and Tramp	15 - 20
D7067	Mickey's Christmas Carol	15 - 20
D7068	One Hundred and One Dalmatians	15 - 20
D7069	Rescuers	15 - 20
D7070	Snow White	15 - 20

Jungle Book, France

D7080	Mowgli, looking at girl	25 - 40
D7081	Mowgli, talking to King Louie	25 - 40
D7082	Mowgli as an infant & Bagherra	25 - 40
D7083	Mowgli, wrapped by Kaa w/Shere Khan	25 - 40
D7084	Mowgli, w/Col. Hathi	25 - 40
D7085	Mowgli & Baloo	25 - 40

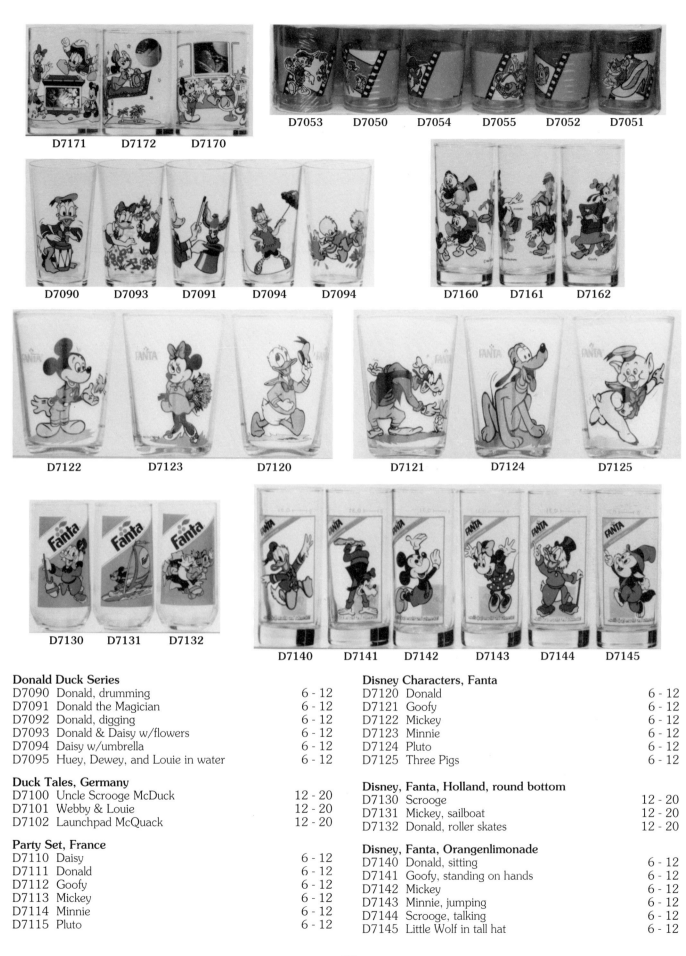

D7171   D7172   D7170

D7053   D7050   D7054   D7055   D7052   D7051

D7090   D7093   D7091   D7094   D7094

D7160   D7161   D7162

D7122   D7123   D7120

D7121   D7124   D7125

D7130   D7131   D7132

D7140   D7141   D7142   D7143   D7144   D7145

Donald Duck Series

D7090 Donald, drumming	6 - 12
D7091 Donald the Magician	6 - 12
D7092 Donald, digging	6 - 12
D7093 Donald & Daisy w/flowers	6 - 12
D7094 Daisy w/umbrella	6 - 12
D7095 Huey, Dewey, and Louie in water	6 - 12

Duck Tales, Germany

D7100 Uncle Scrooge McDuck	12 - 20
D7101 Webby & Louie	12 - 20
D7102 Launchpad McQuack	12 - 20

Party Set, France

D7110 Daisy	6 - 12
D7111 Donald	6 - 12
D7112 Goofy	6 - 12
D7113 Mickey	6 - 12
D7114 Minnie	6 - 12
D7115 Pluto	6 - 12

Disney Characters, Fanta

D7120 Donald	6 - 12
D7121 Goofy	6 - 12
D7122 Mickey	6 - 12
D7123 Minnie	6 - 12
D7124 Pluto	6 - 12
D7125 Three Pigs	6 - 12

Disney, Fanta, Holland, round bottom

D7130 Scrooge	12 - 20
D7131 Mickey, sailboat	12 - 20
D7132 Donald, roller skates	12 - 20

Disney, Fanta, Orangenlimonade

D7140 Donald, sitting	6 - 12
D7141 Goofy, standing on hands	6 - 12
D7142 Mickey	6 - 12
D7143 Minnie, jumping	6 - 12
D7144 Scrooge, talking	6 - 12
D7145 Little Wolf in tall hat	6 - 12

D7150   D7151   D7152   D7153   D7154   D7155   D7180   D7182   D7181

D7183   D7184   D7185

D7190   D7191   D7192

D7267   D7269   D7270   D7250   D7251   D7252

Disney, Fanta

D7150	Donald, painting	6 - 12
D7151	Donald, winking	6 - 12
D7152	Goofy	6 - 12
D7153	Mickey, looking through zipper	6 - 12
D7154	Mickey, dreaming of Minnie	6 - 12
D7155	Mickey	6 - 12

Disney, Germany

D7160	Onkel Doagohert & Tick, Track & Trick (Uncle Scrooge & Huey, Dewey, & Louie)	15 - 25
D7161	Donald Duck, Daniel Dusentrieb, Stroichi & Daisey Duck	15 - 25
D7162	Minni Mausm, Goofy, & Micky Maus	15 - 25

Disney Hologram Series, Coke, Japan

D7170	Mickey & Donald at helm of spaceship, hologram of spaceship on screen	60 - 100
D7171	Donald & Daisy opening treasure chest, hologram of jewels in chest	60 - 100
D7172	Mickey & Minnie on flying carpet, hologram of pyramids & camels on moon	60 - 100

Little Mermaid, "La Petite Serene", France

D7180	Ariel, sitting	15 - 20
D7181	Ariel, swimming	15 - 20
D7182	Ariel, on rock	15 - 20

Mickey Set, Fanta, Japan

Have reflectors that change.

D7183	Mickey, hunting	15 - 20
D7184	Mickey & Minnie as magicians	15 - 20
D7185	Mickey on roller skates	15 - 20

Disney Characters, Coke/McDonald's, Japan

D7190	Donald, magnifying glass (hologram)	20 - 40
D7191	Mickey as Sorcerer's Apprentice	15 - 20
D7192	Alice in Wonderland Characters	15 - 20

Donald Duck Set, Coke, France

All have heads of Donald on one side and a scene on the other.

D7200	Donald, screaming	15 - 25
D7201	Donald, fighting	15 - 25

68

D7202	Donald, talking	15 - 25
D7203	Donald, tipping hat	15 - 25
D7204	Donald, angry	15 - 25
D7205	Donald, hat off	15 - 25

La Bande a Picsou, Coke
D7250	#1	20 - 25
D7251	#2	20 - 25
D7252	#3	20 - 25
D7253	#4	20 - 25

Disney Foreign Singles
D7259	**Bambi, France**	**18 - 24**
D7260	Three Pigs, Coke, Schweinchen Schlau	10 - 20
D7261	Bambi, Coke, France	10 - 20
D7262	Cap & Capper, Coke, France	10 - 20
D7263	Oliver and Co., Coke, France	10 - 20
D7264	Disney Christmas, Coke, France	10 - 20
D7265	Shere Khan, Coke, France	10 - 20
D7266	Surfing Mickey, Coke, France	10 - 20
D7267	Colonel Hathi, Coke, France	10 - 20
D7268	Mickey & Minnie, back to back, Holland this was a mustard container	25 - 40
D7269	Tinkerbell, GB Euro-Disney GB 9s a restaurant	25 - 35
D7270	Mickey pointing at himself, 1950s	25 - 40
D7271	Donald, Kirin Lemon	20 - 30
D7272	Mickey Mouse - Tokyo, 1987	15 - 20

Sports Goofy Set, France
D7300	Goofy, accepting trophy	25 - 40
D7301	Goofy, hitting soccer ball	25 - 40
D7302	Goofy, kicking soccer ball	25 - 40
D7303	Goofy as a goalie	25 - 40

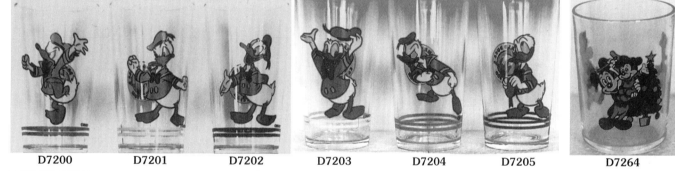

D7260   D7261   D7262

D7259   D7263   D7268

D7200   D7201   D7202   D7203   D7204   D7205   D7264

D7301   D7300   D7302   D7303

D7750   D7751   D7752   D7753

DOGS
D7750	Curbstone Setter	3 - 6
D7751	English Setter	3 - 6
D7752	St. Bernard	3 - 6
D7753	Scottish Terrier	3 - 6

DOMINO'S PIZZA
| D7800 | High ball glass | 4 - 8 |

DOUGHBOY, 1991
This mail-away glass shows the Pillsbury doughboy with different musical instruments around the glass.

| D7875 | Doughboy | 5 - 10 |

DR. PEPPER

D8000	Lady sipping from mug	2 - 4
D8001	Cherubs Kiss	2 - 4
D8005	Sepia Lady, flare	3 - 5
D8006	Hot Air Balloon	2 - 4
D8010	King of the Beverages, 1978, opaque	2 - 4
D8011	King of the Beverages, 1978, transparent	3 - 5
D8012	King of the Beverages, 1979, opaque	2 - 4
D8015	Rainbow	2 - 5
D8020	San Antonio Fiesta	3 - 5
D8025	Building, flare	3 - 5
D8027	100th Celebration	3 - 5
D8030	Dr. Pepper in etched panel, clear glass	3 - 5
D8033	Bell shape glass, white letters, "DR. PEPPER"	5 - 7
D8034	Red design on frosted glass, "DR. PEPPER"	3 - 5
D8040	"Be A Pepper" red & white	2 - 5
D8041	Yellow & white tulips	3 - 5
D8042	Dr. Pepper, red & white logo	3 - 5
D8043	King of Beverages, in diamond design	5 - 8
D8044	Dr. Pepper - modern	2 - 4

DR. SEUSS

D8500	Seuss Navy	8 - 15

DR. WHO

D8550	76 Totters Lane	8 - 15

DRACULA (see UNIVERSAL MONSTERS)

DROOPY (see MGM)

DUDLEY DO-RIGHT (see WARD)

DYNOMUTT (see HANNA BARBERA)

E.T. – THE EXTRA TERRESTRIAL, AAFES, 1982
Army & Air Force Exchange Service & Universal Studios

E1000	To the Space Ship	5 - 15
E1001	"I'll be Right Here"	5 - 15
E1002	"Be Good"	5 - 15
E1003	"E.T. Phone Home"	5 - 15

E.T. COLLECTOR SERIES, Pizza Hut/Universal Studios, 1982

E1004	"Be Good"	4 - 8
E1005	"Home"	4 - 8
E1006	"I'll be Right Here"	4 - 8
E1007	"Phone Home"	4 - 8

D8000   D8001   D8005   D8006

D7800

D8500

D8550

D8010   D8012   D8011

D8015   D8043   D8041   D8044

E1000   E1001   E1002   E1003

E1004   E1005   E1006   E1007

70

E4924   E4925   E8000   E5001   E5002   E5003   E5004

E.T. THE EXTRA TERRESTRIAL, MCA Home Video, Pepsi

Released in 1988 in conjunction with the release of the video. Coupons were accumulated at the video shop from rentals – mail coupons and postage and Pepsi UPC label to Pepsi.

E1010	E.T.'s finger glows	12 - 20
E1011	E.T. dressed up in disguise	12 - 20
E1012	Gertie kisses E.T.	12 - 20
E1013	E.T. rides with Elliott	12 - 20
E1014	Elliott hugs E.T.	12 - 20
E1015	E.T. and Elliott say goodbye	12 - 20

ELMER FUDD (see WARNER BROTHERS)

ELVIS

E4924	Elvis, on the rocks	15 - 20
E4925	Elvis, Memphis Tennassee	?

ENDANGERED SPECIES COLLECTOR SERIES, Burger Chef, 1978

E5001	Bald Eagle	8 - 12
E5002	Giant Panda	8 - 12
E5003	Orang-Utan	8 - 12
E5004	Tiger	8 - 12

Other "Endangered Species" sets different from the above were sold in gift shops & houseware departments at department stores.

ESSO OIL

E7000	Freddie Flamingo	5 - 10
E7001	Kid Koalo	5 - 10
E7002	Match-Point Mert	5 - 10
E7003	Parallel Panda	5 - 10

EXXON

E8000	"Put a Tiger in Your Tank", in diff languages	4 - 6

F&V COOKIES

F0500	Cookie Clown	2 - 5

FAMOUS CITIES

F0800	Rio De Janeiro	5 - 7
F0801	Singapore	5 - 7
F0802	Cairo	5 - 7
F0803	Paris	5 - 7
F0804	Rome	5 - 7
F0805	San Francisco	5 - 7
F0806	London	5 - 7
F0807	Detroit	5 - 7
F0808	Washington D.C.	5 - 7

FANTASTIC FOUR (see SUPER HEROES)

FANTASY GLASSES

F1000	Cowboys	6 - 10
F1001	Indians	6 - 10
F1002	Pirates	6 - 10
F1003	Spacemen	6 - 10
F1004	Vikings	6 - 10

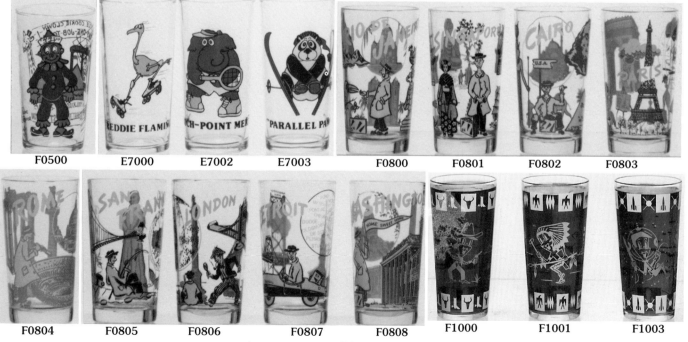

F0500   E7000   E7002   E7003   F0800   F0801   F0802   F0803

F0804   F0805   F0806   F0807   F0808   F1000   F1001   F1003

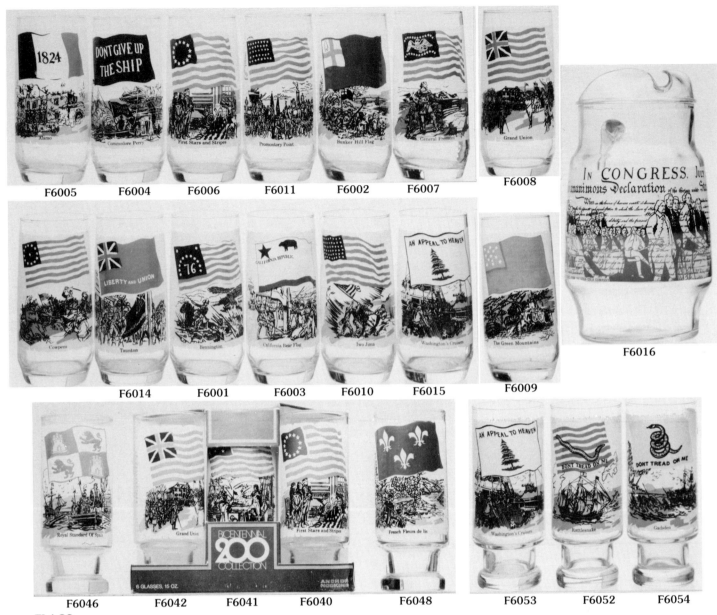

F6005 F6004 F6006 F6011 F6002 F6007 F6008

F6014 F6001 F6003 F6010 F6015 F6009 F6016

F6046 F6042 F6041 F6040 F6048 F6053 F6052 F6054

FLAGS

NATIONAL FLAG FOUNDATION and HERITAGE COLLECTOR SERIES, The Coca-Cola Co., 1976

These glasses and a companion pitcher were distributed by Herfy's.

F6000 Alamo	6 - 10
F6001 Bennington	6 - 10
F6002 Bunker Hill	6 - 10
F6003 California Bear	6 - 10
F6004 Commodore Perry	6 - 10
F6005 Cowpens	6 - 10
F6006 First Stars & Stripes	6 - 10
F6007 General Fremont	6 - 10
F6008 Grand Union	6 - 10
F6009 The Green Mountains	6 - 10
F6010 Iwo Jima	6 - 10
F6011 Promontory Point	6 - 10
F6012 Rattlesnake	6 - 10
F6013 Star Spangled Banner	6 - 10
F6014 Taunton	6 - 10
F6015 Washington Cruisers	6 - 10
F6016 Pitcher	15 - 20

These same Don Hewitt designs were used again on a pedestal shape glass, sold in packages of 6, 2 of each of 3 designs.

Series 1 "Early Flags"

F6040 First Stars & Stripes	6 - 12
F6041 Star Spangled Banner	6 - 12
F6042 Grand Union	6 - 12

Series 2 "The Revolution"

F6043 Bunker Hill	6 - 12
F6044 The Green Mountains	6 - 12
F6045 Taunton	6 - 12

Series 3 "Discover"

F6046 Royal Standard of Spain	6 - 12
F6047 British Union	6 - 12
F6048 French Fleur-de-lis	6 - 12

Series 4 "From Yorktown West"

F6049 Alamo	6 - 12
F6050 General Fremont	6 - 12
F6051 Commodore Perry	6 - 12

| F6045 | F6043 | F6044 | F6050 | F6049 | | F6055 | F6057 | F6056 |

| F6071 | F6076 | F6075 | F6077 | F6070 | F6072 | F8000 | F8001 | F8002 |

Series 5 "Revolution at Sea"
F6052	Rattlesnake	6 - 12
F6053	Washington's Cruisers	6 - 12
F6054	Gadsden	6 - 12

Series 6 "Flags of Freedom"
F6055	Bennington	6 - 12
F6056	Serapis	6 - 12
F6057	Guilford Courthouse	6 - 12

Series 7 "The Continent and Beyond"
F6058	Moon Landing	6 - 12
F6059	Admiral Peary	6 - 12
F6069	Promontory Point	6 - 12

The Pittsburgh Press sponsored eight of these glasses in a series they called "Americana" in 1974. They bear the Pittsburgh Press logo on the reverse. Pittsburgh is also the home office of the National Flag Foundation.

F6070	Bunker Hill	6 - 10
F6071	Commodore Perry	6 - 10
F6072	Confederate Battle Flag	6 - 10
F6073	First Stars & Stripes	6 - 10
F6074	Iwo Jima	6 - 10

F6075	Gadsden	6 - 10
F6076	Star Spangled Banner	6 - 10
F6077	Moon Landing	6 - 10

FLASH, THE (see SUPER HEROES)

FLINTSTONES (see HANNA BARBERA)

FOGHORN LEGHORN (see WARNER BROTHERS)

FOOTBALL (see SPORTS)

FRANKENSTEIN (see UNIVERSAL MONSTERS)

FRIENDLY MONSTERS
F8000	Charmin Charlie	5 - 10
F8001	Friendly Freddy Fright	5 - 10
F8002	Haunty Hanna	5 - 10
F8003	Buzzy Bunny	5 - 10
F8004	Pig	5 - 10

FUDDRUCKERS
F9000	Lady w/sandwich, mug	5 - 8

| G1000 | G1001 | G1002 | G1003 | | G1040 | G1042 | G1043 |

GARFIELD, McDonald's, 1978 copyright date/distributed in 1987

G1000	Poetry in Motion	5 - 8
G1001	Are We Having Fun Yet	5 - 8
G1002	Home James	5 - 8
G1003	Just Me & the Road	5 - 8

GARFIELD MUGS, McDonald's, 1978 copyright date/distributed in 1987

G1010	"I'm easy to get along with when things go my way"	1 - 3
G1011	"Use your friends wisely"	1 - 3
G1012	"I'm not one who rises to the occasion"	1 - 3
G1013	"It's not a pretty life but someone has to live it"	1 - 3

GARFIELD MUGS, McDonald's, 1978 copyright date

G1020	"And what will you fellas have for breakfast"	2 - 4
G1021	"Such a beautiful sunset, and me without a horse"	2 - 4
G1022	"This is the only alarm clock I need to set"	2 - 4
G1023	"I'd like mornings if they started later"	2 - 4

GARFIELD, Single Glasses

G1040	Garfield soda bottle, "Goosh"	5 - 8
G1041	Garfield on ice, "Wheee"	5 - 8
G1042	Garfield blowing bubbles	5 - 8
G1043	Garfield holding balloons	5 - 8
G1044	Garfield juice glass	5 - 8
G1045	Gardield w/straw, "Slurp"	5 - 8

GARFIELD CAFE

G1075	Garfield Cafe, 2 different sizes	5 - 8

GHOSTBUSTERS, Sunoco, Canada, 1989

This set shows different ghosts and the car from *Ghostbusters II*. There is a set issued in Japan distributed by Coke using the same characters, plus the human characters.

G2000	Slimer takes the wheel	3 - 6
G2001	Tony Scoleri sees the sights	3 - 6
G2002	Ecto-1A to the rescue	3 - 6
G2003	Smiling Slimer	3 - 6
G2004	Six Eyes is trapped	3 - 6
G2005	Nunzio Scoleri The Unsinkable	3 - 6

Ghostbusters, Coke, Japan, frosted

G2006	Ghostbusters symbol	25 - 50
G2007	Symbol & live characters	25 - 50
G2008	Symbol & ghost	25 - 50

GHOSTBUSTERS II

G2010	Ghostbusters II Logo	3 - 6
G2011	Ghostbusters II Logo, tumbler	3 - 6
G2020	Mug, Coke, Japan	12 - 25

GINO'S PIZZA & SPAGHETTI HOUSE

G2775	Gino's Gets ...	5 - 8

GO GO GOPHER (see LEONARDO TTV)

F9000

G1041   G1045

G1010   G1011   G1012   G1013   G1023

G1075 – Size variations

G2000   G2001   G2002   G2003   G2004   G2005

G2008   G2006   G2007

G2020

G2010   G2011

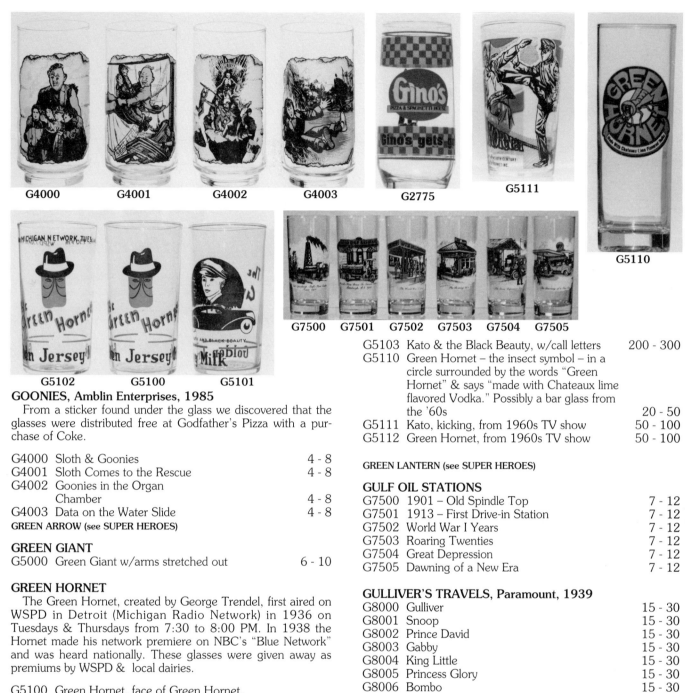

G4000   G4001   G4002   G4003   G2775   **G5111**

G5110

G5102   G5100   G5101

G7500   G7501   G7502   G7503   G7504   G7505

GOONIES, Amblin Enterprises, 1985
From a sticker found under the glass we discovered that the glasses were distributed free at Godfather's Pizza with a purchase of Coke.

G4000	Sloth & Goonies	4 - 8
G4001	Sloth Comes to the Rescue	4 - 8
G4002	Goonies in the Organ Chamber	4 - 8
G4003	Data on the Water Slide	4 - 8

GREEN ARROW (see SUPER HEROES)

GREEN GIANT
G5000	Green Giant w/arms stretched out	6 - 10

GREEN HORNET
The Green Hornet, created by George Trendel, first aired on WSPD in Detroit (Michigan Radio Network) in 1936 on Tuesdays & Thursdays from 7:30 to 8:00 PM. In 1938 the Hornet made his network premiere on NBC's "Blue Network" and was heard nationally. These glasses were given away as premiums by WSPD & local dairies.

G5100	Green Hornet, face of Green Hornet, Golden Jersey Milk, no radio call letters on glass	100 - 250
G5101	Kato & The Black Beauty Golden Jersey Milk, no radio call letters	100 - 250
G5102	Green Hornet, "WDPD 7:30 PM, Michigan Network, Tues-Thurs, 7:30 PM"	200 - 300

G5103	Kato & the Black Beauty, w/call letters	200 - 300
G5110	Green Hornet – the insect symbol – in a circle surrounded by the words "Green Hornet" & says "made with Chateaux lime flavored Vodka." Possibly a bar glass from the '60s	20 - 50
G5111	Kato, kicking, from 1960s TV show	50 - 100
G5112	Green Hornet, from 1960s TV show	50 - 100

GREEN LANTERN (see SUPER HEROES)

GULF OIL STATIONS
G7500	1901 – Old Spindle Top	7 - 12
G7501	1913 – First Drive-in Station	7 - 12
G7502	World War I Years	7 - 12
G7503	Roaring Twenties	7 - 12
G7504	Great Depression	7 - 12
G7505	Dawning of a New Era	7 - 12

GULLIVER'S TRAVELS, Paramount, 1939
G8000	Gulliver	15 - 30
G8001	Snoop	15 - 30
G8002	Prince David	15 - 30
G8003	Gabby	15 - 30
G8004	King Little	15 - 30
G8005	Princess Glory	15 - 30
G8006	Bombo	15 - 30
G8007	Twinkle Toes	15 - 30
G8008	Snitch	15 - 30
G8009	Sneak	15 - 30

GULLIVER'S TRAVELS, Paramount, 1939
Smaller jar size

G8000 - G8004

G8013   G8012   G8011

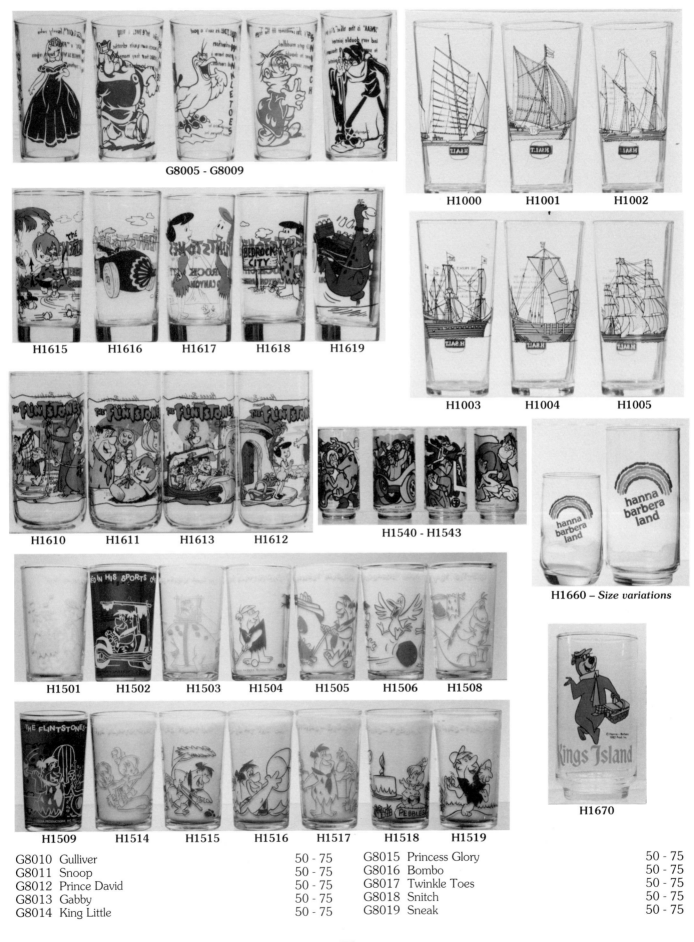

G8005 - G8009

H1000   H1001   H1002

H1615   H1616   H1617   H1618   H1619

H1003   H1004   H1005

H1610   H1611   H1613   H1612

H1540 - H1543

hanna barbera land

H1660 – *Size variations*

H1501   H1502   H1503   H1504   H1505   H1506   H1508

Kings Island

H1509   H1514   H1515   H1516   H1517   H1518   H1519

H1670

G8010	Gulliver	50 - 75	G8015 Princess Glory	50 - 75
G8011	Snoop	50 - 75	G8016 Bombo	50 - 75
G8012	Prince David	50 - 75	G8017 Twinkle Toes	50 - 75
G8013	Gabby	50 - 75	G8018 Snitch	50 - 75
G8014	King Little	50 - 75	G8019 Sneak	50 - 75

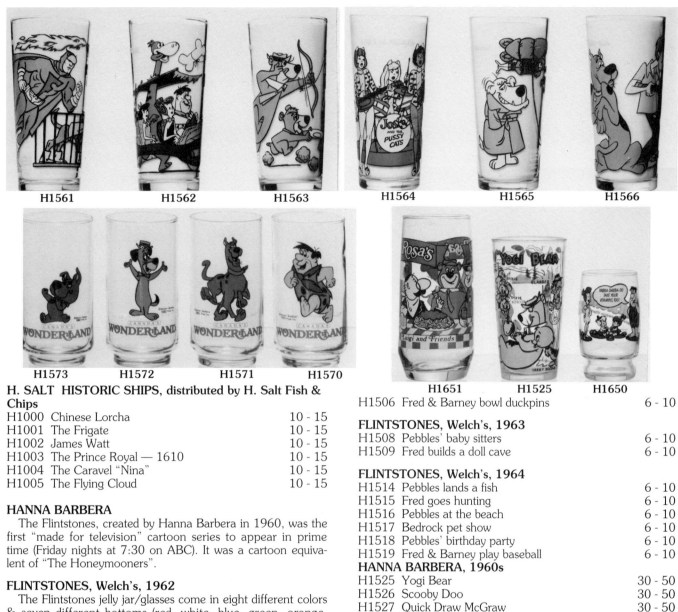

H1561   H1562   H1563   H1564   H1565   H1566

H1573   H1572   H1571   H1570

H1651   H1525   H1650

H. SALT HISTORIC SHIPS, distributed by H. Salt Fish & Chips

H1000	Chinese Lorcha	10 - 15
H1001	The Frigate	10 - 15
H1002	James Watt	10 - 15
H1003	The Prince Royal — 1610	10 - 15
H1004	The Caravel "Nina"	10 - 15
H1005	The Flying Cloud	10 - 15

HANNA BARBERA

The Flintstones, created by Hanna Barbera in 1960, was the first "made for television" cartoon series to appear in prime time (Friday nights at 7:30 on ABC). It was a cartoon equivalent of "The Honeymooners".

FLINTSTONES, Welch's, 1962

The Flintstones jelly jar/glasses come in eight different colors & seven different bottoms (red, white, blue, green, orange, pink, aqua, yellow). The pressed characters under the glass were Pebbles, Bamm Bamm, Fred, Wilma, Barney, Betty & Dino.

H1501	Having a ball	6 - 10
H1502	Fred in his sports car	6 - 10
H1503	Fred & his pals at work	6 - 10
H1504	Fred & Barney play golf	6 - 10
H1505	Fred's newest invention	

H1506	Fred & Barney bowl duckpins	6 - 10

FLINTSTONES, Welch's, 1963

H1508	Pebbles' baby sitters	6 - 10
H1509	Fred builds a doll cave	6 - 10

FLINTSTONES, Welch's, 1964

H1514	Pebbles lands a fish	6 - 10
H1515	Fred goes hunting	6 - 10
H1516	Pebbles at the beach	6 - 10
H1517	Bedrock pet show	6 - 10
H1518	Pebbles' birthday party	6 - 10
H1519	Fred & Barney play baseball	6 - 10

HANNA BARBERA, 1960s

H1525	Yogi Bear	30 - 50
H1526	Scooby Doo	30 - 50
H1527	Quick Draw McGraw	30 - 50
H1528	Huckleberry Hound	15 - 20

HANNA BARBERA T.V. CARTOON CHARACTERS, 7-11, 1976

More to this set may exist.

H1540	Scooby Doo	30 - 60
H1541	Speed Buggy	30 - 60
H1542	Hong Kong Fuey	30 - 60
H1543	Grape Ape	30 - 60

H1600   H1601   H1602   H1603   H1630   H1631   H1632   H1633

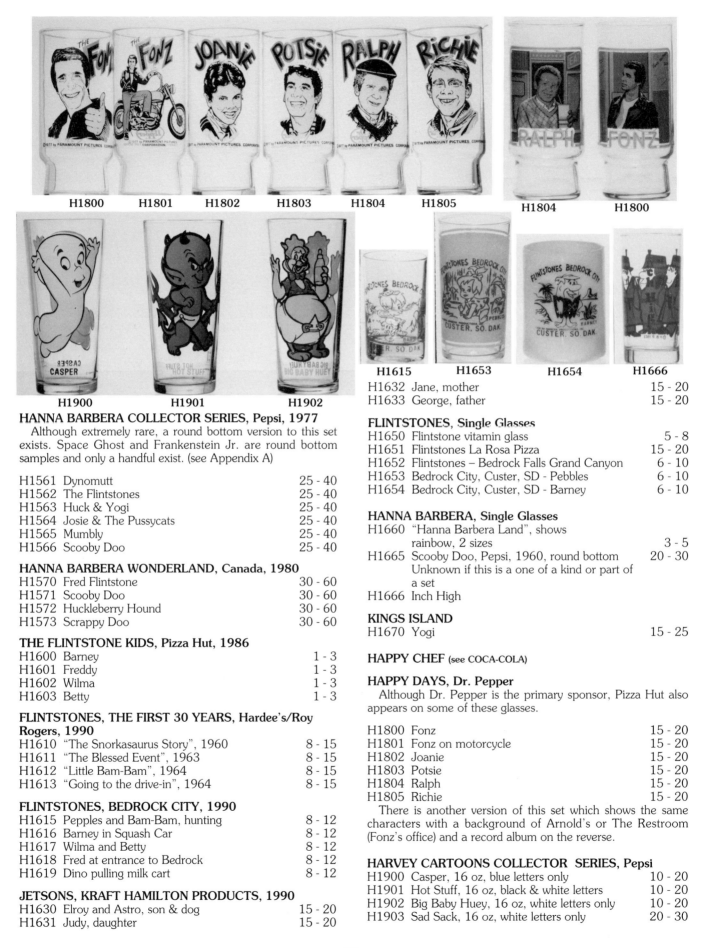

H1800 H1801 H1802 H1803 H1804 H1805

H1804 H1800

H1900 H1901 H1902

H1615 H1653 H1654 H1666

HANNA BARBERA COLLECTOR SERIES, Pepsi, 1977

Although extremely rare, a round bottom version to this set exists. Space Ghost and Frankenstein Jr. are round bottom samples and only a handful exist. (see Appendix A)

H1561	Dynomutt	25 - 40
H1562	The Flintstones	25 - 40
H1563	Huck & Yogi	25 - 40
H1564	Josie & The Pussycats	25 - 40
H1565	Mumbly	25 - 40
H1566	Scooby Doo	25 - 40

HANNA BARBERA WONDERLAND, Canada, 1980

H1570	Fred Flintstone	30 - 60
H1571	Scooby Doo	30 - 60
H1572	Huckleberry Hound	30 - 60
H1573	Scrappy Doo	30 - 60

THE FLINTSTONE KIDS, Pizza Hut, 1986

H1600	Barney	1 - 3
H1601	Freddy	1 - 3
H1602	Wilma	1 - 3
H1603	Betty	1 - 3

FLINTSTONES, THE FIRST 30 YEARS, Hardee's/Roy Rogers, 1990

H1610	"The Snorkasaurus Story", 1960	8 - 15
H1611	"The Blessed Event", 1963	8 - 15
H1612	"Little Bam-Bam", 1964	8 - 15
H1613	"Going to the drive-in", 1964	8 - 15

FLINTSTONES, BEDROCK CITY, 1990

H1615	Pepples and Bam-Bam, hunting	8 - 12
H1616	Barney in Squash Car	8 - 12
H1617	Wilma and Betty	8 - 12
H1618	Fred at entrance to Bedrock	8 - 12
H1619	Dino pulling milk cart	8 - 12

JETSONS, KRAFT HAMILTON PRODUCTS, 1990

H1630	Elroy and Astro, son & dog	15 - 20
H1631	Judy, daughter	15 - 20
H1632	Jane, mother	15 - 20
H1633	George, father	15 - 20

FLINTSTONES, Single Glasses

H1650	Flintstone vitamin glass	5 - 8
H1651	Flintstones La Rosa Pizza	15 - 20
H1652	Flintstones – Bedrock Falls Grand Canyon	6 - 10
H1653	Bedrock City, Custer, SD - Pebbles	6 - 10
H1654	Bedrock City, Custer, SD - Barney	6 - 10

HANNA BARBERA, Single Glasses

H1660	"Hanna Barbera Land", shows rainbow, 2 sizes	3 - 5
H1665	Scooby Doo, Pepsi, 1960, round bottom Unknown if this is a one of a kind or part of a set	20 - 30
H1666	Inch High	

KINGS ISLAND

H1670	Yogi	15 - 25

HAPPY CHEF (see COCA-COLA)

HAPPY DAYS, Dr. Pepper

Although Dr. Pepper is the primary sponsor, Pizza Hut also appears on some of these glasses.

H1800	Fonz	15 - 20
H1801	Fonz on motorcycle	15 - 20
H1802	Joanie	15 - 20
H1803	Potsie	15 - 20
H1804	Ralph	15 - 20
H1805	Richie	15 - 20

There is another version of this set which shows the same characters with a background of Arnold's or The Restroom (Fonz's office) and a record album on the reverse.

HARVEY CARTOONS COLLECTOR SERIES, Pepsi

H1900	Casper, 16 oz, blue letters only	10 - 20
H1901	Hot Stuff, 16 oz, black & white letters	10 - 20
H1902	Big Baby Huey, 16 oz, white letters only	10 - 20
H1903	Sad Sack, 16 oz, white letters only	20 - 30

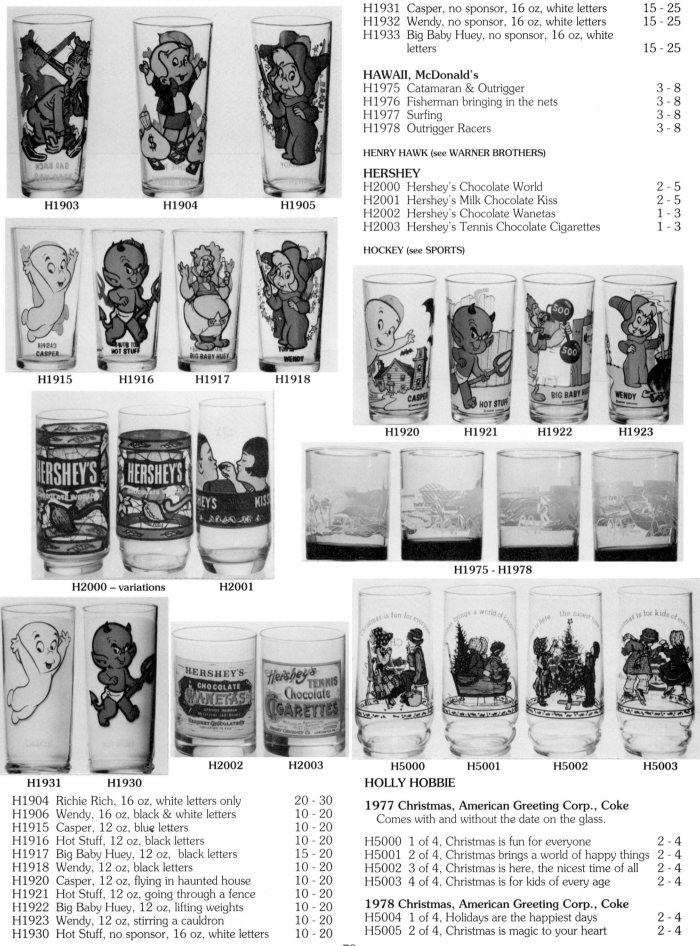

H1903	H1904	H1905

H1915	H1916	H1917	H1918

H2000 – variations	H2001

H1931	H1930

H2002	H2003

H1931	Casper, no sponsor, 16 oz, white letters	15 - 25
H1932	Wendy, no sponsor, 16 oz, white letters	15 - 25
H1933	Big Baby Huey, no sponsor, 16 oz, white letters	15 - 25

HAWAII, McDonald's

H1975	Catamaran & Outrigger	3 - 8
H1976	Fisherman bringing in the nets	3 - 8
H1977	Surfing	3 - 8
H1978	Outrigger Racers	3 - 8

HENRY HAWK (see WARNER BROTHERS)

HERSHEY

H2000	Hershey's Chocolate World	2 - 5
H2001	Hershey's Milk Chocolate Kiss	2 - 5
H2002	Hershey's Chocolate Wanetas	1 - 3
H2003	Hershey's Tennis Chocolate Cigarettes	1 - 3

HOCKEY (see SPORTS)

H1920	H1921	H1922	H1923

H1975 - H1978

H5000	H5001	H5002	H5003

HOLLY HOBBIE

1977 Christmas, American Greeting Corp., Coke
Comes with and without the date on the glass.

H5000	1 of 4, Christmas is fun for everyone	2 - 4
H5001	2 of 4, Christmas brings a world of happy things	2 - 4
H5002	3 of 4, Christmas is here, the nicest time of all	2 - 4
H5003	4 of 4, Christmas is for kids of every age	2 - 4

1978 Christmas, American Greeting Corp., Coke

H5004	1 of 4, Holidays are the happiest days	2 - 4
H5005	2 of 4, Christmas is magic to your heart	2 - 4

H1904	Richie Rich, 16 oz, white letters only	20 - 30
H1906	Wendy, 16 oz, black & white letters	10 - 20
H1915	Casper, 12 oz, blue letters	10 - 20
H1916	Hot Stuff, 12 oz, black letters	10 - 20
H1917	Big Baby Huey, 12 oz, black letters	15 - 20
H1918	Wendy, 12 oz, black letters	10 - 20
H1920	Casper, 12 oz, flying in haunted house	10 - 20
H1921	Hot Stuff, 12 oz, going through a fence	10 - 20
H1922	Big Baby Huey, 12 oz, lifting weights	10 - 20
H1923	Wendy, 12 oz, stirring a cauldron	10 - 20
H1930	Hot Stuff, no sponsor, 16 oz, white letters	10 - 20

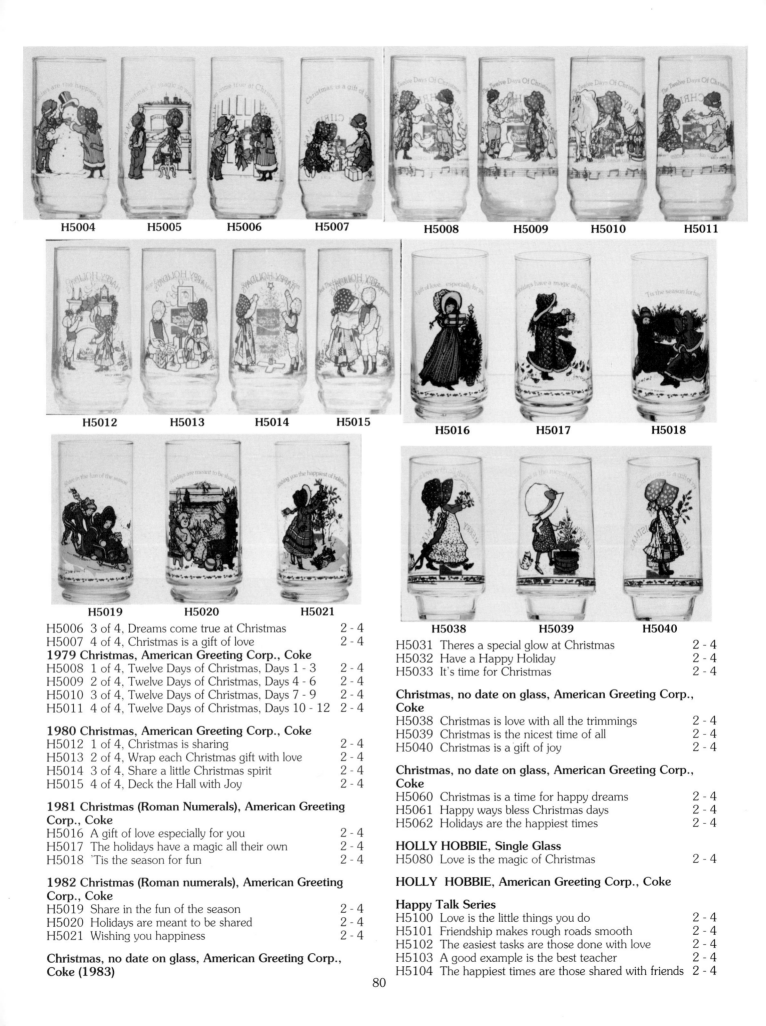

H5004 H5005 H5006 H5007

H5008 H5009 H5010 H5011

H5012 H5013 H5014 H5015

H5016 H5017 H5018

H5019 H5020 H5021

H5038 H5039 H5040

H5006 3 of 4, Dreams come true at Christmas	2 - 4
H5007 4 of 4, Christmas is a gift of love	2 - 4

1979 Christmas, American Greeting Corp., Coke

H5008 1 of 4, Twelve Days of Christmas, Days 1 - 3	2 - 4
H5009 2 of 4, Twelve Days of Christmas, Days 4 - 6	2 - 4
H5010 3 of 4, Twelve Days of Christmas, Days 7 - 9	2 - 4
H5011 4 of 4, Twelve Days of Christmas, Days 10 - 12	2 - 4

1980 Christmas, American Greeting Corp., Coke

H5012 1 of 4, Christmas is sharing	2 - 4
H5013 2 of 4, Wrap each Christmas gift with love	2 - 4
H5014 3 of 4, Share a little Christmas spirit	2 - 4
H5015 4 of 4, Deck the Hall with Joy	2 - 4

1981 Christmas (Roman Numerals), American Greeting Corp., Coke

H5016 A gift of love especially for you	2 - 4
H5017 The holidays have a magic all their own	2 - 4
H5018 'Tis the season for fun	2 - 4

1982 Christmas (Roman numerals), American Greeting Corp., Coke

H5019 Share in the fun of the season	2 - 4
H5020 Holidays are meant to be shared	2 - 4
H5021 Wishing you happiness	2 - 4

Christmas, no date on glass, American Greeting Corp., Coke (1983)

H5031 Theres a special glow at Christmas	2 - 4
H5032 Have a Happy Holiday	2 - 4
H5033 It's time for Christmas	2 - 4

Christmas, no date on glass, American Greeting Corp., Coke

H5038 Christmas is love with all the trimmings	2 - 4
H5039 Christmas is the nicest time of all	2 - 4
H5040 Christmas is a gift of joy	2 - 4

Christmas, no date on glass, American Greeting Corp., Coke

H5060 Christmas is a time for happy dreams	2 - 4
H5061 Happy ways bless Christmas days	2 - 4
H5062 Holidays are the happiest times	2 - 4

HOLLY HOBBIE, Single Glass

H5080 Love is the magic of Christmas	2 - 4

HOLLY HOBBIE, American Greeting Corp., Coke

Happy Talk Series

H5100 Love is the little things you do	2 - 4
H5101 Friendship makes rough roads smooth	2 - 4
H5102 The easiest tasks are those done with love	2 - 4
H5103 A good example is the best teacher	2 - 4
H5104 The happiest times are those shared with friends	2 - 4

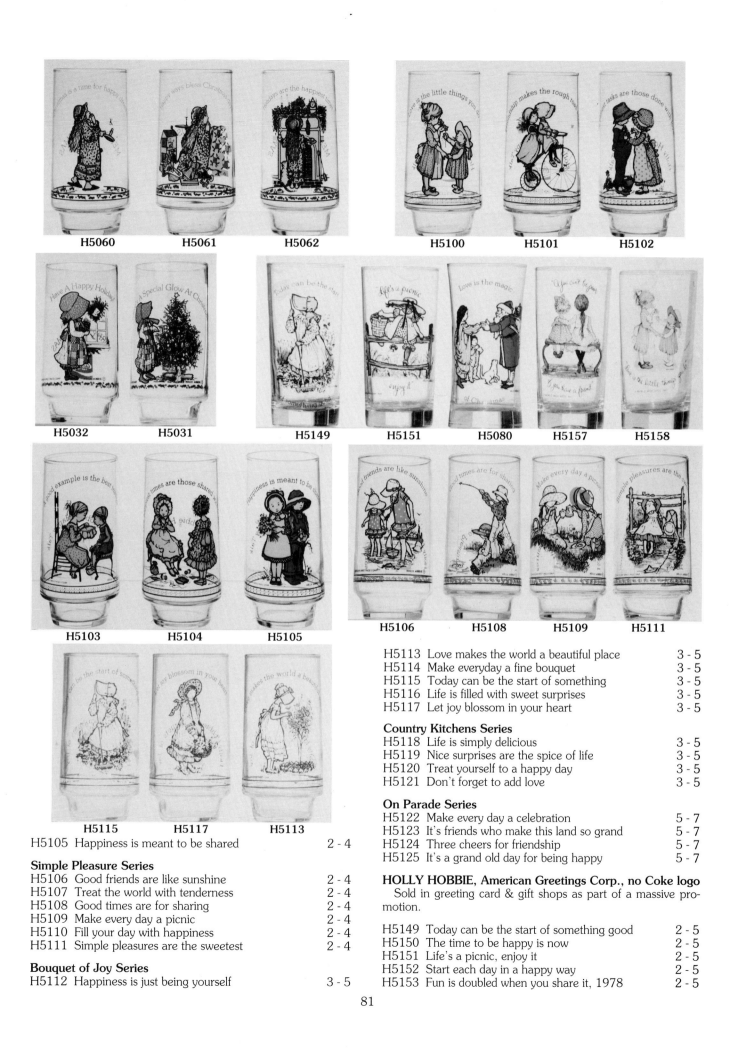

H5060	H5061	H5062

H5100	H5101	H5102

H5032	H5031

H5149	H5151	H5080	H5157	H5158

H5103	H5104	H5105

H5106	H5108	H5109	H5111

H5115	H5117	H5113

H5105 Happiness is meant to be shared   2 - 4

Simple Pleasure Series
H5106 Good friends are like sunshine   2 - 4
H5107 Treat the world with tenderness   2 - 4
H5108 Good times are for sharing   2 - 4
H5109 Make every day a picnic   2 - 4
H5110 Fill your day with happiness   2 - 4
H5111 Simple pleasures are the sweetest   2 - 4

Bouquet of Joy Series
H5112 Happiness is just being yourself   3 - 5

H5113 Love makes the world a beautiful place   3 - 5
H5114 Make everyday a fine bouquet   3 - 5
H5115 Today can be the start of something   3 - 5
H5116 Life is filled with sweet surprises   3 - 5
H5117 Let joy blossom in your heart   3 - 5

Country Kitchens Series
H5118 Life is simply delicious   3 - 5
H5119 Nice surprises are the spice of life   3 - 5
H5120 Treat yourself to a happy day   3 - 5
H5121 Don't forget to add love   3 - 5

On Parade Series
H5122 Make every day a celebration   5 - 7
H5123 It's friends who make this land so grand   5 - 7
H5124 Three cheers for friendship   5 - 7
H5125 It's a grand old day for being happy   5 - 7

HOLLY HOBBIE, American Greetings Corp., no Coke logo
   Sold in greeting card & gift shops as part of a massive promotion.

H5149 Today can be the start of something good   2 - 5
H5150 The time to be happy is now   2 - 5
H5151 Life's a picnic, enjoy it   2 - 5
H5152 Start each day in a happy way   2 - 5
H5153 Fun is doubled when you share it, 1978   2 - 5

H5122   H5123   H5124   H5125

H5170

H5155 H5153 H5154 H5156   H5171

H5350   H5205   H5201

H5200   H5203   H5204   H5202

H5300   H5301   H5302

H5154	The world is full of happy surprises, 1978	2 - 5
H5155	Light hearted ways make happy days, 1978	2 - 5
H5156	Special friends give the heart a lift, 1978	2 - 5
H5157	You can't be poor if you have a friend	2 - 5
H5158	Love is the little things you do	2 - 5
H5159	Happiness starts in sunny hearts	2 - 5
H5160	Title unknown	2 - 5
H5170	Boxed set of 8 glasses – 4 different colors, 2 of each. Glass says "Start each day in a happy way", set	12 - 15
H5171	Single glass from above box	2 - 4

HONEY BUNNY (see WARNER BROTHERS)

HOOK'S DRUGS

Hook's Drugs maintains soda fountains in a few of the company's locations reminiscent of the days when neighborhood drug stores were the major sellers of ice cream and soft drinks. The company drug store museums at the Indiana State Fairgrounds in Indianapolis and historic Nashville, Indiana are the two largest such stores.

H5200	"Hook's Soda"	2 - 5
H5201	"Hook's Historic Drug Store and Pharmacy	

	Museum"	2 - 5
H5202	"The 1900 J.A. Hook's Drug Store"	2 - 5
H5203	"Hook's Historic Drug Store", yellow	2 - 5
H5204	"Hook's Historic Drug Store", red	2 - 5
H5205	"Hook's Historic Drug Store" white	2 - 5

Also see DISNEY – Donald Duck's Birthday series at D2700

HOPALONG CASSIDY (see WESTERN HEROES)

HORSE RACING (see SPORTS)

HOT DOG CASTLE, 1977

H5300	Abilene Past	6 - 8
H5301	Abilene Present	6 - 8
H5302	Abilene Future	6 - 8

HOT SAM'S, Pepsi

H5350	Hot Sam's Restaurant	20 - 30

HOT STUFF (see HARVEY CARTOONS)

HOWARD THE DUCK (see SUPER HEROES)

HOWDY DOODY, Welch's, Kagran

H6000	Kagran – Clarabell gets a kick out of a circus mule	15 - 25

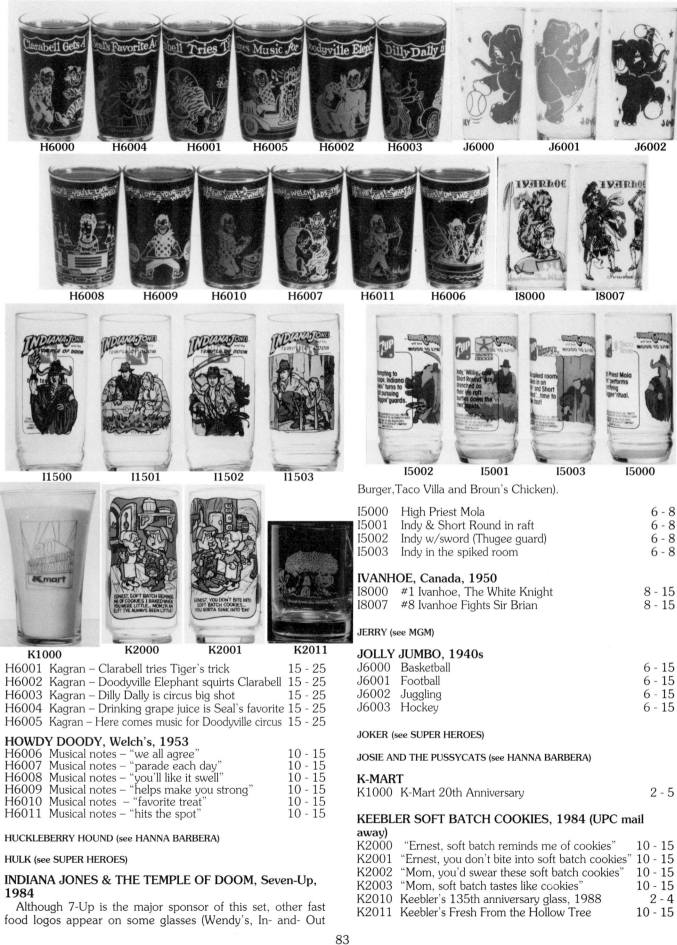

| H6000 | H6004 | H6001 | H6005 | H6002 | H6003 | J6000 | J6001 | J6002 |

| H6008 | H6009 | H6010 | H6007 | H6011 | H6006 | I8000 | I8007 |

| I1500 | I1501 | I1502 | I1503 | | I5002 | I5001 | I5003 | I5000 |

| K1000 | K2000 | K2001 | K2011 |

Burger, Taco Villa and Broun's Chicken).

I5000	High Priest Mola	6 - 8
I5001	Indy & Short Round in raft	6 - 8
I5002	Indy w/sword (Thugee guard)	6 - 8
I5003	Indy in the spiked room	6 - 8

IVANHOE, Canada, 1950
| I8000 | #1 Ivanhoe, The White Knight | 8 - 15 |
| I8007 | #8 Ivanhoe Fights Sir Brian | 8 - 15 |

JERRY (see MGM)

JOLLY JUMBO, 1940s
J6000	Basketball	6 - 15
J6001	Football	6 - 15
J6002	Juggling	6 - 15
J6003	Hockey	6 - 15

JOKER (see SUPER HEROES)

JOSIE AND THE PUSSYCATS (see HANNA BARBERA)

K-MART
| K1000 | K-Mart 20th Anniversary | 2 - 5 |

KEEBLER SOFT BATCH COOKIES, 1984 (UPC mail away)
K2000	"Ernest, soft batch reminds me of cookies"	10 - 15
K2001	"Ernest, you don't bite into soft batch cookies"	10 - 15
K2002	"Mom, you'd swear these soft batch cookies"	10 - 15
K2003	"Mom, soft batch tastes like cookies"	10 - 15
K2010	Keebler's 135th anniversary glass, 1988	2 - 4
K2011	Keebler's Fresh From the Hollow Tree	10 - 15

H6001	Kagran – Clarabell tries Tiger's trick	15 - 25
H6002	Kagran – Doodyville Elephant squirts Clarabell	15 - 25
H6003	Kagran – Dilly Dally is circus big shot	15 - 25
H6004	Kagran – Drinking grape juice is Seal's favorite	15 - 25
H6005	Kagran – Here comes music for Doodyville circus	15 - 25

HOWDY DOODY, Welch's, 1953
H6006	Musical notes – "we all agree"	10 - 15
H6007	Musical notes – "parade each day"	10 - 15
H6008	Musical notes – "you'll like it swell"	10 - 15
H6009	Musical notes – "helps make you strong"	10 - 15
H6010	Musical notes – "favorite treat"	10 - 15
H6011	Musical notes – "hits the spot"	10 - 15

HUCKLEBERRY HOUND (see HANNA BARBERA)

HULK (see SUPER HEROES)

INDIANA JONES & THE TEMPLE OF DOOM, Seven-Up, 1984

Although 7-Up is the major sponsor of this set, other fast food logos appear on some glasses (Wendy's, In- and- Out

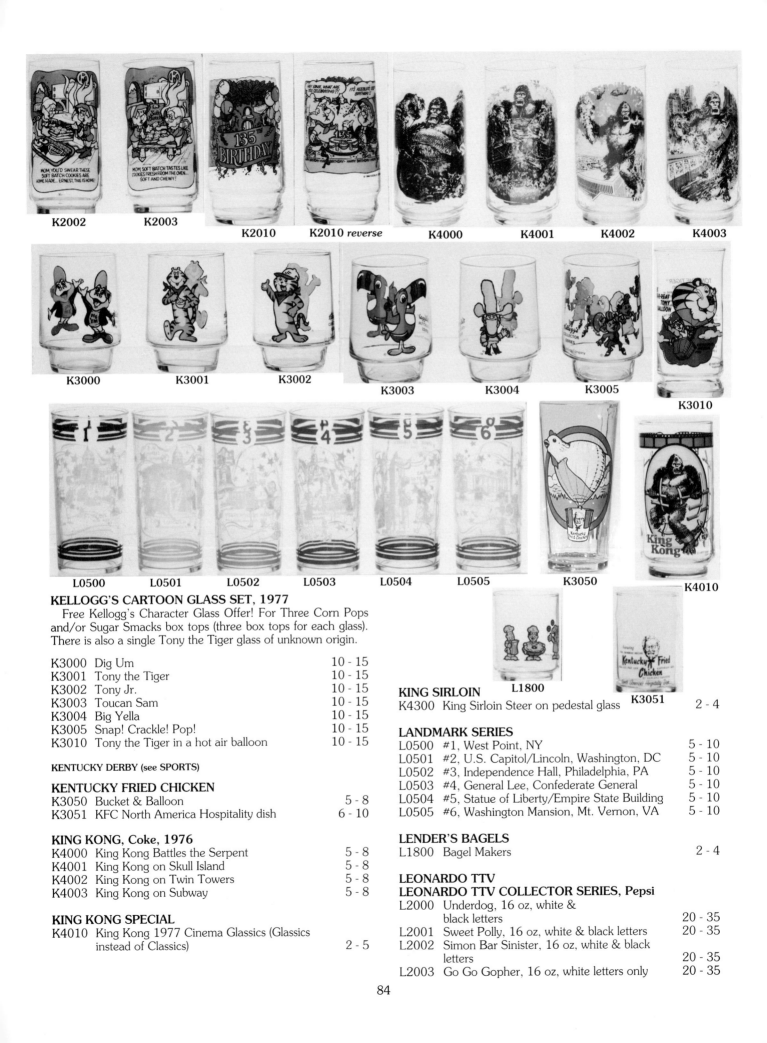

K2002   K2003   K2010   K2010 *reverse*   K4000   K4001   K4002   K4003

K3000   K3001   K3002   K3003   K3004   K3005   K3010

L0500   L0501   L0502   L0503   L0504   L0505   K3050   K4010

L1800   K3051

KELLOGG'S CARTOON GLASS SET, 1977
Free Kellogg's Character Glass Offer! For Three Corn Pops and/or Sugar Smacks box tops (three box tops for each glass). There is also a single Tony the Tiger glass of unknown origin.

K3000	Dig Um	10 - 15
K3001	Tony the Tiger	10 - 15
K3002	Tony Jr.	10 - 15
K3003	Toucan Sam	10 - 15
K3004	Big Yella	10 - 15
K3005	Snap! Crackle! Pop!	10 - 15
K3010	Tony the Tiger in a hot air balloon	10 - 15

KENTUCKY DERBY (see SPORTS)

KENTUCKY FRIED CHICKEN
K3050	Bucket & Balloon	5 - 8
K3051	KFC North America Hospitality dish	6 - 10

KING KONG, Coke, 1976
K4000	King Kong Battles the Serpent	5 - 8
K4001	King Kong on Skull Island	5 - 8
K4002	King Kong on Twin Towers	5 - 8
K4003	King Kong on Subway	5 - 8

KING KONG SPECIAL
K4010	King Kong 1977 Cinema Glassics (Glassics instead of Classics)	2 - 5

KING SIRLOIN
K4300	King Sirloin Steer on pedestal glass	2 - 4

LANDMARK SERIES
L0500	#1, West Point, NY	5 - 10
L0501	#2, U.S. Capitol/Lincoln, Washington, DC	5 - 10
L0502	#3, Independence Hall, Philadelphia, PA	5 - 10
L0503	#4, General Lee, Confederate General	5 - 10
L0504	#5, Statue of Liberty/Empire State Building	5 - 10
L0505	#6, Washington Mansion, Mt. Vernon, VA	5 - 10

LENDER'S BAGELS
L1800	Bagel Makers	2 - 4

LEONARDO TTV
LEONARDO TTV COLLECTOR SERIES, Pepsi
L2000	Underdog, 16 oz, white & black letters	20 - 35
L2001	Sweet Polly, 16 oz, white & black letters	20 - 35
L2002	Simon Bar Sinister, 16 oz, white & black letters	20 - 35
L2003	Go Go Gopher, 16 oz, white letters only	20 - 35

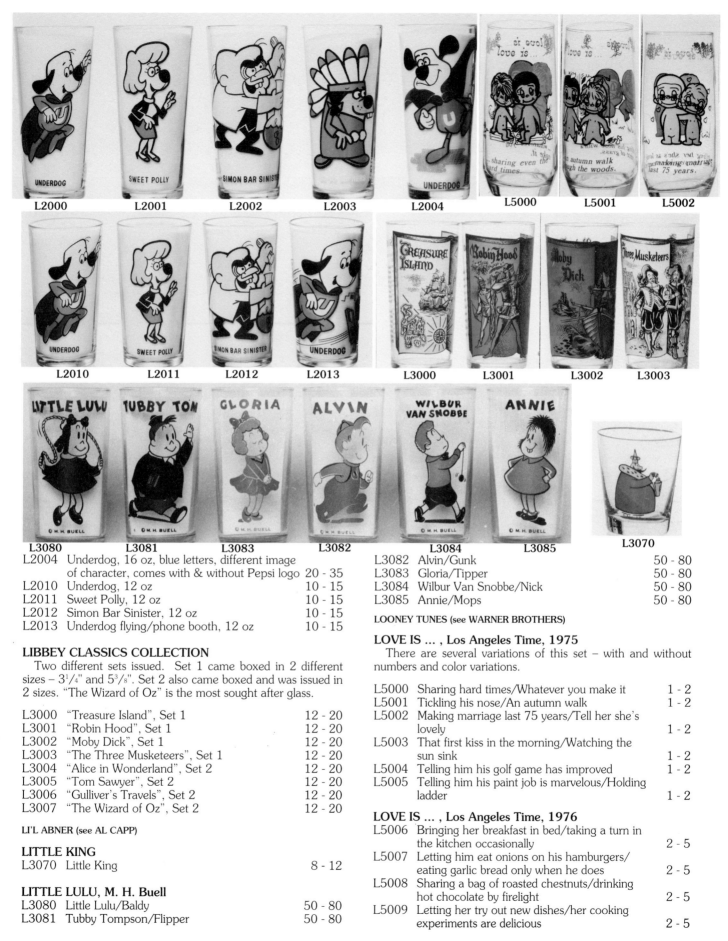

UNDERDOG	SWEET POLLY	SIMON BAR SINISTER	
L2000	L2001	L2002	L2003

UNDERDOG	
L2004	

L5000 L5001 L5002

UNDERDOG	SWEET POLLY	SIMON BAR SINISTER	UNDERDOG
L2010	L2011	L2012	L2013

TREASURE ISLAND Robin Hood Moby Dick Three Musketeers
L3000 L3001 L3002 L3003

LITTLE LULU TUBBY TOM GLORIA ALVIN WILBUR VAN SNOBBE ANNIE
L3080 L3081 L3083 L3082 L3084 L3085

L3070

L2004	Underdog, 16 oz, blue letters, different image of character, comes with & without Pepsi logo	20 - 35
L2010	Underdog, 12 oz	10 - 15
L2011	Sweet Polly, 12 oz	10 - 15
L2012	Simon Bar Sinister, 12 oz	10 - 15
L2013	Underdog flying/phone booth, 12 oz	10 - 15

LIBBEY CLASSICS COLLECTION

Two different sets issued. Set 1 came boxed in 2 different sizes – 3¼" and 5⅜". Set 2 also came boxed and was issued in 2 sizes. "The Wizard of Oz" is the most sought after glass.

L3000	"Treasure Island", Set 1	12 - 20
L3001	"Robin Hood", Set 1	12 - 20
L3002	"Moby Dick", Set 1	12 - 20
L3003	"The Three Musketeers", Set 1	12 - 20
L3004	"Alice in Wonderland", Set 2	12 - 20
L3005	"Tom Sawyer", Set 2	12 - 20
L3006	"Gulliver's Travels", Set 2	12 - 20
L3007	"The Wizard of Oz", Set 2	12 - 20

LI'L ABNER (see AL CAPP)

LITTLE KING

L3070	Little King	8 - 12

LITTLE LULU, M. H. Buell

L3080	Little Lulu/Baldy	50 - 80
L3081	Tubby Tompson/Flipper	50 - 80

L3082	Alvin/Gunk	50 - 80
L3083	Gloria/Tipper	50 - 80
L3084	Wilbur Van Snobbe/Nick	50 - 80
L3085	Annie/Mops	50 - 80

LOONEY TUNES (see WARNER BROTHERS)

LOVE IS ... , Los Angeles Time, 1975

There are several variations of this set – with and without numbers and color variations.

L5000	Sharing hard times/Whatever you make it	1 - 2
L5001	Tickling his nose/An autumn walk	1 - 2
L5002	Making marriage last 75 years/Tell her she's lovely	1 - 2
L5003	That first kiss in the morning/Watching the sun sink	1 - 2
L5004	Telling him his golf game has improved	1 - 2
L5005	Telling him his paint job is marvelous/Holding ladder	1 - 2

LOVE IS ... , Los Angeles Time, 1976

L5006	Bringing her breakfast in bed/taking a turn in the kitchen occasionally	2 - 5
L5007	Letting him eat onions on his hamburgers/ eating garlic bread only when he does	2 - 5
L5008	Sharing a bag of roasted chestnuts/drinking hot chocolate by firelight	2 - 5
L5009	Letting her try out new dishes/her cooking experiments are delicious	2 - 5

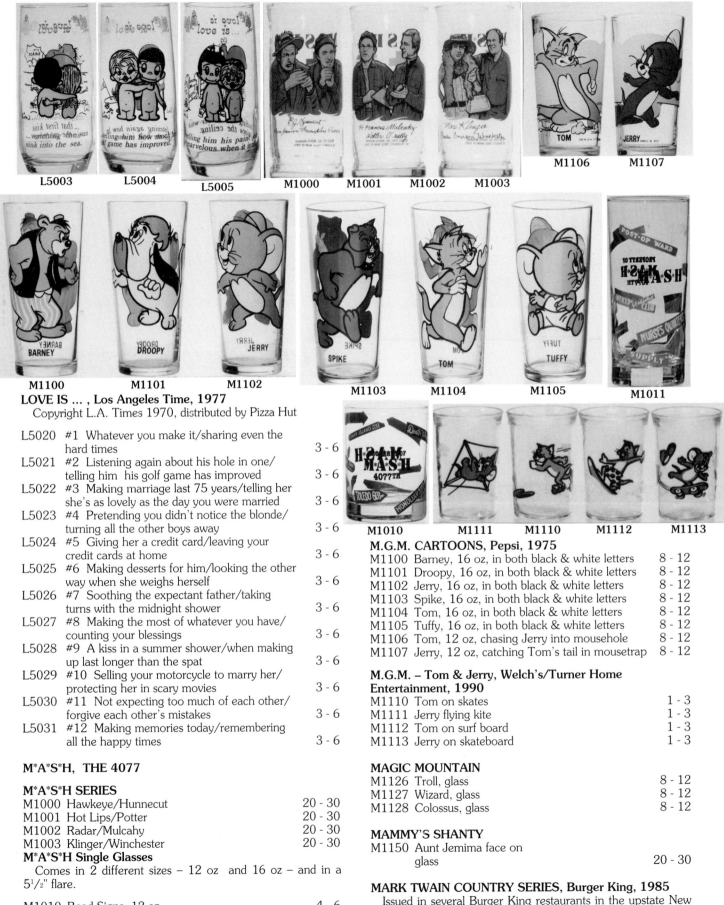

L5003   L5004   L5005   M1000   M1001   M1002   M1003

M1106   M1107

BARNEY   DROOPY   JERRY
M1100   M1101   M1102

SPIKE   TOM   TUFFY
M1103   M1104   M1105   M1011

M1010   M1111   M1110   M1112   M1113

LOVE IS ... , Los Angeles Time, 1977
Copyright L.A. Times 1970, distributed by Pizza Hut

L5020	#1 Whatever you make it/sharing even the hard times	3 - 6
L5021	#2 Listening again about his hole in one/telling him his golf game has improved	3 - 6
L5022	#3 Making marriage last 75 years/telling her she's as lovely as the day you were married	3 - 6
L5023	#4 Pretending you didn't notice the blonde/turning all the other boys away	3 - 6
L5024	#5 Giving her a credit card/leaving your credit cards at home	3 - 6
L5025	#6 Making desserts for him/looking the other way when she weighs herself	3 - 6
L5026	#7 Soothing the expectant father/taking turns with the midnight shower	3 - 6
L5027	#8 Making the most of whatever you have/counting your blessings	3 - 6
L5028	#9 A kiss in a summer shower/when making up last longer than the spat	3 - 6
L5029	#10 Selling your motorcycle to marry her/protecting her in scary movies	3 - 6
L5030	#11 Not expecting too much of each other/forgive each other's mistakes	3 - 6
L5031	#12 Making memories today/remembering all the happy times	3 - 6

M*A*S*H, THE 4077

M*A*S*H SERIES

M1000	Hawkeye/Hunnecut	20 - 30
M1001	Hot Lips/Potter	20 - 30
M1002	Radar/Mulcahy	20 - 30
M1003	Klinger/Winchester	20 - 30

M*A*S*H Single Glasses
Comes in 2 different sizes – 12 oz and 16 oz – and in a 5 1/2" flare.

M1010	Road Signs, 12 oz	4 - 6
M1011	Building Signs, 16 oz	4 - 6

M.G.M. CARTOONS, Pepsi, 1975

M1100	Barney, 16 oz, in both black & white letters	8 - 12
M1101	Droopy, 16 oz, in both black & white letters	8 - 12
M1102	Jerry, 16 oz, in both black & white letters	8 - 12
M1103	Spike, 16 oz, in both black & white letters	8 - 12
M1104	Tom, 16 oz, in both black & white letters	8 - 12
M1105	Tuffy, 16 oz, in both black & white letters	8 - 12
M1106	Tom, 12 oz, chasing Jerry into mousehole	8 - 12
M1107	Jerry, 12 oz, catching Tom's tail in mousetrap	8 - 12

M.G.M. – Tom & Jerry, Welch's/Turner Home Entertainment, 1990

M1110	Tom on skates	1 - 3
M1111	Jerry flying kite	1 - 3
M1112	Tom on surf board	1 - 3
M1113	Jerry on skateboard	1 - 3

MAGIC MOUNTAIN

M1126	Troll, glass	8 - 12
M1127	Wizard, glass	8 - 12
M1128	Colossus, glass	8 - 12

MAMMY'S SHANTY

M1150	Aunt Jemima face on glass	20 - 30

MARK TWAIN COUNTRY SERIES, Burger King, 1985
Issued in several Burger King restaurants in the upstate New York area. Came in a box with open windows for the glasses to show through. Value in original box is much higher.

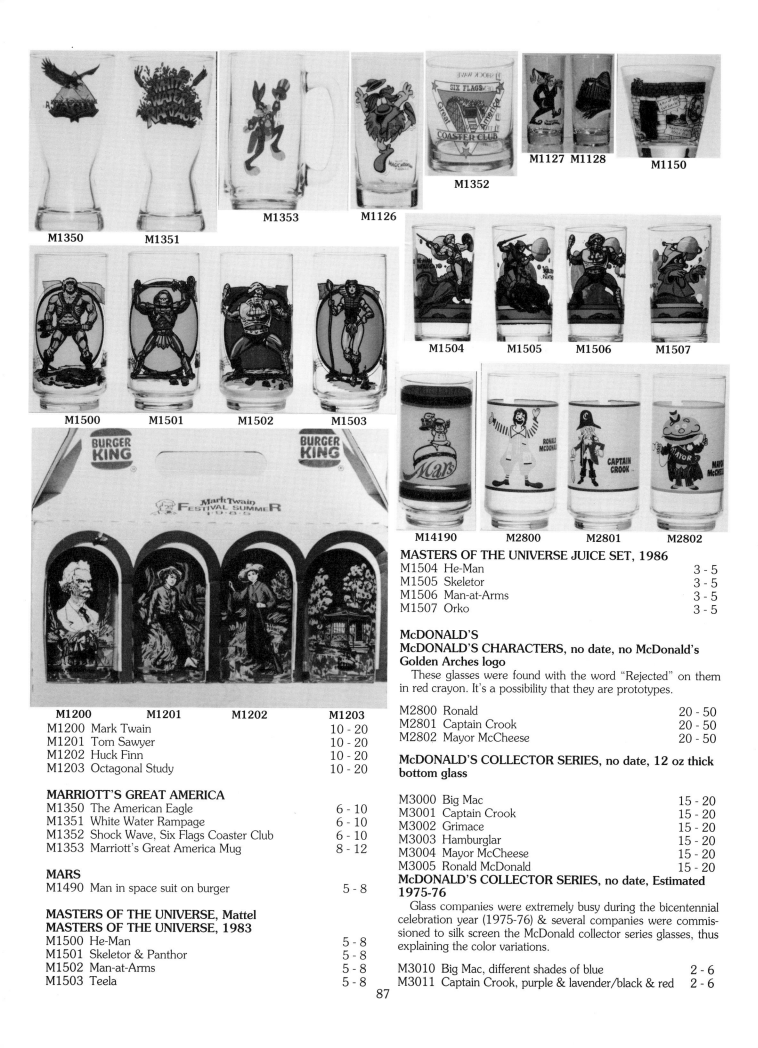

M1350   M1351   M1353   M1126   M1352   M1127 M1128   M1150

M1504   M1505   M1506   M1507

M1500   M1501   M1502   M1503

M14190   M2800   M2801   M2802

M1200   M1201   M1202   M1203

M1200 Mark Twain	10 - 20
M1201 Tom Sawyer	10 - 20
M1202 Huck Finn	10 - 20
M1203 Octagonal Study	10 - 20

MARRIOTT'S GREAT AMERICA
M1350 The American Eagle	6 - 10
M1351 White Water Rampage	6 - 10
M1352 Shock Wave, Six Flags Coaster Club	6 - 10
M1353 Marriott's Great America Mug	8 - 12

MARS
M1490 Man in space suit on burger	5 - 8

MASTERS OF THE UNIVERSE, Mattel
MASTERS OF THE UNIVERSE, 1983
M1500 He-Man	5 - 8
M1501 Skeletor & Panthor	5 - 8
M1502 Man-at-Arms	5 - 8
M1503 Teela	5 - 8

MASTERS OF THE UNIVERSE JUICE SET, 1986
M1504 He-Man	3 - 5
M1505 Skeletor	3 - 5
M1506 Man-at-Arms	3 - 5
M1507 Orko	3 - 5

McDONALD'S
McDONALD'S CHARACTERS, no date, no McDonald's Golden Arches logo

These glasses were found with the word "Rejected" on them in red crayon. It's a possibility that they are prototypes.

M2800 Ronald	20 - 50
M2801 Captain Crook	20 - 50
M2802 Mayor McCheese	20 - 50

McDONALD'S COLLECTOR SERIES, no date, 12 oz thick bottom glass

M3000 Big Mac	15 - 20
M3001 Captain Crook	15 - 20
M3002 Grimace	15 - 20
M3003 Hamburglar	15 - 20
M3004 Mayor McCheese	15 - 20
M3005 Ronald McDonald	15 - 20

McDONALD'S COLLECTOR SERIES, no date, Estimated 1975-76

Glass companies were extremely busy during the bicentennial celebration year (1975-76) & several companies were commissioned to silk screen the McDonald collector series glasses, thus explaining the color variations.

M3010 Big Mac, different shades of blue	2 - 6
M3011 Captain Crook, purple & lavender/black & red	2 - 6

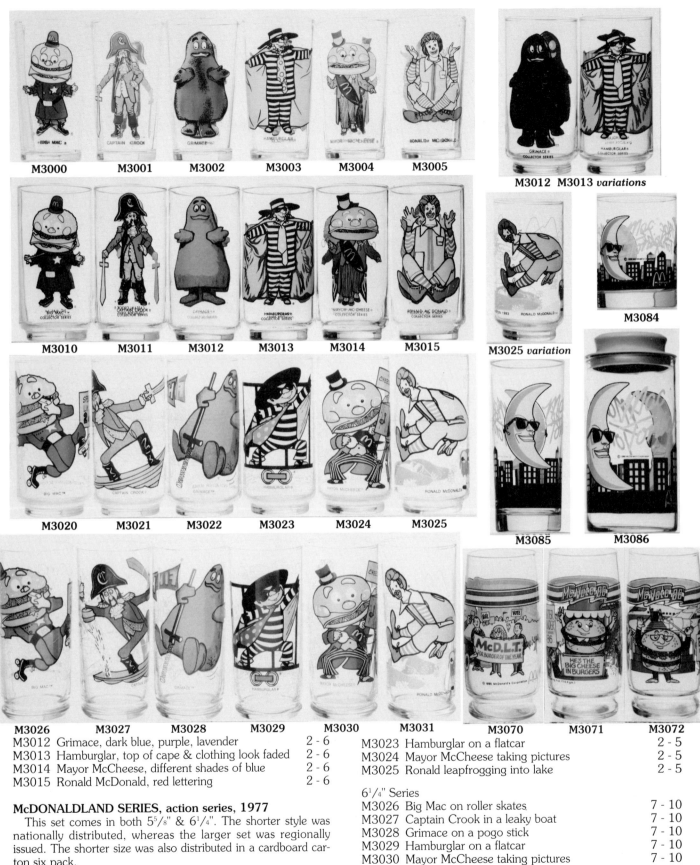

M3000 M3001 M3002 M3003 M3004 M3005

M3012 M3013 *variations*

M3010 M3011 M3012 M3013 M3014 M3015

M3025 *variation*

M3084

M3020 M3021 M3022 M3023 M3024 M3025

M3085 M3086

M3026 M3027 M3028 M3029 M3030 M3031 M3070 M3071 M3072

M3012 Grimace, dark blue, purple, lavender	2 - 6	
M3013 Hamburglar, top of cape & clothing look faded	2 - 6	
M3014 Mayor McCheese, different shades of blue	2 - 6	
M3015 Ronald McDonald, red lettering	2 - 6	

McDONALDLAND SERIES, action series, 1977

This set comes in both 5⅝" & 6¼". The shorter style was nationally distributed, whereas the larger set was regionally issued. The shorter size was also distributed in a cardboard carton six pack.

5⅝" Series
M3020 Big Mac on roller skates	2 - 5
M3021 Captain Crook in a leaky boat	2 - 5
M3022 Grimace on a pogo stick	2 - 5

M3023 Hamburglar on a flatcar	2 - 5
M3024 Mayor McCheese taking pictures	2 - 5
M3025 Ronald leapfrogging into lake	2 - 5

6¼" Series
M3026 Big Mac on roller skates	7 - 10
M3027 Captain Crook in a leaky boat	7 - 10
M3028 Grimace on a pogo stick	7 - 10
M3029 Hamburglar on a flatcar	7 - 10
M3030 Mayor McCheese taking pictures	7 - 10
M3031 Ronald leapfrogging into lake	7 - 10

There is a 1983 version of the above set with the same images in a 6¼" size. Also a 5" glass of Ronald with the 1983 date & the same image as above with some color variation.

88

| M3032 | M3033 | M3034 | M3035 | M3036 | M3037 |

M4102   M3100   M3101

| M3080 | M3081 | M3082 | M3083 | M3102 | M3103 |

| M3095 | M3096 | M3097 | M3098 |

ADVENTURELAND SERIES, action series, 1980

M3032	Big Mac Nets The Hamburglar	15 - 20
M3033	Captain Crook Sails The Bounding Main	15 - 20
M3034	Grimace Climbs A Mountain	15 - 20
M3035	Hamburglar Hooks The Hamburgers	15 - 20
M3036	Mayor McCheese Rides A Runaway Train	15 - 20
M3037	Ronald McDonald Saves The Falling Stars	15 - 20

McVOTE '86, 1986

M3070	McD.L.T	12 - 16
M3071	Quarter Pounder	12 - 16
M3072	Big Mac	12 - 16

SMOKE COLOR MUGS, sports series, embossed images

M3080	Captain Crook, baseball	4 - 10
M3081	Grimace, basketball	4 - 10
M3082	Ronald, football	4 - 10
M3083	Hamburglar, hockey	4 - 10

MAC TONIGHT, 1988

M3084	12 oz on the rocks glass	6 - 8
M3085	16 oz	6 - 8
M3086	32 oz cooler	6 - 8
M3087	Mac at piano, black mug	8 - 10
M3088	Mac singing w/mike, black mug	8 - 10

McDONALD'S CHARACTERS, co-sponsor Coca-Cola, Canada

M3095	Birdie	6 - 8
M3096	Hamburglar	6 - 8
M3097	Grimace	6 - 8
M3098	Ronald	6 - 8

THE NUTCRACKER, McDonald's, 1990

M3100	The Nutcracker led the toys to battle against the army of mice	5 - 12
M3101	Marie cried out with delight, "A nutcracker! Godfather, he is so beautiful."	5 - 12
M3102	Marie and the prince glided across the dance floor in Toyland	5 - 12
M3103	"The Sugar Plum fairy lives here in the Land of Sweets," said the Nutcracker	5 - 12

McDONALD'S, embossed bottom, 1983

Same action scenes as 1977 series

M3200	Ronald	20 - 30
M3201	Big Mac	20 - 30
M3202	Grimace	20 - 30
M3203	Hamburglar	20 - 30

McDONALD'S Single Glasses

McDonald's issued glasses to commemorate a corporation event such as grand openings, store managers' conventions, dedications or regional celebrations.

M4000	1975 "Hamburger U. 10,000 students"	7 - 10
M4005	1977 Store Managers' Convention	10 - 12
M4006	1978 Store Managers' Convention	10 - 12
M4010	1981 Agency Convention	10 - 12
M4015	Juice Glass, frosted, golden arches	2 - 4
M4020	Juice Glass, w/yellow & white daisies	2 - 4
M4025	1982 Grand Opening Gen. De Gaulle, Canada	7 - 10
M4030	4000th Store, Canada	7 - 10
M4035	"Good Morning" milk glass mug, "many happy returns"	1 - 2
M4036	"Good Morning" milk glass mug, maple leaf	2 - 3
M4040	Drink Coca-Cola & McD – red, black, yellow, Canada	7 - 10
M4041	Chesaning, MI Showboat City, pedestal glass	8 - 10
M4045	St. Mary's of Nazareth Hospital Center	8 - 10
M4050	Toledo Zoo	7 - 10
M4060	Texas "Hook 'em Horns"	7 - 10
M4065	Happy Holidays – Mary Lou Retton pictured	6 - 12
M4066	Gold Medal Mary Lou Retton	6 - 12

M4101   M4103

M4041

M6001   M6002   M6003   M6005

M4015   M4050   M4089

M4040   M4090   M4067   M6010

M4067	1984 Olympics, Sam the Eagle, Swimming	6 - 12
M4089	McDonald's Of Harrison "Triple A's"	6 - 12
M4090	Big Mac contents in 6 different languages	7 - 10

ESPANA, 1982, McDonald's and Coke

M4100	Crowd running	25 - 30
M4101	Crowd waving	25 - 30
M4102	Bus with Coke	25 - 30
M4103	Crowd in stands	25 - 30

MEASURING GLASSES, 1930s through 1950s
Most of this type of glass are valued at 5–25.

M5000	Frigidaire beaker measure, 5¼", red	4 - 8
M5001	Phospho-soda measure, 3½", red	4 - 8
M5002	Edward Don & Co	4 - 8
M5003	Gamble's 23rd Anniversary	4 - 8
M5004	Gamble's, 1947	4 - 8
M5005	Speed Queen	4 - 8
M5006	Frigidaire, 5 colors	4 - 8
M5007	Toastmaster	6 - 10
M5008	GE speed cooking ranges	6 - 10
M5009	DON, red	4 - 8
M5010	Mulhey's, orange	4 - 8
M5011	Compliments of Edward Barret County Clerk, Democrat	6 - 10
M5012	Western Stores, 31 Years of Leadership	4 - 8
M5013	Federal Savings and Loan Ins. Corp.	6 - 10
M5014	Bireley's non-carbonated beverage	6 - 10
M5015	Gamble's, green, no date	4 - 8
M5016	Jiffy, red	4 - 8

M5017	Plainview Farms Dairy	6 - 10
M5018	Red Owl Food Store	4 - 8
M5019	National Food Store	4 - 8
M5020	Des Plaines Elks, 1966, 10th Anniversary	6 - 10
M5021	Bireley's, plain	4 - 8
M5022	R.F. Pastina	6 - 8
M5023	GE keyboard ranges	4 - 8
M5024	Master Mix Dealer	6 - 10
M5025	Badcock Home Furnishing Center	6 - 10
M5026	Phospho-soda, Fleet, small	6 - 10
M5027	You get a full measure from DON	4 - 8
M5028	Atlas Mason Jars, Lids and Caps	6 - 10
M5029	Ed Don and Co., 50,000 to 1, Don has your needs	4 - 8
M5030	Duke Power	4 - 8
M5031	Drink Cheer Up	4 - 8
M5032	Speed Queen, Big Q	4 - 8
M5033	Volkenants Appliance Stores	4 - 8
M5034	Gamble's 20 Years of Progress	4 - 8
M5035	GE P7 oven cleans itself	4 - 8
M5036	Hot Point refrigerator with water and ice	4 - 8

MIGHTY MOUSE (see TERRYTOONS)

MISSIONS, Historical, Coke

M6000	Santa Barbara	6 - 10
M6001	San Xavier	6 - 10
M6002	San Gabriel	6 - 10
M6003	San Juan Bautista	6 - 10
M6004	San Antonio de Valero	6 - 10
M6005	San Carlos Borromeo	6 - 10

M5000   M5000 reverse   M5000   M5000   M5000   M5000   M5000   M5000   M5000   M5000

| M5010 | M5012 | M5013 | M5014 | M5015 | M5016 | M5019 | M5017 | M5018 | M5020 |

| M5010 | M5012 | M5013 | M5014 | M5015 | M5016 | M5019 | M5017 | M5018 | M5020 | M5020 |

| M5032 | reverse | M5034 | M5035 | M5004 | M7300 | M7301 | M7302 | M7303 |

| M7000 | M7002 | M7003 | M7004 | M7005 | M7006 |

| M7500 | M7501 |

A small frosted glass set of 6 California missions exists. It was sold in gift shops at & around the missions. Some were duplicates of the Coke set. San Jose was one variation. It is not known if this was an additional glass or a replacement for one of the originals. Texas and Arizona mission glasses also exist.

M6010 San Jose   3 - 6

MONARCH FOODS

Luke and Lucy were part of Monarch's Finer Foods Fall Fiesta.

M7000	Luke sipping lemonade, Lucy taking off her shoe	8 - 15
M7001	Luke & Lucy having a picnic	8 - 15
M7002	Luke posing w/Indian , Lucy taking a picture	8 - 15
M7003	Luke playing Santa Claus	8 - 15
M7004	Luke at the circus, Lucy in center ring	8 - 15
M7005	Luke and Lucy with snowman	8 - 15
M7006	Luke and Lucy ice skating	8 - 15

MONOPOLY COLLECTOR SERIES, Arby's, 1985
M7300 Just Visiting   4 - 6

M7301 Free Parking   4 - 6
M7302 Go To Jail   4 - 6
M7303 Collect $200   4 - 6

MONSTERS (see UNIVERSAL MONSTERS)

MORRIS THE CAT (cat food)
M7500 Morris On Glass Is Like Sterling On Silver   6 - 10
M7501 There's Something Irresistible About This Glass 6 - 10

MOTHER'S PIZZA PASTA RESTAURANT, Canada, Coke
M7800	1 of 6, Couple on motorcycle	8 - 12
M7801	2 of 6, Airplane & train	8 - 12
M7802	3 of 6, Flapper girl	8 - 12
M7803	4 of 6, Delivery truck	8 - 12
M7804	5 of 6, Baseball player	8 - 12
M7805	6 of 6, Trumpet player & cop	8 - 12

Single Glass
M7810 Mother's Pizza Pasta   5 - 8

MOUNT ST. HELENS VOLCANO
M7950 Mt. St. Helens Volcano   2 - 4

M7950

M7800   M7801   M7802   M7803   M7804   M7805

M7810   M8002   M8001 *variations*   M8005   N2000   N2001   N2002

MOVIE STARS (see ACTORS)

MR. MAGOO

This series comes in a jar style glass & a thin glass in three different sizes & color combinations.

M8000	1961 Magoo tipping hat to a fire hydrant/ shows him holding balloons	8 - 12
M8001	1962 Magoo walking into a manhole calling a taxi/shows him riding a horse backwards	8 - 12
M8002	1963 Skiing backwards/"Where's the beach?"	8 - 12
M8003	1964 Magoo in an old car saying "Road hog"/ shows him riding a cow backwards	8 - 15
M8004	Magoo riding backwards on a horse	8 - 15
M8005	Magoo/Road Hog parachuting	8 - 15

MR. TACO

M8100	Mr. Taco, Mexican man	1 - 3

MUMBLY (see HANNA BARBERA)

MUMMY (see UNIVERSAL MONSTERS)

MUPPETS INC., Jim Hensen

THE GREAT MUPPET CAPER, McDonald's, 1981

M9000	Happiness Hotel	1 - 3
M9001	Kermit the Frog	1 - 3
M9002	Miss Piggy	1 - 3
M9003	The Great Gonzo	1 - 3

M8003   M8005 variation   M9020   M9022

THE MUPPETS – From Sesame Street

M9010	16 oz glass, all characters	1 - 3
M9011	12 oz glass	1 - 3
M9012	Juice Glass	1 - 3
M9013	Mug	1 - 3

MUPPET BABIES, Kraft, 1989

M9020	Miss Piggy	5 - 8
M9021	Kermit	5 - 8
M9022	Gonzo and Animal	5 - 8
M9023	Fossie Bear	5 - 8

MUTANT (see UNIVERSAL MONSTERS)

NATASHA (see WARD)

M9000   M9001   M9002   M9003   M9010   M9011   M9012   M9013

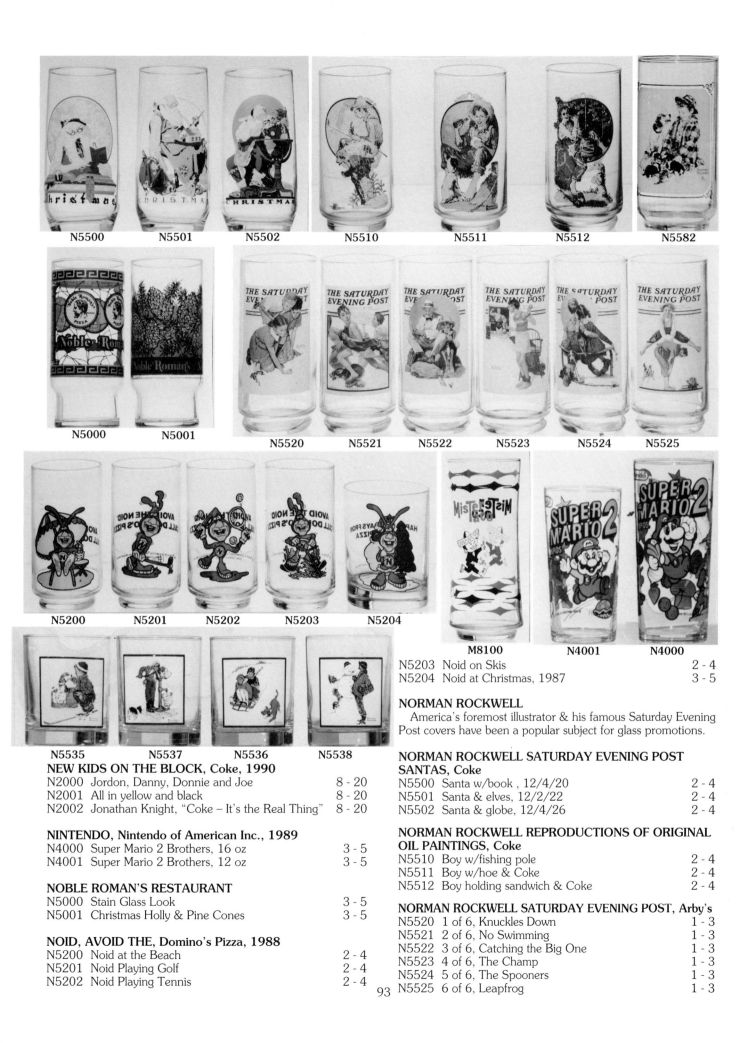

N5500　N5501　N5502　N5510　N5511　N5512　N5582

N5000　N5001　N5520　N5521　N5522　N5523　N5524　N5525

N5200　N5201　N5202　N5203　N5204

M8100　N4001　N4000

N5535　N5537　N5536　N5538

N5203	Noid on Skis	2 - 4
N5204	Noid at Christmas, 1987	3 - 5

NORMAN ROCKWELL

America's foremost illustrator & his famous Saturday Evening Post covers have been a popular subject for glass promotions.

NORMAN ROCKWELL SATURDAY EVENING POST SANTAS, Coke

N5500	Santa w/book , 12/4/20	2 - 4
N5501	Santa & elves, 12/2/22	2 - 4
N5502	Santa & globe, 12/4/26	2 - 4

NORMAN ROCKWELL REPRODUCTIONS OF ORIGINAL OIL PAINTINGS, Coke

N5510	Boy w/fishing pole	2 - 4
N5511	Boy w/hoe & Coke	2 - 4
N5512	Boy holding sandwich & Coke	2 - 4

NORMAN ROCKWELL SATURDAY EVENING POST, Arby's

N5520	1 of 6, Knuckles Down	1 - 3
N5521	2 of 6, No Swimming	1 - 3
N5522	3 of 6, Catching the Big One	1 - 3
N5523	4 of 6, The Champ	1 - 3
N5524	5 of 6, The Spooners	1 - 3
N5525	6 of 6, Leapfrog	1 - 3

NEW KIDS ON THE BLOCK, Coke, 1990

N2000	Jordon, Danny, Donnie and Joe	8 - 20
N2001	All in yellow and black	8 - 20
N2002	Jonathan Knight, "Coke – It's the Real Thing"	8 - 20

NINTENDO, Nintendo of American Inc., 1989

N4000	Super Mario 2 Brothers, 16 oz	3 - 5
N4001	Super Mario 2 Brothers, 12 oz	3 - 5

NOBLE ROMAN'S RESTAURANT

N5000	Stain Glass Look	3 - 5
N5001	Christmas Holly & Pine Cones	3 - 5

NOID, AVOID THE, Domino's Pizza, 1988

N5200	Noid at the Beach	2 - 4
N5201	Noid Playing Golf	2 - 4
N5202	Noid Playing Tennis	2 - 4

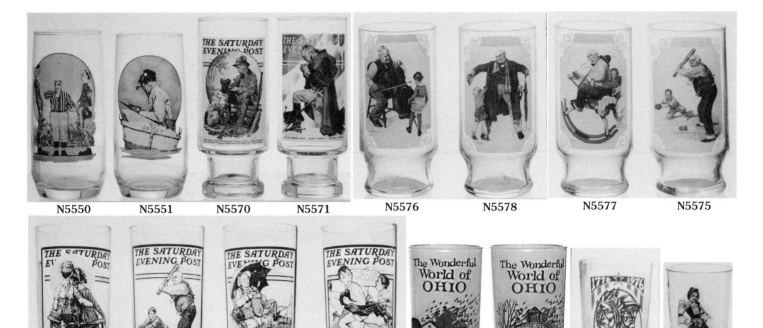

N5550   N5551   N5570   N5571   N5576   N5578   N5577   N5575

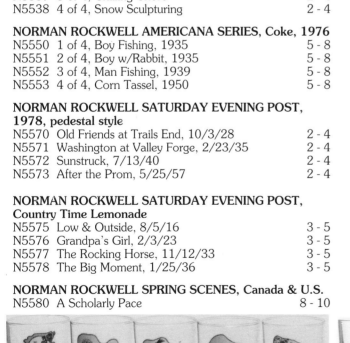

N5590   N5591   N5592   N5593   O1950   O1951   O2000   N8005

NORMAN ROCKWELL WINTER SCENES, Arby's & Pepsi, 1979

N5535	1 of 4, A Boy Meets His Dog	2 - 4
N5536	2 of 4, Downhill Daring	2 - 4
N5537	3 of 4, Chilling Chore	2 - 4
N5538	4 of 4, Snow Sculpturing	2 - 4

NORMAN ROCKWELL AMERICANA SERIES, Coke, 1976

N5550	1 of 4, Boy Fishing, 1935	5 - 8
N5551	2 of 4, Boy w/Rabbit, 1935	5 - 8
N5552	3 of 4, Man Fishing, 1939	5 - 8
N5553	4 of 4, Corn Tassel, 1950	5 - 8

NORMAN ROCKWELL SATURDAY EVENING POST, 1978, pedestal style

N5570	Old Friends at Trails End, 10/3/28	2 - 4
N5571	Washington at Valley Forge, 2/23/35	2 - 4
N5572	Sunstruck, 7/13/40	2 - 4
N5573	After the Prom, 5/25/57	2 - 4

NORMAN ROCKWELL SATURDAY EVENING POST, Country Time Lemonade

N5575	Low & Outside, 8/5/16	3 - 5
N5576	Grandpa's Girl, 2/3/23	3 - 5
N5577	The Rocking Horse, 11/12/33	3 - 5
N5578	The Big Moment, 1/25/36	3 - 5

NORMAN ROCKWELL SPRING SCENES, Canada & U.S.

N5580	A Scholarly Pace	8 - 10

N5581	Beguiling Buttercups	8 - 10
N5582	Pride of Parenthood	8 - 10
N5583	A Young Mans Fancy	8 - 10

NORMAN ROCKWELL SUMMER SCENES, Arby's & Coke, 1987

Although the Coke trademark does not appear on the glass, the store sign advertised the sale of a glass for 49 cents with the purchase of a sandwich & a classic Coke (or other soft drink).

N5590	Sunset	1 - 3
N5591	Gramps at the Plate	1 - 3
N5592	Gone Fishing	1 - 3
N5593	No Swimming	1 - 3

NUDES, 1940s

These glasses show a dressed woman on the outside of the glass and the same woman nude on the inside.

N8000	Woman smoking	5 - 8
N8001	Woman telephoning	5 - 8
N8002	Woman walking	5 - 8
N8003	Woman reading	5 - 8
N8004	Woman w/flowers	5 - 8

There is also a set showing women in their native costumes on the outside of the glass and the back of the same woman nude on the inside.

N8005	Woman standing	5 - 8

N8000   N8001   N8002   N8003   N8004

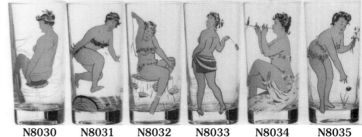

N8030   N8031   N8032   N8033   N8034   N8035

O3000   O3001   O3002   O3003   O3004   O3005   O3029   O3031

O3025   O3027   O3028   O3026   O3030   O3032   O3034

Full Figured Nudes

A set by Duane Dryers featuring a scantily clothed full-figured lady.

N8030	Helga on stool	5 - 8
N8031	Helga on log	5 - 8
N8032	Helga scratching back	5 - 8
N8033	Helga w/towel	5 - 8
N8034	Helga w/flute	5 - 8
N8035	Helga picking flowers	5 - 8

OHIO, The Wonderful World of

O1950	Marietta, Campus Martius Museum	5 - 8
O1951	Greenville, Fort Recovery State Memorial	5 - 8

OHIO BICENTENNIAL, Pepsi

O2000	Tecumseh/Johnny Appleseed	8 - 12
O2001	Fort Amanda/Fort Findlay	8 - 12
O2002	Miami-Erie Canal	8 - 12

OHIO & OKLAHOMA INDIANS, Knox Industries, 1959 giveaway

Ohio Indians

O3000	Blue Jacket - Shawnee	5 - 10
O3001	Chief Logan - Mingo	5 - 10
O3002	Cornstalk - Shawnee	5 - 10
O3003	Little Turtle - Miami	5 - 10
O3004	Pontiac - Ottawa	5 - 10
O3005	The Prophet - Shawnee	5 - 10
O3006	Tecumseh - Shawnee	5 - 10
O3007	White Eyes - Delaware	5 - 10
O3008	Wood carrier to the above set	10 - 15
O3009	Pitcher to the above set	20 - 25

Oklahoma Indians

The Oklahoma Indians were designed by Acee Blue Eagle, one of the world's greatest Indian artist. He was commissioned by Knox Industries to produce 8 paintings to be reproduced on 15 oz tumblers.

O3025	Geronimo - Apache	5 - 10
O3026	Quanah Parker - Comanche	5 - 10
O3027	Hen-Toh - Wyandot	5 - 10
O3028	Running Horse - Kiowa	5 - 10
O3029	Dull Knife - Cheyenne	5 - 10
O3030	Ruling His Sun - Pawnee	5 - 10
O3031	Bacon Rind - Osage	5 - 10
O3032	Sequoyah - Cherokee	5 - 10
O3033	Wood Carrier to the above set	10 - 15
O3034	Pitcher to the above set	20 - 25
O3035	Original Mailing Carton	10 - 15

OLYMPICS

SAM THE EAGLE (L.A. Olympics), Coke, 1984

Sam the Eagle was designed by Disney artists and given to the American Olympics Committee. There were many variations of this set using different events, issued in different countries. All sponsored by Coke.

A 6" size (0.41 liter) issued in England, but distributed in L.A. during the Olympics.

O4000	Sam w/torch	10 - 15
O4001	Sam jumping hurdles	10 - 15
O4002	Sam swimming	10 - 15
O4003	Sam kayaking	10 - 15
O4004	Sam waving	10 - 15
O4005	Sam soccer	10 - 15

O4006–The above 6 glasses were issued in a 5" (0.31
O4011 liter) version and distributed in Germany only, ea. 9 - 12

A set with color olympic rings as coasters was issued in Japan.

O4012	Sam kicking ball	15 - 20
O4013	Sam on gym horse	15 - 20
O4014	Sam diving	15 - 20
O4015	Sam holding torch	15 - 20
O4016	Sam lifting weights	15 - 20
O4017	Title unknown	15 - 20

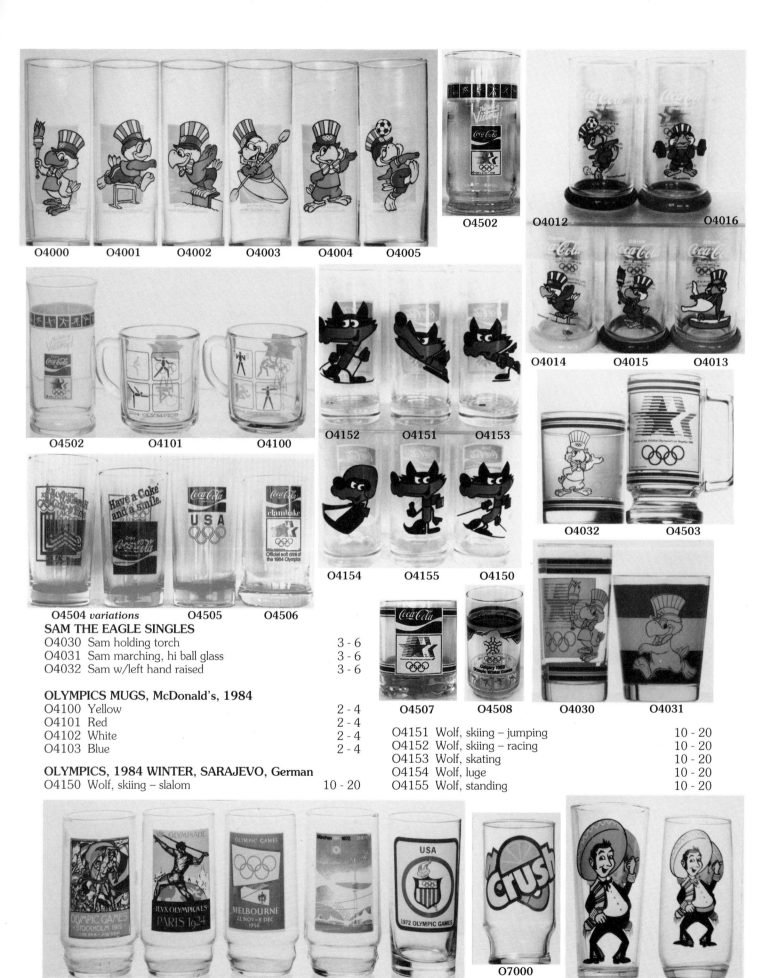

O4000   O4001   O4002   O4003   O4004   O4005

O4502

O4012   O4016

O4014   O4015   O4013

O4502   O4101   O4100

O4152   O4151   O4153

O4032   O4503

O4154   O4155   O4150

O4504 *variations*   O4505   O4506

O4507   O4508   O4030   O4031

SAM THE EAGLE SINGLES

O4030	Sam holding torch	3 - 6
O4031	Sam marching, hi ball glass	3 - 6
O4032	Sam w/left hand raised	3 - 6

OLYMPICS MUGS, McDonald's, 1984

O4100	Yellow	2 - 4
O4101	Red	2 - 4
O4102	White	2 - 4
O4103	Blue	2 - 4

OLYMPICS, 1984 WINTER, SARAJEVO, German

O4150	Wolf, skiing – slalom	10 - 20
O4151	Wolf, skiing – jumping	10 - 20
O4152	Wolf, skiing – racing	10 - 20
O4153	Wolf, skating	10 - 20
O4154	Wolf, luge	10 - 20
O4155	Wolf, standing	10 - 20

O4600 *variations*   96   O4500   O7000   P1200   P1201

P1000   P1001

P1015   P1014   P1013   P1012   P1016   P1400

P1002   P1003

P1410   P1411   P1412   P1413

P1435
both sides shown

P1404   P1402   P1403

OLYMPIC SINGLES

O4500	1972 Olympic Games	2 - 5
O4501	National Sports Festival, 1982, Coke	3 - 6
O4502	The Taste of Victory, 1984, Coke	3 - 6
O4503	Games of the XXIII Olympiad, 1984	3 - 6
O4504	Have a Coke and Smile, Coke, 2 diff sizes	10 - 15
O4505	USA, Coke	10 - 15
O4506	1984 Olympics Clambake	10 - 20
O4507	1984 Olympics, hi-ball	5 - 10
O4508	1988 Calgary, Coke, German	5 - 10

There is a set of at least 12 glasses with the official posters of various Olympiads.

O4600	Poster Glasses of the Olympics, 12, each	3 - 6

Glasses as souvenirs of the Olympic Games have been popular since the late '20s; however, they are difficult to find. Most of these glasses remain in the host country.

ORANGE CRUSH

O7000	Orange Crush, the soft drink trademark	4 - 6
O7001	Orange Crush, the Denver Bronco nickname	2 - 4

PAC MAN

PAC MAN SERIES, Bally, AAFES, 1980

P1000	Bashful	4 - 6
P1001	Pokey	4 - 6
P1002	Speedy	4 - 6
P1003	Shadow	4 - 6

PAC MAN COLLECTOR SERIES, Bally, 1980

P1010	Pac Man, Arby's 1980	2 - 4
P1011	Ms Pac Man, 1981	2 - 4
P1012	Pac Man Mug	2 - 4
P1013	Pac Man, tall flare top	2 - 4
P1014	Pac Man, short flare	2 - 4
P1015	Pac Man, short straight	2 - 4
P1016	Pac Man Mug, gobble ghost design	2 - 4

PANCHO'S MEXICAN RESTAURANT

P1200	Pancho, Pepsi logo	5 - 7
P1201	Pancho, round bottom	3 - 5

PEABODY (MR.) (see WARD)

PEANUTS CHARACTERS

P1400	Snoopy & Woodstock, slim	4 - 6
P1401	Snoopy, giant mug	8 - 12
P1402	Snoopy on lemon	3 - 6
P1403	Snoopy – Juice, Juice, Juice	3 - 6
P1404	Snoopy on apple	3 - 6
P1405	Snoopy, "Life is too short"	4 - 8
P1406	Snoopy, "This has been a good day"	4 - 8
P1407	Snoopy, dessert juice glass	4 - 8
P1408	Snoopy & Woodstock, mug	8 - 12

SPORTS SNOOPY, Dolly Madison, 1980s

P1415	Baseball	8 - 12
P1416	Tennis	8 - 12
P1417	Golf	8 - 12
P1418	Football	8 - 12

SNOOPY VOTE SET, Dolly Madison, 1980s

P1420	"Back the Beagle"	8 - 12
P1421	"The People's Choice"	8 - 12
P1422	"Put Snoopy in the White House"	8 - 12
P1423	"Vote For the American Beagle"	8 - 12

CAMP SNOOPY, McDonald's, released in 1983

Note: the dates on the glasses indicate the copyright dates for the individual characters, not the issue date.

P1401   P1430   P1431   P1432   P1433   P1434

P1450 variations

P1408   P1420   P1421   P1422   P1423   P1460   P1455

P1430	Charlie Brown – "Rats! Why is Having Fun Always So Much Work?"	2 - 4
P1431	Snoopy – "Civilization is Overrated"	2 - 4
P1432	Lucy – "There's No Excuse For Not Being Properly Prepared"	2 - 4
P1433	Snoopy – "Morning People Are Hard To Love"	2 - 4
P1434	Linus – "The Struggle For Security is No Picnic"	2 - 4
P1435	Charlie Brown – "Good Grief. McDonald's "Camp Snoopy" glasses are coming"	

This trailer glass was given to McDonald's restaurants to encourage them to order an ample supply of "Camp Snoopy" glasses in the summer of '83. The lure must have worked – "Camp Snoopy" glasses are by far the most common of the character glasses. The trailer glass, however, is worth whatever a collector wants to pay for it. At a glass show, I couldn't lure it away from its owner with a $50 offer.

SNOOPY and food
P1450	"Snoopy's Kitchen", different sizes	5 - 8
P1455	Snoopy, spaghetti scene, different sizes	5 - 8
P1460	Snoopy hamburger & hot dog scene, 4 diff sizes	5 - 8
P1465	Snoopy "Too Much Root Beer"	5 - 8
P1466	Snoopy "Big Apple"	5 - 8
P1470	Snoopy & Lemon	5 - 8

SNOOPY and the gang in an activity
P1480	Charlie & gang flying a kite	3 - 5
P1481	Lucy & the gang at lemonade stand	3 - 5

P1490   P1492   P1491   P1493

P1480   P1481   P1483   P1465

P1482	Lucy & Charlie "Never Underestimate a Pretty Face"	3 - 5
P1483	Lucy jumping rope	3 - 5

SNOOPY, pedestal glass
P1490	Cheers	1 - 3
P1491	Surprise	1 - 3
P1492	Love	1 - 3
P1493	Super Star	1 - 3

SNOOPY, Kraft's Jelly, 1988
P1500	Charlie flying a kite	1 - 2
P1501	Snoopy on surfboard	1 - 2
P1502	Lucy on a swing	1 - 2
P1503	Snoopy in pool	1 - 2

PENGUIN (see SUPER HEROES)

PEPE LE PEW (see WARNER BROTHERS)

PEPSI COLA (also see BICENTENNIAL, CHRISTMAS, COLLEGES, COUNTRY KITCHEN, DISNEY, HANNA BARBERA, WALTER LANTZ, LEONARDO TTV, M.G.M., TERRYTOONS, PANCHO'S, POPEYE, RINGLING BROTHERS CIRCUS, NORMAN ROCKWELL, SONIC, SPORTS, SUPER HEROES, TACO TIME, VISUAL CREATIONS, JAY WARD, WARNER BROTHERS)

PEPSI REPRODUCTION ADVERTISEMENT, circa 1900, black and white ads
P2100	"After A Hard Game"	7 - 10
P2101	"Down On The Beach"	7 - 10
P2102	"Drink At The Fountain"	7 - 10
P2103	"Barney Oldfield"	7 - 10

P1500   P1501   P1502   P1503

P2100   P2101   P2102   P2103

P2110   P2111   P2112   P2113

P2180   P2173

P2126   P2125   P2128   P2150   P2178   P2177   P2176

PEPSI CIRCA SET, trademark changes through the years

P2110	1906	7 - 10
P2111	1950	7 - 10
P2112	1962	7 - 10
P2113	1973	7 - 10
P2114	1987	7 - 10

PEPSI STAIN GLASS LOOK, Tiffany

P2125	Pepsi Cola, 6", red & blue	3 - 6
P2126	Pepsi Cola, 5", red & blue	3 - 6
P2127	Pepsi Cola, 3", red & blue	5 - 7
P2128	Pepsi Cola Pitcher to the above	10 - 12
P2130	Pepsi Cola 75th Anniversary Commemorative Set, in presentation box. Box contains shaker and 12 glasses. Six 8 oz glasses & six 12 oz glasses, dated 1898, 1905, 1906, 1950, 1962 & 1973.	
	Set	100 - 150
	Individual Glasses	5 - 8
	Shaker	15 - 25
P2150	"Golden Harvest", mason jar, 1 pint, "PEPSI"	8 - 10
P2151	"Pepsi Cola" in fancy white tole work design	2 - 4
P2154	"Pepsi Cola" matching pitcher to above	10 - 12

P2155	"Pepsi Cola", flare glass sold as set of 4 w/tray	12 - 20
P2158	"Pepsi Cola", 20 Pepsi logos of different countries, gold trim, crushed glass look	8 - 12
P2159	"Pepsi Cola", same as above, taller, no gold, painted on	6 - 12
P2160	"Pepsi Cola 1876-1976", 14 oz set of 4, tray	15 - 20
P2170	"Pepsi", poinsettia	6 - 10
P2172	"Pepsi Cola", bottle cap design, 4$\frac{1}{2}$"	6 - 10
P2173	"Pepsi Cola", bottle cap design, 5$\frac{1}{2}$"	6 - 10
P2175	"Diet Pepsi", 14 oz, tall slender glass	6 - 10
P2176	"Diet Pepsi One Calorie", tall slender	6 - 10
P2177	"Pepsi Light", blue	2 - 5
P2178	"Pepsi Light", all green	3 - 8
P2180	"Pepsi Cola", goblet	2 - 5
P2181	"Pepsi Cola", pedestal	2 - 5
P2185	"Pepsi Cola", girl sipping from a glass	2 - 5
P2186	"Pepsi Cola", 7" pedestal	2 - 5
P2188	"Pepsi Cola", diamond leaded glass design	2 - 4
P2189	Pitcher to match diamond design	10 - 15
P2190	Carafe to match diamond design	5 - 8
P2195	"Pepsi Cola", diamond design, "Union Station"	6 - 10
P2196	"Pepsi Cola", 32 oz, vertical design	2 - 4

P2151	P2154	P2155

P2400	P2401	P2402	P2403

P2130

P2198	"Pepsi", modern, single arch	1 - 3
P2199	"Pepsi", modern, three arches	1 - 3
P2200	"Pepsi 100th Anniversary"	3 - 5
P2210	Pepsi, "Now you see it, now you don't"	2 - 4
P2211	Pepsi, "200 years of feelin' free"	2 - 4
P2215	Pepsi Second Annual Sales Rally, 1959	6 - 8
P2216	"Catch the Pepsi Spirit"	4 - 8

PEPSI, Single Glasses

P2230	Pepsi Cola w/syrup line	6 - 10
P2231	Uh huh, diet Pepsi	4 - 8
P2232	Pepsi-Cola in triangle	4 - 8

Pepsi, through its local bottling companies, distributed many glasses with the PEPSI trademark celebrating local events.

P2300	Bakersfield College	2 - 4
P2301	Herfy's 20th Anniversary	2 - 4
P2305	KYYX Radio	2 - 4
P2310	University of Arkansas Razorbacks	3 - 5
P2315	Multi-Language "Merry Christmas"	3 - 5
P2320	PCBA Dallas Roundup	2 - 4
P2325	Detroit Grand Prix	3 - 5
P2330	150th Anniversary of Michigan	3 - 5
P2335	Eau Clair, Wisconsin Opening	2 - 4
P2340	America's Cup	3 - 5
P2341	Caterpillar 1 and 2 (tractors), each	5 - 8
P2342	Same as P2341, but "Caterpillar" misspelled	10 - 15

P2350	Washington, DC 1776-1976	2 - 4
P2355	Opening, San Diego	2 - 4
P2360	Opening, Brownwood	2 - 4
P2365	Opening, Corpus Christi	2 - 5
P2370	Viola, California	2 - 4
P2375	Welcome to Las Vegas	5 - 8
P2380	PCBA, Jackson Hole	5 - 10
P2385	Hot Sam's	20 - 30
P2390	Food Service	20 - 30
P2391	Pepsi, Kroger	10 - 15
P2392	Shakey's	6 - 8

WINTER COOL COLLECTION

P2400.	Winter Wonderland	5 - 8
P2401	Diet Pepsi - penguins	5 - 8
P2402	Pepsi, house with snow	5 - 8
P2403	Santa and reindeer	5 - 8

PETER PAN, 1940s

P2500	Peter Pan and the Crocodile, 4"	10 - 15
P2501	Peter Pan and the Fairies, 4"	10 - 15
P2502	Peter Pan and the Mermaids, 4"	10 - 15
P2503	Peter Pan and the Never Bird, 4"	10 - 15
P2504	Peter Pan and the Pirate Captain, 4"	10 - 15
P2505	Peter Pan and his Shadow, 4"	10 - 15

PETUNIA PIG (see WARNER BROTHERS)

PIERRE THE BEAR, LK's

P2158	P2159	P2198	P2199	P2215	P2196	P2211

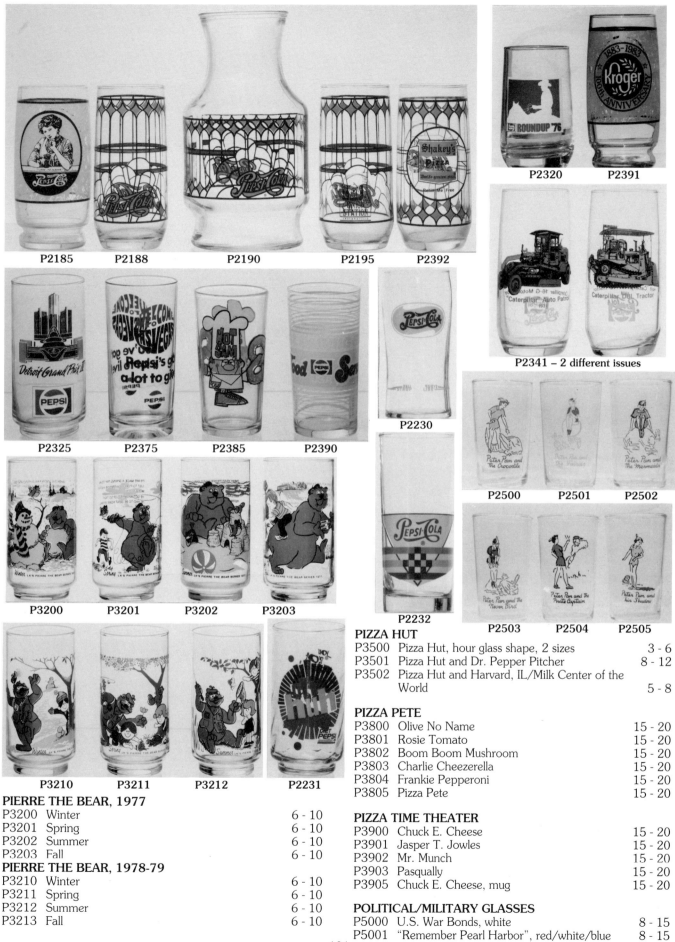

P2185   P2188   P2190   P2195   P2392

P2320   P2391

P2341 – 2 different issues

P2325   P2375   P2385   P2390

P2230

P2500   P2501   P2502

P3200   P3201   P3202   P3203

P2232

P2503   P2504   P2505

P3210   P3211   P3212   P2231

PIERRE THE BEAR, 1977

P3200	Winter	6 - 10
P3201	Spring	6 - 10
P3202	Summer	6 - 10
P3203	Fall	6 - 10

PIERRE THE BEAR, 1978-79

P3210	Winter	6 - 10
P3211	Spring	6 - 10
P3212	Summer	6 - 10
P3213	Fall	6 - 10

PIZZA HUT

P3500	Pizza Hut, hour glass shape, 2 sizes	3 - 6
P3501	Pizza Hut and Dr. Pepper Pitcher	8 - 12
P3502	Pizza Hut and Harvard, IL/Milk Center of the World	5 - 8

PIZZA PETE

P3800	Olive No Name	15 - 20
P3801	Rosie Tomato	15 - 20
P3802	Boom Boom Mushroom	15 - 20
P3803	Charlie Cheezerella	15 - 20
P3804	Frankie Pepperoni	15 - 20
P3805	Pizza Pete	15 - 20

PIZZA TIME THEATER

P3900	Chuck E. Cheese	15 - 20
P3901	Jasper T. Jowles	15 - 20
P3902	Mr. Munch	15 - 20
P3903	Pasqually	15 - 20
P3905	Chuck E. Cheese, mug	15 - 20

POLITICAL/MILITARY GLASSES

P5000	U.S. War Bonds, white	8 - 15
P5001	"Remember Pearl Harbor", red/white/blue	8 - 15

P3900   P3901   P3902   P3903   P6020   P6021   P6022   P6023

P6050   P3500 – 2 sizes   P3501   P6010   P6011   P6012

P6030   P6031   P6032   P6033   P6013   P6014   P6015

P5000   P5002   P5001

P5992   P5003   P5004   P5979   P5978   P5977   P5976   P5980

P6040	**P6041**	**P6042**	**P6043**
P5002	"V" for Victory, blue		8 - 15
P5003	Good Times for Everyone		10 - 20
P5004	Toss Your Hat in the Ring		10 - 20

1940s Cottage Cheese Glasses

P5010	Destroyer Selfridge, blue	15 - 30
P5011	20-Ton Patrol Bomber, yellow	15 - 30
P5012	Curtis Dive Bomber, red	15 - 30
P5013	155mm Gun, yellow	15 - 30
P5014	Armored Car, green	15 - 30
P5015	U.S. Submarine "S-20", yellow	15 - 30
P5016	U.S. Army M-3 Tank, red	15 - 30
P5017	Parachute Jumpers, red/white/blue	15 - 30

POPEYE

Some of the glasses have the 1929 copyright date on them and some have the 1936 copyright date, depending on when the characters were created. The set was released in the late '30s. Several reverse sides shown.

P5975	Popeye/Oscar	25 - 50
P5976	Popeye/Wimpy	25 - 50
P5977	Popeye/Olive Oil	25 - 50
P5978	Popeye/Jeep	25 - 50
P5979	Popeye/Alice the Goon	25 - 50
P5980	Popeye/Swee' Pea	25 - 50
P5981	Popeye/Sea Hag	25 - 50
P5982	Popeye/Bluto (Brutus)	25 - 50

There is also a line drawing, single color, numbered set of early Popeye glasses showing Popeye in an action scene. The exact number in the set is unknown, but we will assume for now that there are at least 8.

P5992	#3 Popeye/Wimpy	12 - 25

POPEYE – Kollect a Set, Coke, 1975

P6010	Popeye	3 - 5
P6011	Olive Oil	3 - 5
P6012	Wimpy	3 - 5
P6013	Brutus	3 - 5
P6014	Swee' Pea	3 - 5
P6015	Rough House	3 - 5

"Castor Oil", Olive's brother, and a "Geezel" exist in prototype. (see Appendix A)

POPEYE SPORTS SCENES, Popeye's Fried Chicken, 1978

P6020	Popeye	20 - 30
P6021	Olive Oyl	20 - 30
P6022	Brutus	20 - 30
P6023	Swee' Pea	20 - 30

POPEYE'S PALS, Popeye's Fried Chicken, 1979

P6030	Popeye	15 - 25
P6031	Olive Oil	15 - 25
P6032	Brutus	15 - 25
P6033	Swee' Pea	15 - 25

POPEYE'S FRIED CHICKEN – Tenth Anniversary, Pepsi, 1982

P6040	Popeye	15 - 20
P6041	Olive Oil	15 - 20
P6042	Brutus	15 - 20
P6043	Swee' Pea	15 - 20
P6050	Olive Oil, beaker style glass of Olive looking in a mirror, company give-away	10 - 20

POPPLES (Those Kids From Cleveland), Pizza Hut

P6200	Puzzle Popple	3 - 6
P6201	P.C. Popple	3 - 6
P6202	Party Popple	3 - 6
P6203	Puffball Popple	3 - 6
P6220	Popples single glass, juice size	3 - 6

PORKY PIG (see WARNER BROTHERS)

PRESIDENTS

Ohio Born - set

P8000	Rutherford B. Hayes	5 - 10
P8001	James Garfield	5 - 10
P8002	Benjamin Harrison	5 - 10
P8003	William McKinley	5 - 10
P8004	William H. Taft	5 - 10
P8005	Warren G. Harding	5 - 10

P6220

P6200	**P6201**	**P6202**	**P6203**	**R1501**	**R1502**	**R1503**	**R1504**

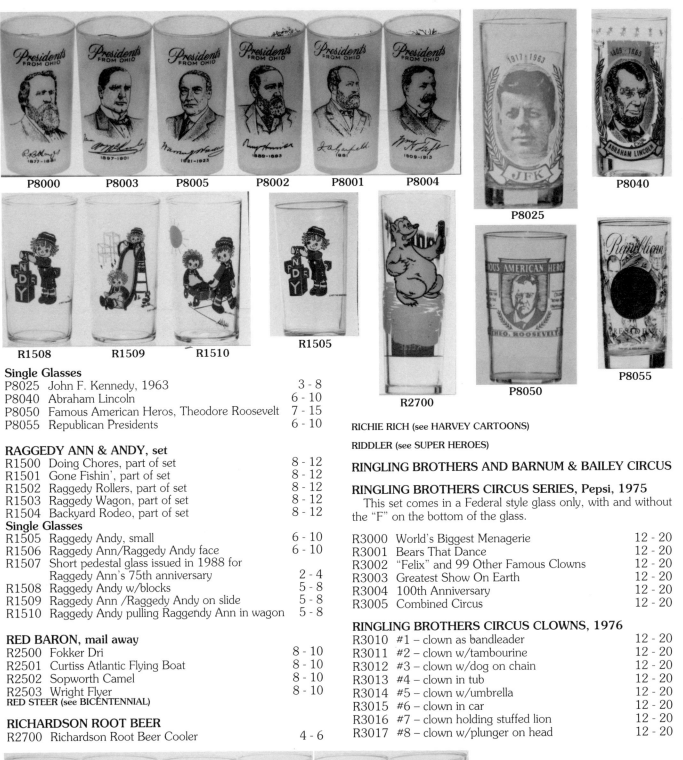

P8000   P8003   P8005   P8002   P8001   P8004

P8025

P8040

R1508   R1509   R1510

R1505

R2700

P8050

P8055

Single Glasses

P8025	John F. Kennedy, 1963	3 - 8
P8040	Abraham Lincoln	6 - 10
P8050	Famous American Heros, Theodore Roosevelt	7 - 15
P8055	Republican Presidents	6 - 10

RAGGEDY ANN & ANDY, set

R1500	Doing Chores, part of set	8 - 12
R1501	Gone Fishin', part of set	8 - 12
R1502	Raggedy Rollers, part of set	8 - 12
R1503	Raggedy Wagon, part of set	8 - 12
R1504	Backyard Rodeo, part of set	8 - 12

Single Glasses

R1505	Raggedy Andy, small	6 - 10
R1506	Raggedy Ann/Raggedy Andy face	6 - 10
R1507	Short pedestal glass issued in 1988 for Raggedy Ann's 75th anniversary	2 - 4
R1508	Raggedy Andy w/blocks	5 - 8
R1509	Raggedy Ann /Raggedy Andy on slide	5 - 8
R1510	Raggedy Andy pulling Raggendy Ann in wagon	5 - 8

RED BARON, mail away

R2500	Fokker Dri	8 - 10
R2501	Curtiss Atlantic Flying Boat	8 - 10
R2502	Sopworth Camel	8 - 10
R2503	Wright Flyer	8 - 10

RED STEER (see BICENTENNIAL)

RICHARDSON ROOT BEER

R2700	Richardson Root Beer Cooler	4 - 6

RICHIE RICH (see HARVEY CARTOONS)

RIDDLER (see SUPER HEROES)

RINGLING BROTHERS AND BARNUM & BAILEY CIRCUS

RINGLING BROTHERS CIRCUS SERIES, Pepsi, 1975

This set comes in a Federal style glass only, with and without the "F" on the bottom of the glass.

R3000	World's Biggest Menagerie	12 - 20
R3001	Bears That Dance	12 - 20
R3002	"Felix" and 99 Other Famous Clowns	12 - 20
R3003	Greatest Show On Earth	12 - 20
R3004	100th Anniversary	12 - 20
R3005	Combined Circus	12 - 20

RINGLING BROTHERS CIRCUS CLOWNS, 1976

R3010	#1 – clown as bandleader	12 - 20
R3011	#2 – clown w/tambourine	12 - 20
R3012	#3 – clown w/dog on chain	12 - 20
R3013	#4 – clown in tub	12 - 20
R3014	#5 – clown w/umbrella	12 - 20
R3015	#6 – clown in car	12 - 20
R3016	#7 – clown holding stuffed lion	12 - 20
R3017	#8 – clown w/plunger on head	12 - 20

R3000   R3001   R3002   R3003   R3004   R3005   R3018   R3019

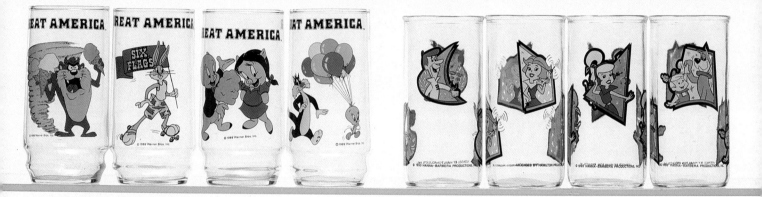

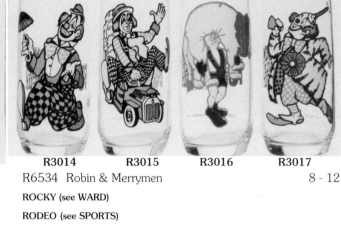

R3010	R3011	R3012	R3013

R3018 Circus World, 12 oz		12 - 20
R3019 Circus World mug		4 - 6

ROAD RUNNER (see WARNER BROTHERS)

ROARING '20s
R6400	Rudolph Valentino
R6401	Ramon Novarro
R6402	Charlie Chaplin
R6403	Lionel Barrymore

ROBIN (see SUPER HEROES)

ROBIN HOOD, Canada
R6500	#1 Robin Hood	10 - 20
R6501	#2 King Richard	10 - 20
R6502	#3 Friar Tuck	10 - 20
R6503	#4 Little John	10 - 20
R6504	#5 Maid Marian	10 - 20
R6505	#6 Will Scarlett	10 - 20
R6506	#7 Prince John	10 - 20
R6507	#8 Sheriff of Nottingham	10 - 20

ROBIN HOOD JELLY GLASSES
R6525	6" Robin standing	5 - 8
R6526	5" Robin standing	5 - 8
R6527	5" Robin kneeling, shooting arrow	5 - 8
R6528	Robin and Little John on log over water	5 - 8

ROBIN HOOD Single Glasses
R6530	Robin Hood & Begging Lady	10 - 15
R6531	Robin Hood, Friar Tuck, Little John	8 - 12
R6532	Robin Hood shooting deer	8 - 12
R6533	Robin & Little John	8 - 12

R3014	R3015	R3016	R3017

R6534 Robin & Merrymen		8 - 12

ROCKY (see WARD)

RODEO (see SPORTS)

ROGER HARGREAVES, Set 2
R7000	Mr. Funny	3 - 6
R7001	Mr. Tickle	3 - 6
R7002	Little Miss Helpful	3 - 6
R7003	Little Miss Shy	3 - 6
Set 2		
R7010	Little Miss Sunshine	3 - 6
R7011	Little Miss Neat	3 - 6
R7012	Mr. Silly	3 - 6
R7013	Mr. Bump	3 - 6

ROUND TABLE PIZZA
R7050	Round Table Pizza	2 - 5
R7051	Classic Auto Set, set of 4: '56 Corvette, '61 Thunderbird, '57 Chevrolet, '59 Cadillac, ea.	5 - 7

ROY ROGERS (see WESTERN HEROES)

SAD SACK (see HARVEY CARTOONS)

SANDY'S DRIVE-IN
S1000	Sandy, dancing	3 - 6
S1001	Sandy, head	3 - 6

SCOOBY DOO (see HANNA BARBERA)

R6401	R6402	R6403	R6404

R6531	R6532	R6533	R6534

P6500	P6502	P6503	P6504	P6505	P6505	R6530

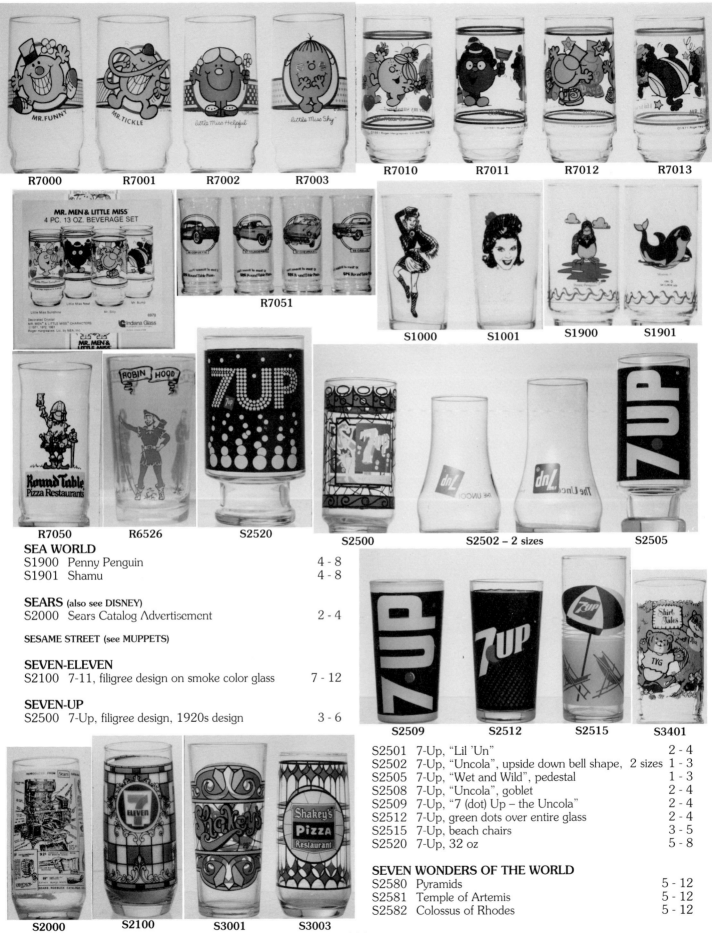

R7000   R7001   R7002   R7003   R7010   R7011   R7012   R7013

R7051   S1000   S1001   S1900   S1901

R7050   R6526   S2520   S2500   S2502 – 2 sizes   S2505

SEA WORLD

S1900	Penny Penguin	4 - 8
S1901	Shamu	4 - 8

SEARS (also see DISNEY)

S2000	Sears Catalog Advertisement	2 - 4

SESAME STREET (see MUPPETS)

SEVEN-ELEVEN

S2100	7-11, filigree design on smoke color glass	7 - 12

SEVEN-UP

S2500	7-Up, filigree design, 1920s design	3 - 6

S2509   S2512   S2515   S3401

S2501	7-Up, "Lil 'Un"	2 - 4
S2502	7-Up, "Uncola", upside down bell shape, 2 sizes	1 - 3
S2505	7-Up, "Wet and Wild", pedestal	1 - 3
S2508	7-Up, "Uncola", goblet	2 - 4
S2509	7-Up, "7 (dot) Up – the Uncola"	2 - 4
S2512	7-Up, green dots over entire glass	2 - 4
S2515	7-Up, beach chairs	3 - 5
S2520	7-Up, 32 oz	5 - 8

SEVEN WONDERS OF THE WORLD

S2580	Pyramids	5 - 12
S2581	Temple of Artemis	5 - 12
S2582	Colossus of Rhodes	5 - 12

S2000   S2100   S3001   S3003

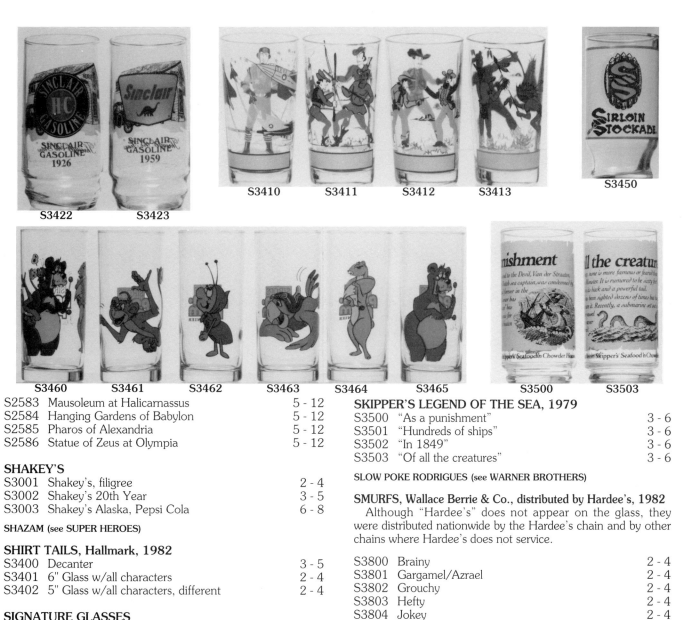

S3422   S3423   S3410   S3411   S3412   S3413   S3450

S3460   S3461   S3462   S3463   S3464   S3465   S3500   S3503

S2583	Mausoleum at Halicarnassus	5 - 12
S2584	Hanging Gardens of Babylon	5 - 12
S2585	Pharos of Alexandria	5 - 12
S2586	Statue of Zeus at Olympia	5 - 12

SHAKEY'S
S3001	Shakey's, filigree	2 - 4
S3002	Shakey's 20th Year	3 - 5
S3003	Shakey's Alaska, Pepsi Cola	6 - 8

SHAZAM (see SUPER HEROES)

SHIRT TAILS, Hallmark, 1982
S3400	Decanter	3 - 5
S3401	6" Glass w/all characters	2 - 4
S3402	5" Glass w/all characters, different	2 - 4

SIGNATURE GLASSES
S3410	Space theme
S3411	Merry Old England theme
S3412	Cowboy theme
S3413	Indian theme

SIMON BAR SINISTER (see LEONARDO TTV)

SINCLAIR GAS STATIONS
In 1990 a set of 4 glasses were issued to celebrate Sinclair's 75th anniversary.

S3420	1916	4 - 8
S3421	1920	4 - 8
S3422	1926	4 - 8
S3423	1959, dinosaur	4 - 8

SIRLOIN STOCKADE
| S3450 | Sirloin Stockade | 2 - 4 |

SIROPS PAM PAM, Cusenier, Holland
S3460	All characters	8 - 10
S3461	Monkey	8 - 10
S3462	Bug	8 - 10
S3463	Parrot	8 - 10
S3464	Mink	8 - 10
S3465	Bear	8 - 10

SKIPPER'S LEGEND OF THE SEA, 1979
S3500	"As a punishment"	3 - 6
S3501	"Hundreds of ships"	3 - 6
S3502	"In 1849"	3 - 6
S3503	"Of all the creatures"	3 - 6

SLOW POKE RODRIGUES (see WARNER BROTHERS)

SMURFS, Wallace Berrie & Co., distributed by Hardee's, 1982
Although "Hardee's" does not appear on the glass, they were distributed nationwide by the Hardee's chain and by other chains where Hardee's does not service.

S3800	Brainy	2 - 4
S3801	Gargamel/Azrael	2 - 4
S3802	Grouchy	2 - 4
S3803	Hefty	2 - 4
S3804	Jokey	2 - 4
S3805	Lazy	2 - 4
S3806	Papa Smurf	2 - 4
S3807	Smurfette	2 - 4

SMURFS, Hardee's, 1983
S3820	Baker Smurf	2 - 4
S3821	Clumsy Smurf	2 - 4
S3822	Handy Smurf	2 - 4
S3823	Harmony Smurf	2 - 4
S3824	Papa Smurf	2 - 4

S3800   S3801   S3802   S3803

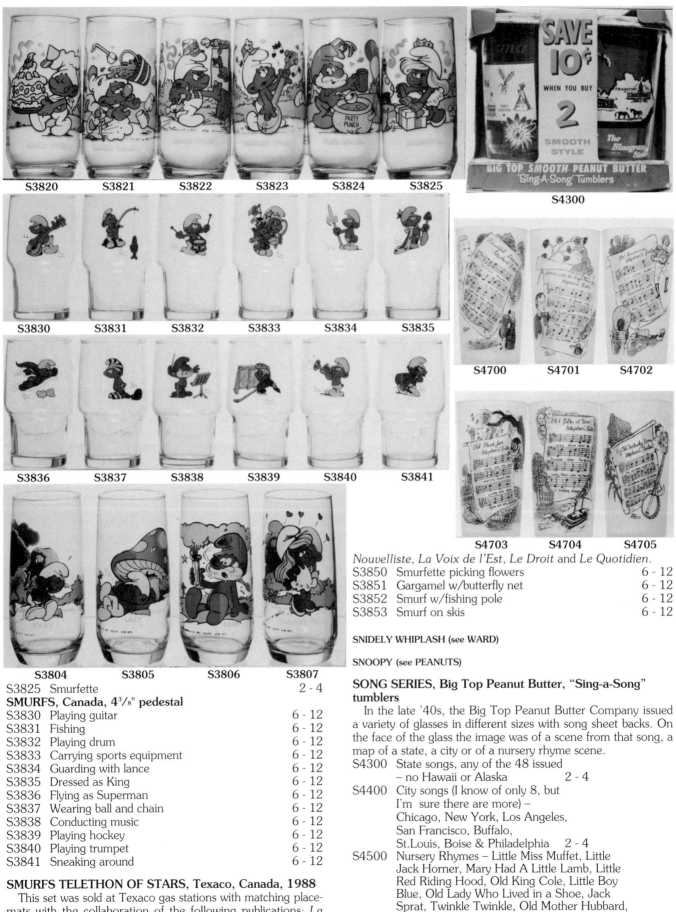

S3820	S3821	S3822	S3823	S3824	S3825
S3830	S3831	S3832	S3833	S3834	S3835
S3836	S3837	S3838	S3839	S3840	S3841

S4300

S4700	S4701	S4702
S4703	S4704	S4705

S3804	S3805	S3806	S3807

S3825 Smurfette   2 - 4

SMURFS, Canada, 4³/₈" pedestal

S3830	Playing guitar	6 - 12
S3831	Fishing	6 - 12
S3832	Playing drum	6 - 12
S3833	Carrying sports equipment	6 - 12
S3834	Guarding with lance	6 - 12
S3835	Dressed as King	6 - 12
S3836	Flying as Superman	6 - 12
S3837	Wearing ball and chain	6 - 12
S3838	Conducting music	6 - 12
S3839	Playing hockey	6 - 12
S3840	Playing trumpet	6 - 12
S3841	Sneaking around	6 - 12

SMURFS TELETHON OF STARS, Texaco, Canada, 1988

This set was sold at Texaco gas stations with matching place-mats with the collaboration of the following publications: *La Presse*, *The Gazette*, *Le Soleil*, *La Tribune*, *Tje Record*, *Le*

Nouvelliste, *La Voix de l'Est*, *Le Droit* and *Le Quotidien*.

S3850	Smurfette picking flowers	6 - 12
S3851	Gargamel w/butterfly net	6 - 12
S3852	Smurf w/fishing pole	6 - 12
S3853	Smurf on skis	6 - 12

SNIDELY WHIPLASH (see WARD)

SNOOPY (see PEANUTS)

SONG SERIES, Big Top Peanut Butter, "Sing-a-Song" tumblers

In the late '40s, the Big Top Peanut Butter Company issued a variety of glasses in different sizes with song sheet backs. On the face of the glass the image was of a scene from that song, a map of a state, a city or of a nursery rhyme scene.

S4300 State songs, any of the 48 issued
       – no Hawaii or Alaska   2 - 4

S4400 City songs (I know of only 8, but
       I'm sure there are more) –
       Chicago, New York, Los Angeles,
       San Francisco, Buffalo,
       St.Louis, Boise & Philadelphia   2 - 4

S4500 Nursery Rhymes – Little Miss Muffet, Little
       Jack Horner, Mary Had A Little Lamb, Little
       Red Riding Hood, Old King Cole, Little Boy
       Blue, Old Lady Who Lived in a Shoe, Jack
       Sprat, Twinkle Twinkle, Old Mother Hubbard,
       Jack Be Nibble, Jack & Jill, Little Bo Peep and

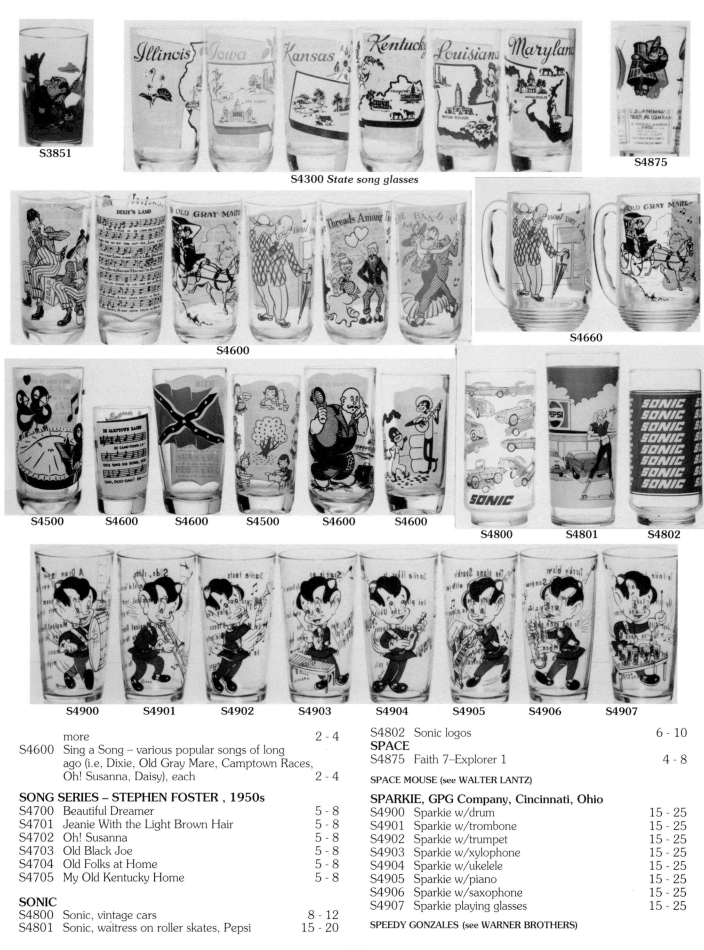

S3851

S4300 *State song glasses*

S4875

S4600

S4660

| S4500 | S4600 | S4600 | S4500 | S4600 | S4600 |

| S4800 | S4801 | S4802 |

| S4900 | S4901 | S4902 | S4903 | S4904 | S4905 | S4906 | S4907 |

	more	2 - 4
S4600	Sing a Song – various popular songs of long ago (i.e, Dixie, Old Gray Mare, Camptown Races, Oh! Susanna, Daisy), each	2 - 4

SONG SERIES – STEPHEN FOSTER , 1950s

S4700	Beautiful Dreamer	5 - 8
S4701	Jeanie With the Light Brown Hair	5 - 8
S4702	Oh! Susanna	5 - 8
S4703	Old Black Joe	5 - 8
S4704	Old Folks at Home	5 - 8
S4705	My Old Kentucky Home	5 - 8

SONIC

S4800	Sonic, vintage cars	8 - 12
S4801	Sonic, waitress on roller skates, Pepsi	15 - 20
S4802	Sonic logos	6 - 10

SPACE

S4875	Faith 7–Explorer 1	4 - 8

SPACE MOUSE (see WALTER LANTZ)

SPARKIE, GPG Company, Cincinnati, Ohio

S4900	Sparkie w/drum	15 - 25
S4901	Sparkie w/trombone	15 - 25
S4902	Sparkie w/trumpet	15 - 25
S4903	Sparkie w/xylophone	15 - 25
S4904	Sparkie w/ukelele	15 - 25
S4905	Sparkie w/piano	15 - 25
S4906	Sparkie w/saxophone	15 - 25
S4907	Sparkie playing glasses	15 - 25

SPEEDY GONZALES (see WARNER BROTHERS)

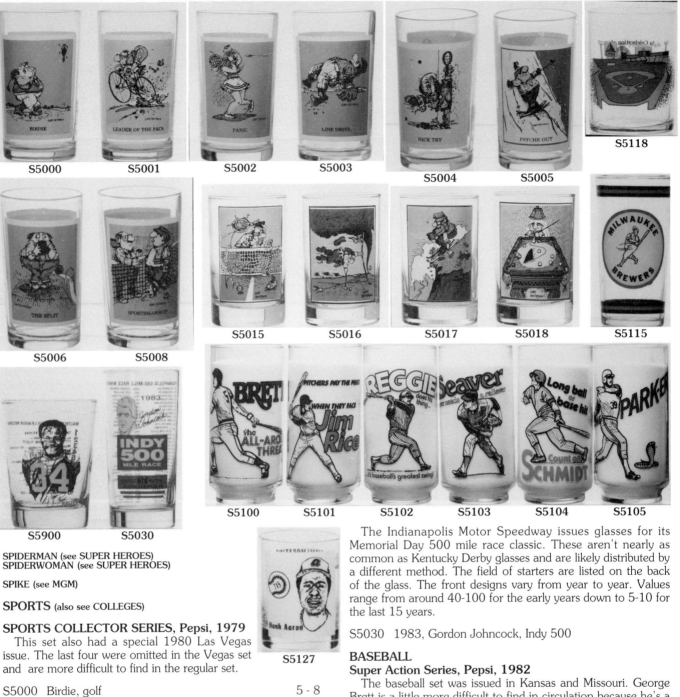

S5000   S5001   S5002   S5003   S5004   S5005   S5118

S5006   S5008   S5015   S5016   S5017   S5018   S5115

S5900   S5030   S5100   S5101   S5102   S5103   S5104   S5105

S5127

SPIDERMAN (see SUPER HEROES)
SPIDERWOMAN (see SUPER HEROES)

SPIKE (see MGM)

SPORTS (also see COLLEGES)

SPORTS COLLECTOR SERIES, Pepsi, 1979
This set also had a special 1980 Las Vegas issue. The last four were omitted in the Vegas set and are more difficult to find in the regular set.

S5000	Birdie, golf	5 - 8
S5001	Leader of the Pack, bicycling	5 - 8
S5002	Panic, tennis	5 - 8
S5003	Line Drive, baseball	5 - 8
S5004	Nice Try, racquetball	5 - 8
S5005	Psyche Out, skiing	5 - 8
S5006	The Split	10 - 12
S5007	Heads Up	10 - 12
S5008	Sportsmanship	10 - 12
S5009	Backlash	10 - 12

THOUGHT FACTORY COLLECTOR SERIES, Arby's, 1982

S5015	Luck Out, tennis	3 - 5
S5016	Dedication, golf	3 - 5
S5017	First Flake, skiing	3 - 5
S5018	Pool Shark, pool	3 - 5

AUTO RACING

The Indianapolis Motor Speedway issues glasses for its Memorial Day 500 mile race classic. These aren't nearly as common as Kentucky Derby glasses and are likely distributed by a different method. The field of starters are listed on the back of the glass. The front designs vary from year to year. Values range from around 40-100 for the early years down to 5-10 for the last 15 years.

S5030   1983, Gordon Johncock, Indy 500

BASEBALL

Super Action Series, Pepsi, 1982
The baseball set was issued in Kansas and Missouri. George Brett is a little more difficult to find in circulation because he's a native of Kansas and most Kansas dwellers hold on to him.

S5100	George Brett	30 - 50
S5101	Jim Rice	30 - 50
S5102	Reggie Jackson	30 - 50
S5103	Tom Seaver	30 - 50
S5104	Mike Schmidt	30 - 50
S5105	Dave Parker	30 - 50

Single Glasses

S5115	Milwaukee Brewers	5 - 8
S5116	Cincinnati Reds, Tresler Comet Auto	5 - 8
S5117	Brewers, Unocal '76, mitt w/ball	5 - 8
S5118	Fenway Park, Citgo/Red Sox	5 - 8
S5125	Pete Rose, Gold Star Chili	5 - 8
S5127	Hank Aaron, 715 Home Run	6 - 10

Milwaukee Brewers, McDonald's, 1982

S5125    S5130   S5131   S5132   S5133    S5138    S5117   S5116

S5140   S5141   S5142

S5143   S5144   S5145

S5170   S5171   S5172   S5173

S5150   S5151   S5152   S5153    S5160   S5161   S5162   S5163

S5141	2 of 6, Rick Dempsey	6 - 10
S5142	3 of 6, Eddie Murray	6 - 10
S5143	4 of 6, Storm Davis	6 - 10
S5144	5 of 6, Fred Lynn	6 - 10
S5145	6 of 6, Mike Boddicker	6 - 10

Pittsburgh Pirates, Elby's, Coca-Cola

S5150	Jim Gott & Jose Lind	5 - 8
S5151	Mike La Valliere & Barry Bonds	5 - 8
S5152	Bobby Bonilla & Doug Drabek	5 - 8
S5153	Mike Dunne & Andy Van Slyke	5 - 8

Detroit Tigers, Little Caesar's, 1984

S5160	Trammell, Rozema, Johnson	8 - 12
S5161	Lemon, Hernandez, Wilcox	8 - 12
S5162	Gibson, Lopez, Morris	8 - 12

| S5163 | Petry, Parrish, Whitaker | 8 - 12 |

Detroit Tigers '88 (mascot)

S5170	Tiger holding scoreboard	8 - 12
S5171	Tiger catching fly ball	8 - 12
S5172	Tiger at bat	8 - 12
S5173	Tiger waving pennant	8 - 12

**Detroit Tigers (Aren't You Hungry?), "First 4 Sports",
Burger King**

  This set shows a tiger with an object in his mouth that is a rep-

S5130	Paul Molitor & Pete Vuckovich	6 - 10
S5131	Robin Yount & Ben Ogilvie	6 - 10
S5132	Gorman Thomas & Cecil Cooper	6 - 10
S5133	Rollie Fingers & Ted Simmons	6 - 10

Milwaukee Brewers, Pepsi/Total

| S5138 | Milwaukee Brewers | 3 - 6 |

Baltimore Orioles, 1984

| S5140 | 1 of 6, Cal Ripken, Jr. | 6 - 10 |

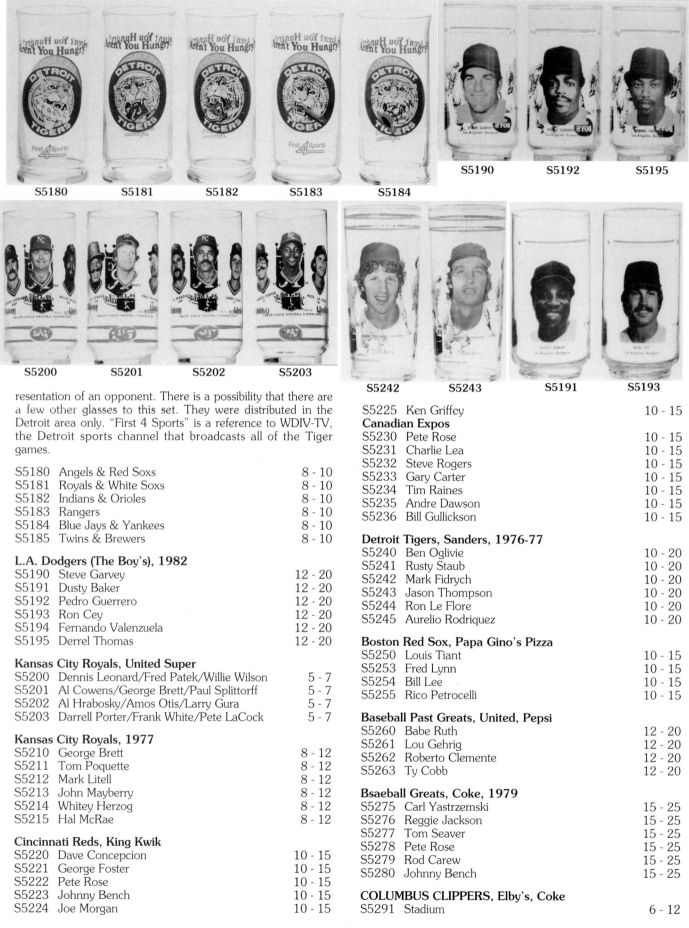

S5180   S5181   S5182   S5183   S5184

S5190   S5192   S5195

S5200   S5201   S5202   S5203

S5242   S5243   S5191   S5193

resentation of an opponent. There is a possibility that there are a few other glasses to this set. They were distributed in the Detroit area only. "First 4 Sports" is a reference to WDIV-TV, the Detroit sports channel that broadcasts all of the Tiger games.

S5180	Angels & Red Soxs	8 - 10
S5181	Royals & White Soxs	8 - 10
S5182	Indians & Orioles	8 - 10
S5183	Rangers	8 - 10
S5184	Blue Jays & Yankees	8 - 10
S5185	Twins & Brewers	8 - 10

L.A. Dodgers (The Boy's), 1982

S5190	Steve Garvey	12 - 20
S5191	Dusty Baker	12 - 20
S5192	Pedro Guerrero	12 - 20
S5193	Ron Cey	12 - 20
S5194	Fernando Valenzuela	12 - 20
S5195	Derrel Thomas	12 - 20

Kansas City Royals, United Super

S5200	Dennis Leonard/Fred Patek/Willie Wilson	5 - 7
S5201	Al Cowens/George Brett/Paul Splittorff	5 - 7
S5202	Al Hrabosky/Amos Otis/Larry Gura	5 - 7
S5203	Darrell Porter/Frank White/Pete LaCock	5 - 7

Kansas City Royals, 1977

S5210	George Brett	8 - 12
S5211	Tom Poquette	8 - 12
S5212	Mark Litell	8 - 12
S5213	John Mayberry	8 - 12
S5214	Whitey Herzog	8 - 12
S5215	Hal McRae	8 - 12

Cincinnati Reds, King Kwik

S5220	Dave Concepcion	10 - 15
S5221	George Foster	10 - 15
S5222	Pete Rose	10 - 15
S5223	Johnny Bench	10 - 15
S5224	Joe Morgan	10 - 15

S5225	Ken Griffey	10 - 15

Canadian Expos

S5230	Pete Rose	10 - 15
S5231	Charlie Lea	10 - 15
S5232	Steve Rogers	10 - 15
S5233	Gary Carter	10 - 15
S5234	Tim Raines	10 - 15
S5235	Andre Dawson	10 - 15
S5236	Bill Gullickson	10 - 15

Detroit Tigers, Sanders, 1976-77

S5240	Ben Oglivie	10 - 20
S5241	Rusty Staub	10 - 20
S5242	Mark Fidrych	10 - 20
S5243	Jason Thompson	10 - 20
S5244	Ron Le Flore	10 - 20
S5245	Aurelio Rodriquez	10 - 20

Boston Red Sox, Papa Gino's Pizza

S5250	Louis Tiant	10 - 15
S5253	Fred Lynn	10 - 15
S5254	Bill Lee	10 - 15
S5255	Rico Petrocelli	10 - 15

Baseball Past Greats, United, Pepsi

S5260	Babe Ruth	12 - 20
S5261	Lou Gehrig	12 - 20
S5262	Roberto Clemente	12 - 20
S5263	Ty Cobb	12 - 20

Bsaeball Greats, Coke, 1979

S5275	Carl Yastrzemski	15 - 25
S5276	Reggie Jackson	15 - 25
S5277	Tom Seaver	15 - 25
S5278	Pete Rose	15 - 25
S5279	Rod Carew	15 - 25
S5280	Johnny Bench	15 - 25

COLUMBUS CLIPPERS, Elby's, Coke

S5291	Stadium	6 - 12

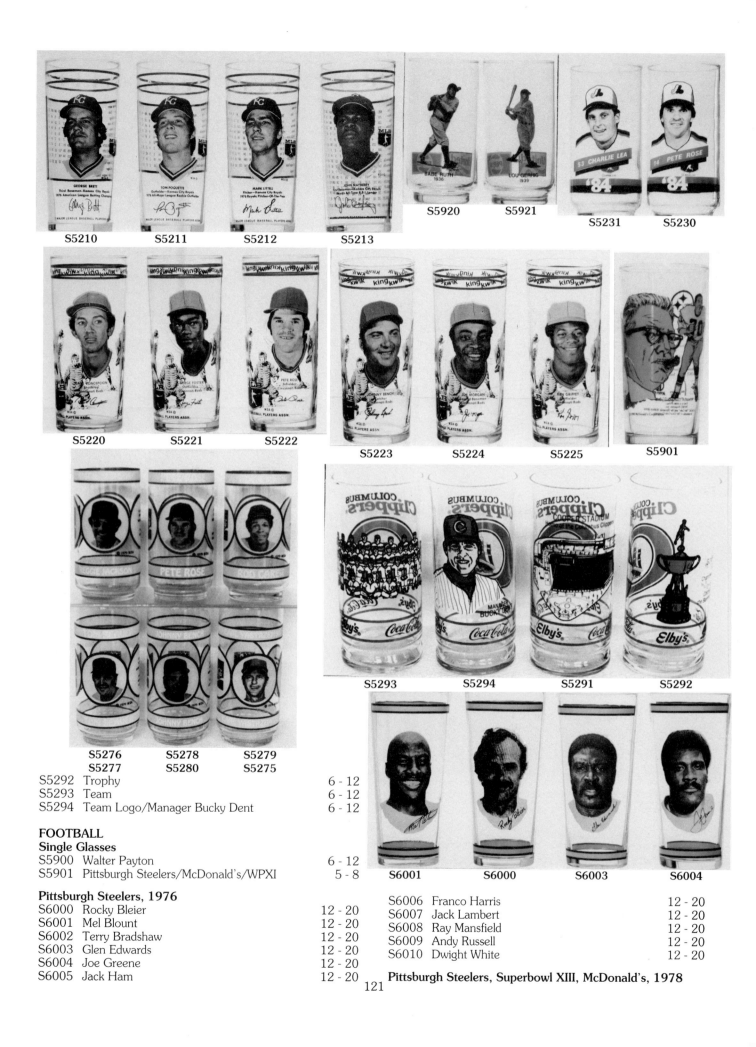

S5210 S5211 S5212 S5213

S5920 S5921

S5231 S5230

S5220 S5221 S5222

S5223 S5224 S5225 S5901

| S5276 | S5278 | S5279 |
| S5277 | S5280 | S5275 |

S5293 S5294 S5291 S5292

S6001 S6000 S6003 S6004

S5292	Trophy	6 - 12
S5293	Team	6 - 12
S5294	Team Logo/Manager Bucky Dent	6 - 12

FOOTBALL
Single Glasses

| S5900 | Walter Payton | 6 - 12 |
| S5901 | Pittsburgh Steelers/McDonald's/WPXI | 5 - 8 |

Pittsburgh Steelers, 1976

S6000	Rocky Bleier	12 - 20
S6001	Mel Blount	12 - 20
S6002	Terry Bradshaw	12 - 20
S6003	Glen Edwards	12 - 20
S6004	Joe Greene	12 - 20
S6005	Jack Ham	12 - 20

S6006	Franco Harris	12 - 20
S6007	Jack Lambert	12 - 20
S6008	Ray Mansfield	12 - 20
S6009	Andy Russell	12 - 20
S6010	Dwight White	12 - 20

Pittsburgh Steelers, Superbowl XIII, McDonald's, 1978

S6006	S6007	S6008	S6009	S6010

S6070   S6071

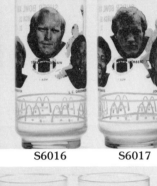

S6015	S6016	S6017	S6018

S6072   S6073

S6110

S6025	S6026	S6028	S6027

S6080	S6081	S6082	S6083

S6030	S6031	S6032	S6033

S6111	S6112	S6113

S6015	Stallworth, Greene, Wagner	5 - 8
S6016	Webster, Bradshaw, Greenwood	5 - 8
S6017	Davis, Lambert, Banaszak	5 - 8
S6018	Shell, Bleier, Ham	5 - 8

Pittsburgh Steelers, Superbowl XIV, McDonald's, 1979

S6025	Bleier, Stallworth, Winston	5 - 8
S6026	Kolb, Lambert, Blount	5 - 8
S6027	Davis, Bradshaw, Ham	5 - 8
S6028	Thorton, Greene, Bahr	5 - 8

Pittsburgh Steelers, "The All Time Greatest Steelers Team", McDonald's, 1982

S6030	#1 - Mullins, Brown, Lambert, Harris, Brady, White	5 - 8
S6031	#2 - Greene, Nickel, Kolb, Bleier, Shell, Ham	5 - 8
S6032	#3 - Gerela, Davis, Wagner, Greenwood, Webster, Swann	5 - 8
S6033	#4 - Blount, Stoutner, Bradshaw, Russell, Stallworth, Butler	5 - 8

Cleveland Browns, Wendy's, 1981

S6050	Brian Sipe	4 - 6
S6051	Doug Dieken	4 - 6

S6060   S6061   S6062   S6063   S6064   S6090   S6091   S6092

S6050   S6051   S6052   S6053

S6093   S6094   S6095

S6216   S6217   S6100   S6102   S6101   S6103   S6104   S6105

| S6052 | Lyle Alzado | 4 - 6 |
| S6053 | Mike Pruitt | 4 - 6 |

Philadelphia Eagles, McDonald's, 1980

S6060	Jaworski, Krepfle	5 - 8
S6061	Carmichael, Logan	5 - 8
S6062	Franklin, Walters	5 - 8
S6063	Montgomery, Campfield	5 - 8
S6064	Bunting, Bergey	5 - 8

Atlanta Falcons, McDonald's/Dr. Pepper as co - sponsor, 1980

S6070	Andrews, Van Note, Kenn	4 - 6
S6071	Thielemann, Butler, Cain	4 - 6
S6072	Bartkowski, Jackson, Jenkins	4 - 6
S6073	Kuykendall, Williams, Curry	4 - 6

Seattle Seahawks, McDonald's, 1979

S6080	Beeson, Eller, Beamon	4 - 6
S6081	Boyd, Gregory, Tuiasosopo	4 - 6
S6082	Raible, Zorn, McCullum	4 - 6
S6083	Smith, Largent, Sims	4 - 6

Green Bay Packers, Pizza Hut

S6090	Willie Davis	5 - 8
S6091	Paul Hornung	5 - 8
S6092	Jerry Kramer	5 - 8
S6093	Ray Nitschke	5 - 8
S6094	Vince Lombardi	5 - 8
S6095	Bart Starr	5 - 8

Denver Broncos, Burger King/Dr. Pepper as co - sponsor, 1977

S6100	Lyle Alzado	8 - 10
S6101	Randy Gradishar	8 - 10
S6102	Tom Jackson	8 - 10
S6103	Craig Morton	8 - 10
S6104	Haven Moses	8 - 10
S6105	Riley Odoms	8 - 10

Denver Broncos, "All Time Greats 25th Anniversary", Pizza Hut and KCNC TV, 1984

S6110	#1 - Odoms, Wright, Smith, Gradishar, Turner, Chavous	8 - 10
S6111	#2 - Johnson, Taylor, Jackson, Swenson, Minor, Little	8 - 10
S6112	#3 - Van Heusen, Morton, Upchurch, Moses, Thompson, Bryan	8 - 10
S6113	#4 - Watson, Tripucka, Alzado, Jackson,	

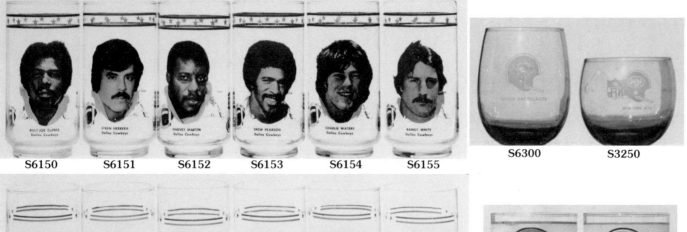

| S6150 | S6151 | S6152 | S6153 | S6154 | S6155 |

S6300   S3250

| S6156 | S6157 | S6160 | S6158 | S6161 | S6159 |

S6450 *various issues*

	Glassic, Gonsoulin	8 - 10

Dallas Cowboys – Set One
S6150	Billy Joe DuPree	8 - 10
S6151	Efren Herrera	8 - 10
S6152	Harvey Martin	8 - 10
S6153	Drew Pearson	8 - 10
S6154	Charlie Waters	8 - 10
S6155	Randy White	8 - 10

Dallas Cowboys – Set Two
S6156	Bob Breunig	8 - 10
S6157	Pat Donovan	8 - 10
S6158	Cliff Harris	8 - 10
S6159	D.D. Lewis	8 - 10
S6160	Robert Newhouse	8 - 10
S6161	Golden Richards	8 - 10

Football Collector Series, American Conference, Welch's, 1976
S6200	Bills, Jets, Patriots, Colts, Dolphins (Eastern Div)	5 - 8
S6201	Chiefs, Raiders, Chargers, Broncos, Buccaneers (Western Div)	5 - 8
S6202	Browns, Steelers, Bengals, Oilers (Central Div)	5 - 8

Football Collector Series, National Conference, Welch's, 1976
S6210	Lions, Packers, Vikings, Bears (Central Div)	5 - 8
S6211	Eagles, Giants, Redskins, Cardinals, Cowboys (Eastern Div)	5 - 8
S6212	Seahawks, Saints, 49ers, Falcons, Rams (Western Div)	5 - 8

Football Helmet Glasses, set of 2, Welch's
| S6216 | American Football Conference Helmet Glass, Welch's on lid – no Buccaneers on glass | 5 - 8 |
| S6217 | National Football Conference Helmet Glass, Welch's on lid – no Seahawks | 5 - 8 |

Football Helmets

The Shell Oil Company, for several years, had released a smoke color roly-poly style glass with an etched football helmet & the team's name. Every team & various championship games are represented. The championship glasses come in the $4^1/_2$" size only, whereas the team helmets come in both the $3^1/_2$" as well as the $4^1/_2$".

S6250	Shell Oil smoke colored football helmet, small	2 - 6
S6300	Shell Oil smoke colored football helmet, large	2 - 6
S6350	Shell Oil smoke colored football helmet, championships	2 - 6
S6400	Shell Oil smoke colored football helmet mug	2 - 6

The Mobil Oil Company issued a series of 28 glasses of all the team helmets in the years 1985, 1986, 1987 & 1988. The glasses vary in size & appearance. The two earlier years were frosted. In some cases Mobil promoted basketball and perhaps other sports (L.A. Lakers, etc.). In 1988 a complete set of 28 clear football helmet glasses could be gotten by frequenting a Mobil station or opening a Mobil credit card.

Teams involved were the Atlanta Falcons, Buffalo Bills, Chicago Bears, Cincinnati Bengals, Cleveland Browns, Dallas Cowboys, Denver Broncos, Detroit Lions, Green Bay Packers, Houston Oilers, Indianapolis Colts, Kansas City Chiefs, Los Angeles Raiders, Los Angeles Rams, Miami Dolphins, Minnesota Vikings, New York Jets, New York Giants, New Orleans Saints, New England Patriots, Phoenix Cardinals, Philadelphia Eagles, Pittsburgh Steelers, San Francisco 49ers, San Diego Chargers, Seattle Seahawks, Tampa Bay Buccaneers and Washington Redskins.

S6450	Short frosted helmet glasses	4 - 6
S6500	Tall frosted helmet glasses	3 - 5
S6550	Short clear helmet glasses	2 - 4
S6600	Tall clear helmet glasses	1 - 3

Burger Chef Football Helmet Series, 1979

Burger Chef was a regional hamburger fast-food chain headquartered in Cincinnati, Ohio. It sold out to the Hardee's chain shortly after these glasses were issued.

| S6620 | Smoke colored glass helmets (assuming 28 teams were issued), each | 4 - 8 |

Nut Mugs

Both the Fisher (Beatrice Company) & Flavor House Products have released a series of "mug of nuts" with dry roasted peanuts in them using NFL football logos & helmets and col-

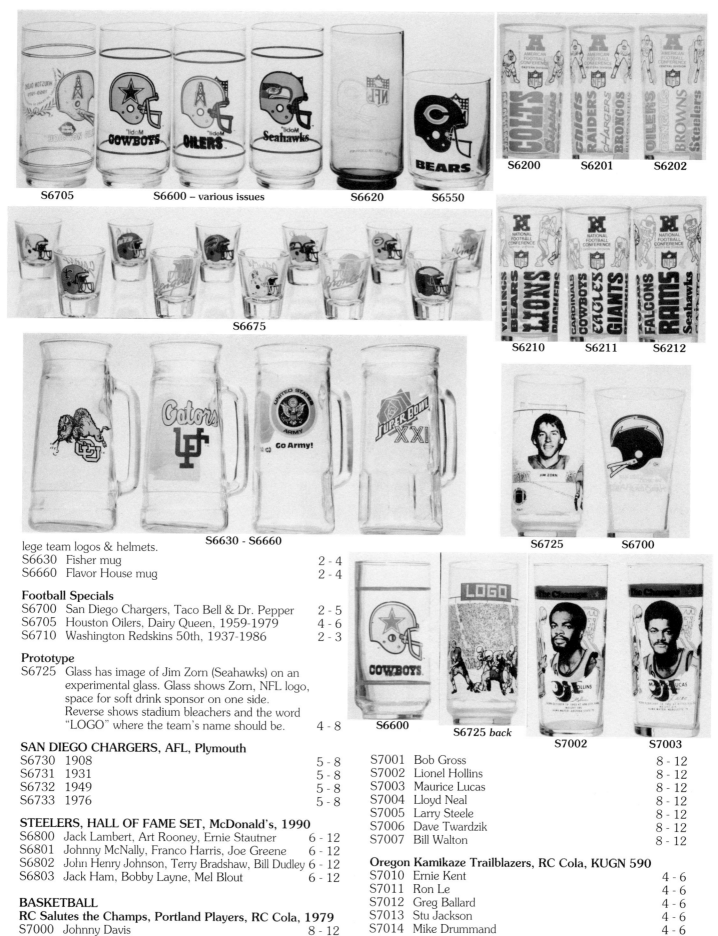

S6705   S6600 – various issues   S6620   S6550

S6200   S6201   S6202

S6210   S6211   S6212

S6630 - S6660

S6725   S6700

lege team logos & helmets.

S6630	Fisher mug	2 - 4
S6660	Flavor House mug	2 - 4

Football Specials

S6700	San Diego Chargers, Taco Bell & Dr. Pepper	2 - 5
S6705	Houston Oilers, Dairy Queen, 1959-1979	4 - 6
S6710	Washington Redskins 50th, 1937-1986	2 - 3

Prototype

S6725   Glass has image of Jim Zorn (Seahawks) on an experimental glass. Glass shows Zorn, NFL logo, space for soft drink sponsor on one side. Reverse shows stadium bleachers and the word "LOGO" where the team's name should be.   4 - 8

SAN DIEGO CHARGERS, AFL, Plymouth

S6730	1908	5 - 8
S6731	1931	5 - 8
S6732	1949	5 - 8
S6733	1976	5 - 8

STEELERS, HALL OF FAME SET, McDonald's, 1990

S6800	Jack Lambert, Art Rooney, Ernie Stautner	6 - 12
S6801	Johnny McNally, Franco Harris, Joe Greene	6 - 12
S6802	John Henry Johnson, Terry Bradshaw, Bill Dudley	6 - 12
S6803	Jack Ham, Bobby Layne, Mel Blout	6 - 12

BASKETBALL

RC Salutes the Champs, Portland Players, RC Cola, 1979

S7000	Johnny Davis	8 - 12

S6600   S6725 *back*

S7002   S7003

S7001	Bob Gross	8 - 12
S7002	Lionel Hollins	8 - 12
S7003	Maurice Lucas	8 - 12
S7004	Lloyd Neal	8 - 12
S7005	Larry Steele	8 - 12
S7006	Dave Twardzik	8 - 12
S7007	Bill Walton	8 - 12

Oregon Kamikaze Trailblazers, RC Cola, KUGN 590

S7010	Ernie Kent	4 - 6
S7011	Ron Le	4 - 6
S7012	Greg Ballard	4 - 6
S7013	Stu Jackson	4 - 6
S7014	Mike Drummand	4 - 6

S7004   S7005   S7006   S7007

S7010 - S7015

S7000   S7001   S7011

S7030   S7031   S7032   S7033

S7020   S7026   S7021

S7022   S7023   S7024   S7025

S7230   S7236   S7235

S7026	Matching pitcher to this set	10 - 15

Seattle Supersonics, Godfather's

S7030	Donaldson/Thompson/Vranes	5 - 8
S7031	Kelser/Shelton/Tolbert	5 - 8
S7032	Smith/Brown/Radford	5 - 8
S7033	Williams/Wilkens/Sikma	5 - 8

Portland Trailblazers, Dairy Queen, 1992

S7035	Clyde Drexler	5 - 10
S7036	Kevin Duckworth	5 - 10
S7037	Jerome Kersey	5 - 10
S7038	Terry Porter	5 - 10
S7039	Cliff Robinson	5 - 10
S7040	Buck Williams	5 - 10

Bulls, Chicago Tribune

S7100	How sweet it is	8 - 12
S7101	On balance ... it's all Bulls	8 - 12
S7102	Jordan finishes off Sixers	8 - 12
S7103	Bulls end Piston reign of terror	8 - 12

S7015	Mark Barwig	4 - 6

Portland Trailblazers, Sunshine Pizza Exchange, 1983-84

S7020	Lever & Paxson	4 - 6
S7021	Carr & Norris	4 - 6
S7022	Drexler & Natt	4 - 6
S7023	Werhoeven & Thompson	4 - 6
S7024	Lamp & Valentine	4 - 6
S7025	Cooper & Piotrowski	4 - 6

S7035   S7036   S7037   S7038   S7039   S7040   S7227

S7100   S7101   S7102   S7103   S7104   S7105   S7106   S7107

S7220   S7221   S7227   S7222   S7223   S7234

S7104	Whew! Bulls do it in OT	8 - 12
S7105	Bulls take finals by the horns	8 - 12
S7106	Bulls stampede to first title	8 - 12
S7107	High five! Bulls are champs	8 - 12

SOCCER
Wichita Wings, MSA KFH 13 AM Radio, "The Voice of the Wings"

S7200	Jeff Bourne	12 - 20
S7201	Andy Chapman	12 - 20
S7202	John Cutbush	12 - 20

S7203	Mike Dowler	12 - 20
S7204	Kevin Kewley	12 - 20
S7205	Jorgen Kristensen	12 - 20
S7206	Norman Piper	12 - 20
S7207	Kim Roentved	12 - 20
S7208	Jimmy Ryan	12 - 20
S7209	Roy Tuner	12 - 20

Soccer, Coke

| S7220 | Pele, Brazil | 15 - 20 |
| S7221 | Wolfgang Weber, West Germany | 15 - 20 |

S7204   S7203   S7208   S7206   S7202   S7209   S7207   S7201   S7205   S7200

127

| S7275 | S7276 | S7277 | S7278 | S7279 | S7280 | S7281 | S7282 | S7283 | S7284 | S7285 | S7286 |

| S7400 | S7401 | S7402 | S7403 |

| | S7223 | S7224 |

| S7420 | S7421 | S7422 | S7423 | | S7237 | | S7229 |

S7222	Espana '82 World Cup, Coke, Germany	10 - 15
S7223	Argentina '78 World Cup, Coke, Germany	10 - 15
S7224	Argentina '78, Coke, Germany	10 - 15
S7225	Mexico World Cup, Coke	10 - 15
S7226	Mundial, 1986, Coke	10 - 15
S7227	European Champ Soccer, 1984, Coke, France	10 - 15
S7228	Mundial, 1982, Coke, France	10 - 15
S7229	Mexico World Cup, 1986, Coke, 2 sizes	10 - 15
S7230	World Cup, 1990, English	10 - 15
S7231	Italian World Cup, 1974	10 - 15
S7232	German World Cup, 1974	10 - 15
S7233	German World Cup, 1974, WM '74	10 - 15
S7234	America's Cup, Australia Defence '87, unissued prototype	30 - 50
S7235	World Cup, 1990, Italian	10 - 15
S7236	World Cup, 1990, German	10 - 15

Soccer – 1990 World Cup, Belgium Team, Coke, Belgium

S7275	De Grijse	10 - 20
S7276	Grun	10 - 20
S7277	Van Der Linden	10 - 20
S7278	Prerud 'Homme	10 - 20
S7279	Gerets	10 - 20
S7280	Van Der Elst	10 - 20
S7281	Versavel	10 - 20
S7282	Clijsters	10 - 20

S7283	Scifo	10 - 20
S7284	Emmers	10 - 20
S7285	Demol	10 - 20
S7286	Ceulemans	10 - 20

HOCKEY

Penguins, Elby's Big Boy, 1989

S7400	Rob Brown	2 - 4
S7401	Paul Coffey	2 - 4
S7402	Mario Lemieux	2 - 4
S7403	Zarley Zalapski	2 - 4

Detroit Red Wings, Little Caesar's Pizza, 1988

S7420	Klima & Burr	4 - 6
S7421	Probert & Kocur	4 - 6
S7422	Gallant & Yzerman	4 - 6
S7423	Hanlon & Stefan	4 - 6

Detroit Red Wings, Pepsi and Total Gas, 1988

S7430	Harold Snepsts	6 - 8
S7431	Brent Ashton	6 - 8
S7432	Steve Yzerman	6 - 8
S7433	Bob Probert	6 - 8

Canadian NHL Glasses

A glass for each different division.

S7430   S7431   S7432   S7433   S7480   S7477   S7476   S7475

S7610   S7611   S7612   S7613   S7755   S7700   S7701   S7702

S7630   S7631   S7632   S7633   S7635   S7634   S7600   S7703   S7704

S7476	Norris Division	6 - 8
S7477	Adams Division	6 - 8
S7478	Smythe Division	6 - 8

NHL Glasses, Coke

S7480	Canadian NHL Hockey	6 - 8

WRESTLING Single Glasses

S7600	Hulk Hogan, 1985 round bottom style	1 - 2
S7601	Hulk Hogan, 7" pedestal	1 - 2

World of Wrestling, Canada (peanut butter), 1989

S7610	Hulkamania	1 - 2
S7611	Macho Madness	1 - 2
S7612	Jake the Snake	1 - 2
S7613	Ultimate Warrior	1 - 2
S7614	Miss Elizabeth	1 - 2

World Wrestling Federation, 1990

S7630	Ax of Demolition/Smash of Demolition	4 - 8
S7631	Brutus the Barber Beefcake	4 - 8
S7632	Hulk Hogan	4 - 8
S7633	Luke the Bushwacker/Butch the Bushwacker	4 - 8
S7634	Macho King Randy Savage	4 - 8
S7635	Ultimate Warrior	4 - 8

RODEO

World Championship Rodeo Series, PRCA National Finals Rodeo, 1979, Oklahoma City, OK

Prior to moving to Las Vegas, NV, the PRCA national finals were held in Oklahoma City.

S7700	Team Roping	3 - 5
S7701	Calf Roping	3 - 5
S7702	Bull Riding	3 - 5
S7703	Steer Wrestling	3 - 5
S7704	Saddle Bronc Riding	3 - 5
S7705	Bareback Riding	3 - 5

**Houston Livestock & Rodeo Show,
Coke & McDonald's, 1983**

S7730	1 of 4, Saddle Bronc Riding & Bareback Riding	8 - 12
S7731	2 of 4, Chuckwagon Racing & Barrel Racing	8 - 12
S7732	3 of 4, Calf Scramble & Rodeo Clown	8 - 12
S7733	4 of 4, Steer Wrestling & Bull Riding	8 - 12

Houston Livestock & Rodeo Show, Coke & McDonald's, 1984

S7740	1 of 4, Bareback Riding & Saddle Bronc Riding	8 - 12
S7741	2 of 4, Chuckwagon Racing & Women's Barrel Racing	8 - 12
S7742	3 of 4, Calf Scrambling & Horse Cutting	8 - 12
S7743	4 of 4, Steer Wrestling & Bull Riding	8 - 12

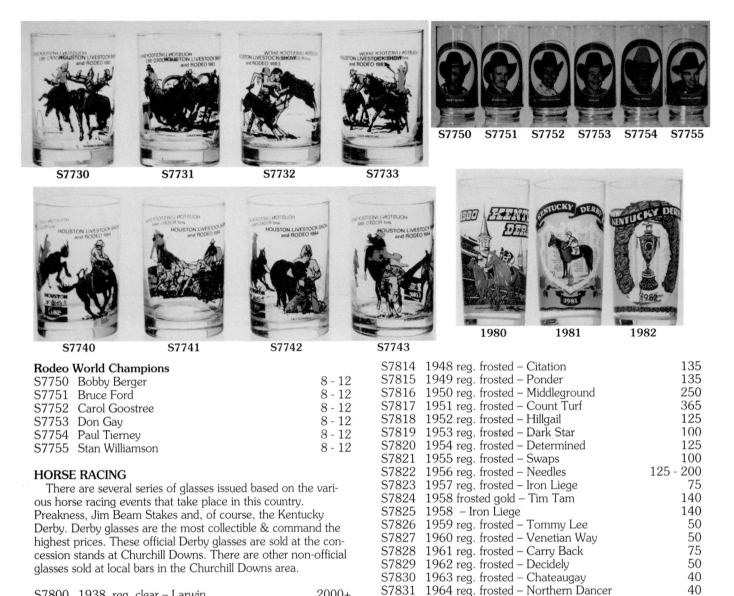

S7730   S7731   S7732   S7733

S7750 S7751 S7752 S7753 S7754 S7755

S7740   S7741   S7742   S7743

1980   1981   1982

Rodeo World Champions

S7750	Bobby Berger	8 - 12
S7751	Bruce Ford	8 - 12
S7752	Carol Goostree	8 - 12
S7753	Don Gay	8 - 12
S7754	Paul Tierney	8 - 12
S7755	Stan Williamson	8 - 12

HORSE RACING

There are several series of glasses issued based on the various horse racing events that take place in this country. Preakness, Jim Beam Stakes and, of course, the Kentucky Derby. Derby glasses are the most collectible & command the highest prices. These official Derby glasses are sold at the concession stands at Churchill Downs. There are other non-official glasses sold at local bars in the Churchill Downs area.

S7800	1938 reg. clear – Larwin	2000+
S7801	1939 reg. clear – Johnstown	2000+
S7802	1940 reg. clear – Gallahadion	2500+
S7803	1940 aluminum – Gallahadion	425
S7804	1941 aluminum – Grandstand	425
S7805	1942 bakelite – Shut Out	1800 - 2000+
S7806	1943 bakelite – Count Fleet	1800 - 2000+
S7807	1944 bakelite – Pensive	1800 - 2000+
S7808	1945 reg. frosted – Hoop Jr.	725
S7809	1945 tall frosted – Hoop Jr.	325
S7810	1945 jigger – Hoop Jr.	700
S7811	1946 short frosted – Assault	40 - 60
S7812	1946 tall frosted – Assault	100
S7813	1947 tall – Jet Pilot	75

S7814	1948 reg. frosted – Citation	135
S7815	1949 reg. frosted – Ponder	135
S7816	1950 reg. frosted – Middleground	250
S7817	1951 reg. frosted – Count Turf	365
S7818	1952 reg. frosted – Hillgail	125
S7819	1953 reg. frosted – Dark Star	100
S7820	1954 reg. frosted – Determined	125
S7821	1955 reg. frosted – Swaps	100
S7822	1956 reg. frosted – Needles	125 - 200
S7823	1957 reg. frosted – Iron Liege	75
S7824	1958 frosted gold – Tim Tam	140
S7825	1958 – Iron Liege	140
S7826	1959 reg. frosted – Tommy Lee	50
S7827	1960 reg. frosted – Venetian Way	50
S7828	1961 reg. frosted – Carry Back	75
S7829	1962 reg. frosted – Decidely	50
S7830	1963 reg. frosted – Chateaugay	40
S7831	1964 reg. frosted – Northern Dancer	40
S7832	1965 reg. frosted – Lucky Debonair	50

From 1966 through 1989 they range from $3.00 to $30.00. There are some errors & color variations that may alter this price range. The 1980 green in color is rare & only 2 are known. The entire glass is green.

S7833	1966 – Kauai	20 - 25
S7834	1967 – Proud Clarion	20 - 25
S7835	1968 – Dancer's Image	20 - 25
S7836	1969 – Majestic Prince	15 - 20
S7837	1970 – Dust Commander	15 - 20
S7838	1971 – Canonero II	15 - 20
S7839	1972 – Riva Ridge	10 - 15

1956   1958   1959   1962   1963   1964   1966 *variation*   1969   1966

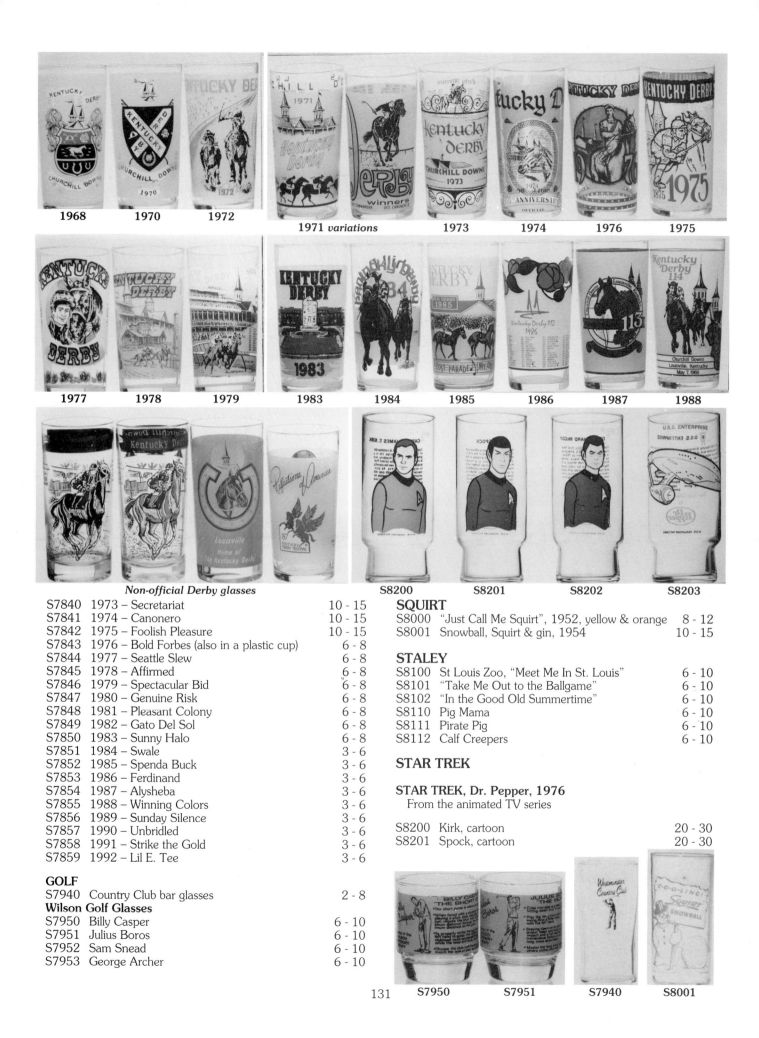

1968   1970   1972

1971 *variations*   **1973   1974   1976   1975**

1977   1978   1979   1983   1984   1985   1986   1987   1988

Non-official Derby glasses

S8200   S8201   S8202   S8203

S7840	1973 – Secretariat	10 - 15
S7841	1974 – Canonero	10 - 15
S7842	1975 – Foolish Pleasure	10 - 15
S7843	1976 – Bold Forbes (also in a plastic cup)	6 - 8
S7844	1977 – Seattle Slew	6 - 8
S7845	1978 – Affirmed	6 - 8
S7846	1979 – Spectacular Bid	6 - 8
S7847	1980 – Genuine Risk	6 - 8
S7848	1981 – Pleasant Colony	6 - 8
S7849	1982 – Gato Del Sol	6 - 8
S7850	1983 – Sunny Halo	6 - 8
S7851	1984 – Swale	3 - 6
S7852	1985 – Spenda Buck	3 - 6
S7853	1986 – Ferdinand	3 - 6
S7854	1987 – Alysheba	3 - 6
S7855	1988 – Winning Colors	3 - 6
S7856	1989 – Sunday Silence	3 - 6
S7857	1990 – Unbridled	3 - 6
S7858	1991 – Strike the Gold	3 - 6
S7859	1992 – Lil E. Tee	3 - 6

GOLF

S7940	Country Club bar glasses	2 - 8

Wilson Golf Glasses

S7950	Billy Casper	6 - 10
S7951	Julius Boros	6 - 10
S7952	Sam Snead	6 - 10
S7953	George Archer	6 - 10

SQUIRT

S8000	"Just Call Me Squirt", 1952, yellow & orange	8 - 12
S8001	Snowball, Squirt & gin, 1954	10 - 15

STALEY

S8100	St Louis Zoo, "Meet Me In St. Louis"	6 - 10
S8101	"Take Me Out to the Ballgame"	6 - 10
S8102	"In the Good Old Summertime"	6 - 10
S8110	Pig Mama	6 - 10
S8111	Pirate Pig	6 - 10
S8112	Calf Creepers	6 - 10

STAR TREK

STAR TREK, Dr. Pepper, 1976
   From the animated TV series

S8200	Kirk, cartoon	20 - 30
S8201	Spock, cartoon	20 - 30

131

S7950   S7951   S7940   S8001

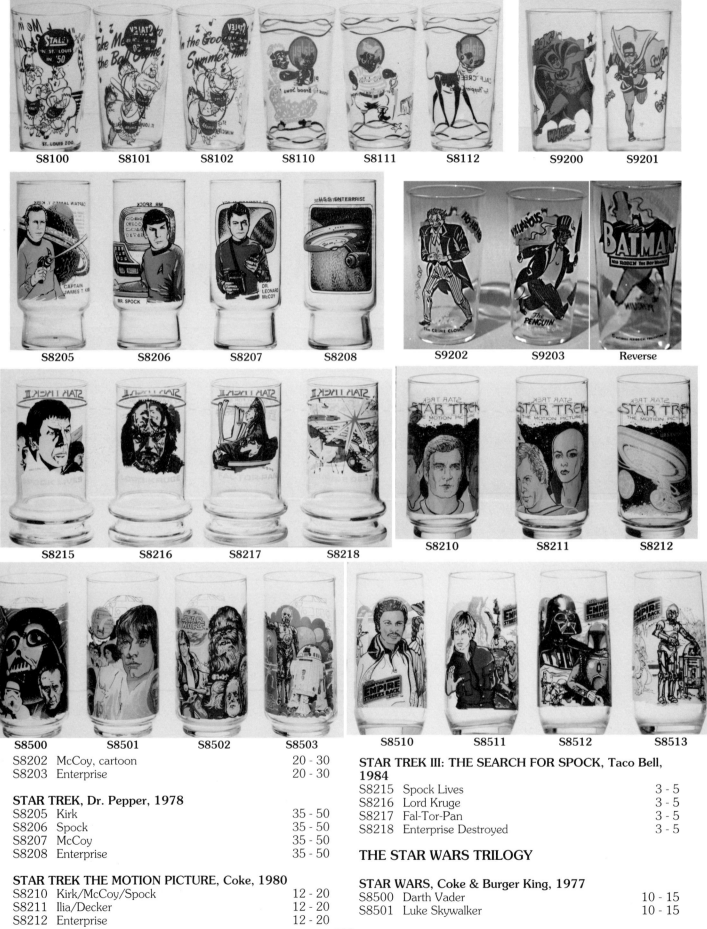

| S8100 | S8101 | S8102 | S8110 | S8111 | S8112 | S9200 | S9201 |

| S8205 | S8206 | S8207 | S8208 | S9202 | S9203 | Reverse |

| S8215 | S8216 | S8217 | S8218 | S8210 | S8211 | S8212 |

| S8500 | S8501 | S8502 | S8503 | S8510 | S8511 | S8512 | S8513 |

| S8202 | McCoy, cartoon | 20 - 30 |
| S8203 | Enterprise | 20 - 30 |

STAR TREK, Dr. Pepper, 1978

S8205	Kirk	35 - 50
S8206	Spock	35 - 50
S8207	McCoy	35 - 50
S8208	Enterprise	35 - 50

STAR TREK THE MOTION PICTURE, Coke, 1980

S8210	Kirk/McCoy/Spock	12 - 20
S8211	Ilia/Decker	12 - 20
S8212	Enterprise	12 - 20

STAR TREK III: THE SEARCH FOR SPOCK, Taco Bell, 1984

S8215	Spock Lives	3 - 5
S8216	Lord Kruge	3 - 5
S8217	Fal-Tor-Pan	3 - 5
S8218	Enterprise Destroyed	3 - 5

THE STAR WARS TRILOGY

STAR WARS, Coke & Burger King, 1977

| S8500 | Darth Vader | 10 - 15 |
| S8501 | Luke Skywalker | 10 - 15 |

132

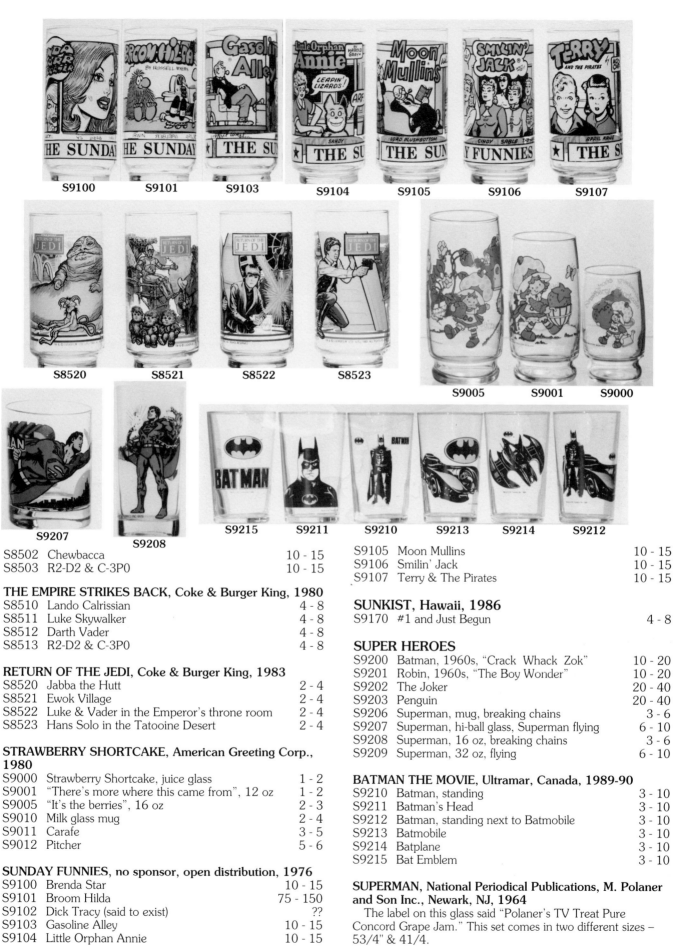

| S9100 | S9101 | S9103 | S9104 | S9105 | S9106 | S9107 |

| S8520 | S8521 | S8522 | S8523 |

| S9005 | S9001 | S9000 |

| S9207 | S9208 |

| S9215 | S9211 | S9210 | S9213 | S9214 | S9212 |

S8502   Chewbacca   10 - 15
S8503   R2-D2 & C-3P0   10 - 15

THE EMPIRE STRIKES BACK, Coke & Burger King, 1980
S8510   Lando Calrissian   4 - 8
S8511   Luke Skywalker   4 - 8
S8512   Darth Vader   4 - 8
S8513   R2-D2 & C-3P0   4 - 8

RETURN OF THE JEDI, Coke & Burger King, 1983
S8520   Jabba the Hutt   2 - 4
S8521   Ewok Village   2 - 4
S8522   Luke & Vader in the Emperor's throne room   2 - 4
S8523   Hans Solo in the Tatooine Desert   2 - 4

STRAWBERRY SHORTCAKE, American Greeting Corp., 1980
S9000   Strawberry Shortcake, juice glass   1 - 2
S9001   "There's more where this came from", 12 oz   1 - 2
S9005   "It's the berries", 16 oz   2 - 3
S9010   Milk glass mug   2 - 4
S9011   Carafe   3 - 5
S9012   Pitcher   5 - 6

SUNDAY FUNNIES, no sponsor, open distribution, 1976
S9100   Brenda Star   10 - 15
S9101   Broom Hilda   75 - 150
S9102   Dick Tracy (said to exist)   ??
S9103   Gasoline Alley   10 - 15
S9104   Little Orphan Annie   10 - 15

S9105   Moon Mullins   10 - 15
S9106   Smilin' Jack   10 - 15
S9107   Terry & The Pirates   10 - 15

SUNKIST, Hawaii, 1986
S9170   #1 and Just Begun   4 - 8

SUPER HEROES
S9200   Batman, 1960s, "Crack Whack Zok"   10 - 20
S9201   Robin, 1960s, "The Boy Wonder"   10 - 20
S9202   The Joker   20 - 40
S9203   Penguin   20 - 40
S9206   Superman, mug, breaking chains   3 - 6
S9207   Superman, hi-ball glass, Superman flying   6 - 10
S9208   Superman, 16 oz, breaking chains   3 - 6
S9209   Superman, 32 oz, flying   6 - 10

BATMAN THE MOVIE, Ultramar, Canada, 1989-90
S9210   Batman, standing   3 - 10
S9211   Batman's Head   3 - 10
S9212   Batman, standing next to Batmobile   3 - 10
S9213   Batmobile   3 - 10
S9214   Batplane   3 - 10
S9215   Bat Emblem   3 - 10

SUPERMAN, National Periodical Publications, M. Polaner and Son Inc., Newark, NJ, 1964
   The label on this glass said "Polaner's TV Treat Pure Concord Grape Jam." This set comes in two different sizes – 53/4" & 41/4.

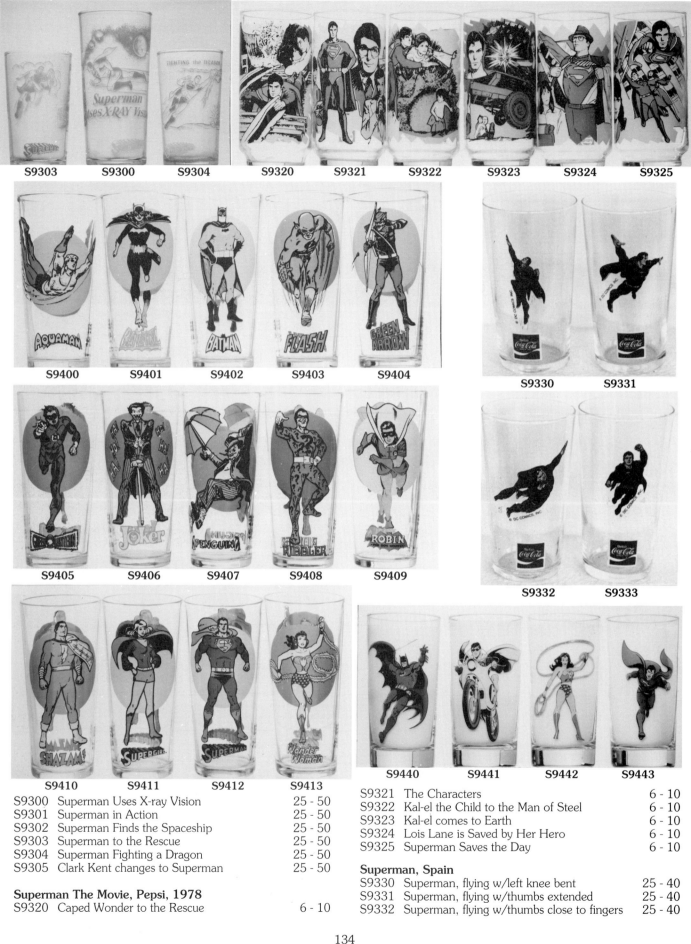

| S9303 | S9300 | S9304 | | S9320 | S9321 | S9322 | | S9323 | S9324 | S9325 |

| S9400 | S9401 | S9402 | S9403 | S9404 |

S9330   S9331

| S9405 | S9406 | S9407 | S9408 | S9409 |

S9332   S9333

| S9410 | S9411 | S9412 | S9413 |

| S9440 | S9441 | S9442 | S9443 |

S9300	Superman Uses X-ray Vision	25 - 50
S9301	Superman in Action	25 - 50
S9302	Superman Finds the Spaceship	25 - 50
S9303	Superman to the Rescue	25 - 50
S9304	Superman Fighting a Dragon	25 - 50
S9305	Clark Kent changes to Superman	25 - 50

Superman The Movie, Pepsi, 1978

S9320	Caped Wonder to the Rescue	6 - 10

S9321	The Characters	6 - 10
S9322	Kal-el the Child to the Man of Steel	6 - 10
S9323	Kal-el comes to Earth	6 - 10
S9324	Lois Lane is Saved by Her Hero	6 - 10
S9325	Superman Saves the Day	6 - 10

Superman, Spain

S9330	Superman, flying w/left knee bent	25 - 40
S9331	Superman, flying w/thumbs extended	25 - 40
S9332	Superman, flying w/thumbs close to fingers	25 - 40

S9433	S9434	S9435

S9420	S9421	S9422	S9423

S9443 *reverse*

S9430	S9431	S9432

S9424	S9425	S9426

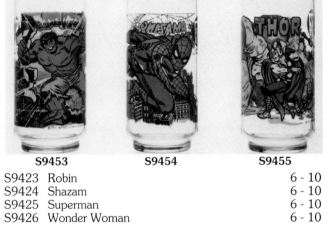

S9450	S9451	S9452

S9453	S9454	S9455

S9333   Superman, flying w/clenched hands   25 - 40

SUPER SERIES (Super Heroes), Pepsi, 1976

This set of 14 comes with both the DC & NPP logos
(Detective Comics & National Periodical Publications). Glasses
bearing the DC logo are valued 25% more.

S9400	Aquaman	8 - 12
S9401	Batgirl	8 - 12
S9402	Batman	12 - 20
S9403	Flash	8 - 12
S9404	Green Arrow	8 - 12
S9405	Green Lantern	20 - 40
S9406	Joker	25 - 50
S9407	Penguin	25 - 50
S9408	Riddler	25 - 50
S9409	Robin	8 - 12
S9410	Shazam	8 - 12
S9411	Supergirl	8 - 12
S9412	Superman	8 - 12
S9413	Wonder Woman	8 - 12

SUPER HEROES Collector Series, Pepsi, 1978

S9420	Aquaman	6 - 10
S9421	Batman	8 - 12
S9422	Flash	6 - 10
S9423	Robin	6 - 10
S9424	Shazam	6 - 10
S9425	Superman	6 - 10
S9426	Wonder Woman	6 - 10

This set comes in both the standard 16 oz Brockway style
glass used by Pepsi as well as the round bottom style. In the
round bottom version it does not include Aquaman.

S9430	Batman	15 - 25
S9431	Flash	15 - 25
S9432	Robin	15 - 25
S9433	Shazam	15 - 25
S9434	Superman	15 - 25
S9435	Wonder Woman	15 - 25

Double Characters Super Heroes, Pepsi

Each of these glasses has a picture of Superman on one side
& another hero on the other (except for the last, which has two
different pictures of Superman).

S9440	Superman/Batman	60 -75
S9441	Superman/Robin	25 - 40
S9442	Superman/Wonder Woman	25 - 40
S9443	Superman/Superman	40 - 60

S9460   S9461   S9463   S9464   S9462

S9601   S9602   S9603

T0091   T0090   T1005   T1025   T1100   T1101

"Beauregard"   "Frawley"   "Harley"   "Irving"

T1030   T1031   T1032   T1033

"Julius"   "Lazlo"   "Mortimer"   "Sigmund"

T1034   T1035   T1036   T1037

Marvel Super Heroes, 7-11 (Seven Eleven), 1977

S9450	Captain America	20 - 35
S9451	Fantastic Four	20 - 35
S9452	Howard the Duck	20 - 35
S9453	Hulk	20 - 35
S9454	Spiderman	20 - 35
S9455	Thor	20 - 35

Marvel Super Heroes, no sponsor, 1978

There may be several more to this set.

S9460	Captain America	45 - 60
S9461	Hulk	45 - 60
S9462	Thor	45 - 60
S9463	Spider-man	45 - 60
S9464	Spider-woman	45 - 60

SUPERIOR COLLECTION SERIES, 1971, "COOL IT"

S9601	Typist	5 - 7
S9602	Cook Out	5 - 7
S9603	Tennis	5 - 7

SWEET POLLY (see LEONARDO TTV)

SYLVESTER (see WARNER BROTHERS)

TG & Y

| T0090 | "The Break" food sign | 3 - 6 |
| T0091 | "The Break" woodland scene | 3 - 6 |

TACO MAYO

| T1005 | Mouse Cot | 6 - 12 |

TACO TIME

| T1025 | Taco Time Cactus | 1 - 3 |

TACO VILLA

The 1977 set is a still of the character, whereas the 1979 shows the character in an action. These glasses are found mostly in Texas.

Taco Villa, 1977

T1030	Beauregard	15 - 25
T1031	Frawley	15 - 25
T1032	Harley	15 - 25
T1033	Irving	15 - 25
T1034	Julius	15 - 25
T1035	Lazlo	15 - 25
T1036	Mortimer	15 - 25
T1037	Sigmund	15 - 25

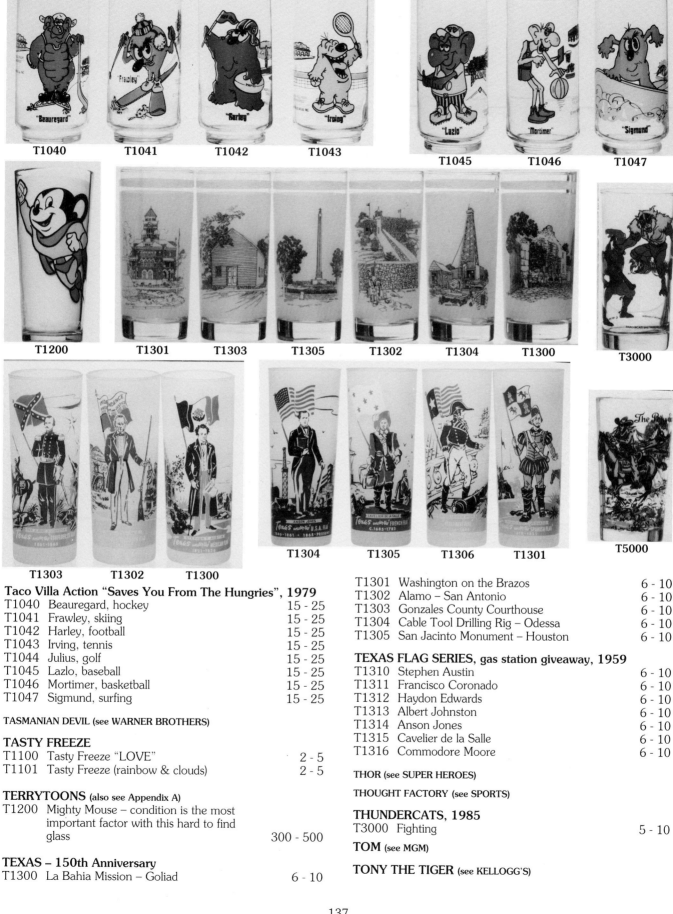

T1040 T1041 T1042 T1043

T1045 T1046 T1047

T1200 T1301 T1303 T1305 T1302 T1304 T1300 T3000

T1303 T1302 T1300

T1304 T1305 T1306 T1301

T5000

Taco Villa Action "Saves You From The Hungries", 1979

T1040	Beauregard, hockey	15 - 25
T1041	Frawley, skiing	15 - 25
T1042	Harley, football	15 - 25
T1043	Irving, tennis	15 - 25
T1044	Julius, golf	15 - 25
T1045	Lazlo, baseball	15 - 25
T1046	Mortimer, basketball	15 - 25
T1047	Sigmund, surfing	15 - 25

TASMANIAN DEVIL (see WARNER BROTHERS)

TASTY FREEZE

T1100	Tasty Freeze "LOVE"	2 - 5
T1101	Tasty Freeze (rainbow & clouds)	2 - 5

TERRYTOONS (also see Appendix A)

T1200	Mighty Mouse – condition is the most important factor with this hard to find glass	300 - 500

TEXAS – 150th Anniversary

T1300	La Bahia Mission – Goliad	6 - 10
T1301	Washington on the Brazos	6 - 10
T1302	Alamo – San Antonio	6 - 10
T1303	Gonzales County Courthouse	6 - 10
T1304	Cable Tool Drilling Rig – Odessa	6 - 10
T1305	San Jacinto Monument – Houston	6 - 10

TEXAS FLAG SERIES, gas station giveaway, 1959

T1310	Stephen Austin	6 - 10
T1311	Francisco Coronado	6 - 10
T1312	Haydon Edwards	6 - 10
T1313	Albert Johnston	6 - 10
T1314	Anson Jones	6 - 10
T1315	Cavelier de la Salle	6 - 10
T1316	Commodore Moore	6 - 10

THOR (see SUPER HEROES)

THOUGHT FACTORY (see SPORTS)

THUNDERCATS, 1985

T3000	Fighting	5 - 10

TOM (see MGM)

TONY THE TIGER (see KELLOGG'S)

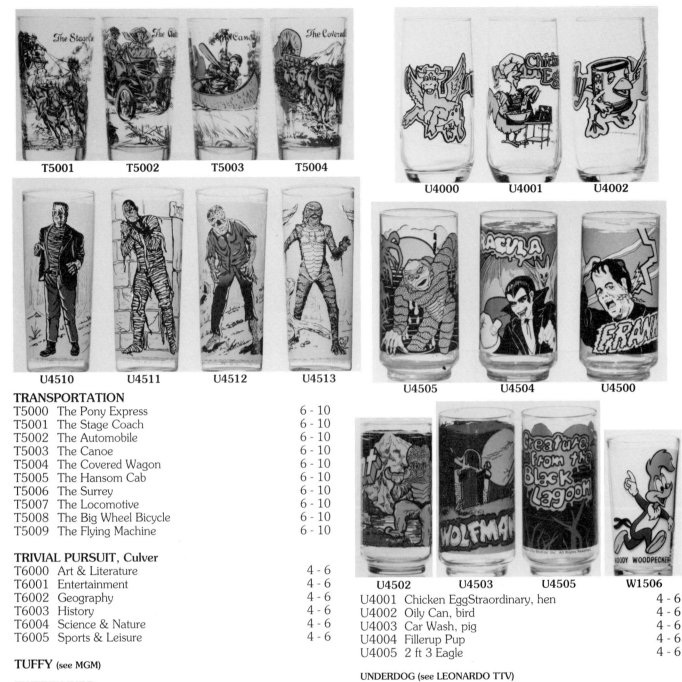

T5001   T5002   T5003   T5004

U4000   U4001   U4002

U4510   U4511   U4512   U4513

U4505   U4504   U4500

TRANSPORTATION

T5000	The Pony Express	6 - 10
T5001	The Stage Coach	6 - 10
T5002	The Automobile	6 - 10
T5003	The Canoe	6 - 10
T5004	The Covered Wagon	6 - 10
T5005	The Hansom Cab	6 - 10
T5006	The Surrey	6 - 10
T5007	The Locomotive	6 - 10
T5008	The Big Wheel Bicycle	6 - 10
T5009	The Flying Machine	6 - 10

TRIVIAL PURSUIT, Culver

T6000	Art & Literature	4 - 6
T6001	Entertainment	4 - 6
T6002	Geography	4 - 6
T6003	History	4 - 6
T6004	Science & Nature	4 - 6
T6005	Sports & Leisure	4 - 6

TUFFY (see MGM)

TWEETY BIRD (see WARNER BROTHERS)

ULTRAMART (ULTRAMAR)

The Ultramart Corporation developed these characters to promote their gasoline stations "Ultramar" in Canada.

U4000	Ultra Moo, cow	4 - 6

U4502   U4503   U4505   W1506

U4001	Chicken EggStraordinary, hen	4 - 6
U4002	Oily Can, bird	4 - 6
U4003	Car Wash, pig	4 - 6
U4004	Fillerup Pup	4 - 6
U4005	2 ft 3 Eagle	4 - 6

UNDERDOG (see LEONARDO TTV)

UNIVERSAL MONSTERS, Universal Studios, 1980

U4500	Frankenstein	50 - 75
U4501	Mummy, said to exist	50 - 75
U4502	Mutant	50 - 75
U4503	Wolfman	50 - 75
U4504	Dracula	50 - 75
U4505	Creature from the Black Lagoon	50 - 75

W1509   W1506   W1508   T6000   T6001   T6002   T6003   T6005

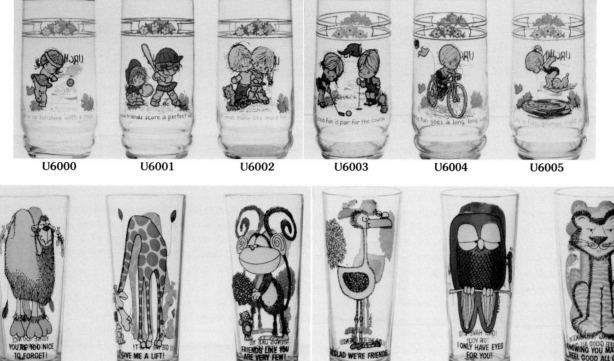

U6000	U6001	U6002	U6003	U6004	U6005

V3000	V3001	V3002	V3003	V3004	V3005

W1500	W1501	W1502	W1503	W1504	W1505

UNIVERSAL MONSTERS, Universal Studios, no date

U4510	Frankenstein	25 - 50
U4511	Mummy	25 - 50
U4512	Wolfman	25 - 50
U4513	Creature from the Black Lagoon	25 - 50

URCHINS, Coke, 1976

U6000	Serve up sunshine with a smile	3 - 6
U6001	Good friends score a perfect hit	3 - 6
U6002	Friends make life more fun	3 - 6
U6003	Good fun is par for the coarse	3 - 6
U6004	A little fun goes a long long way	3 - 6
U6005	Life is fun ... plunge right in	3 - 6

VISUAL CREATIONS, Pepsi, no date

Comes with the Pepsi logo & without. Glasses with the Pepsi logo are valued at 50% more.

V3000	Camel, "You're too nice to forget"	6 - 10
V3001	Giraffe, "You give me a lift"	6 - 10
V3002	Monkey, "Friends like you are very few "	6 - 10
V3003	Ostrich, "I'm glad were friends"	6 - 10
V3004	Owl, "I only have eyes for you"	6 - 10

V3005 Tiger, "Knowing you makes me feel good all over 6 - 10

WALLY WALRUS (see WALTER LANTZ)

WALTER LANTZ
WALTER LANTZ COLLECTOR SERIES, Pepsi, 1977

W1500	Andy Panda, 16 oz, white letters only	75 - 125
W1501	Chilly Willy, 16 oz, white letters only	30 - 50
W1502	Cuddles, 16 oz, white letters only	75 - 125
W1503	Space Mouse, 16 oz, white letters only	100 - 200
W1504	Wally Walrus, 16 oz, white letters only	75 - 125
W1505	Woody Woodpecker, 16 oz, white & black letters	10 - 25
W1506	Chilly Willy, 12 oz, black letters only	10 - 25
W1507	Woody Woodpecker, 12 oz, black letters only	10 - 25
W1508	Chilly Willy painting a snowman, 12 oz	10 - 25
W1509	Woody Woodpecker chasing butterflies, 12 oz	10 - 25

WALTER LANTZ DOUBLE SIDED SERIES, no date, no logo.

Comes in 6¹/₈" & 5⁵/₈".

W1520	Andy Panda/Miranda	20 - 40
W1521	Buzz Buzzard/Space Mouse	20 - 40
W1522	Chilly Willy/Smedley	20 - 40

W1520   W1521   W1522

W2011   W2012   W2013   W2014   W2015

W2000   W2001   W2002

W2005 Snidely Whiplash, 16 oz, black & white letters		15 - 25
W2006 Bullwinkle, 16 oz, brown letters, with & without logo		15 - 25
W2007 Rocky, 16 oz, gray letters & figure, w/logo		50 -100
W2008 Rocky, 16 oz, brown letters & figure, without logo		15 - 25
W2009 Snidely Whiplash, 16 oz, w/green letters, w/logo		15 - 25
W2010 Dudley Do-Right, 16 oz, w/red letters, without logo		15 - 25
W2011 Boris, 12 oz		5 - 20
W2012 Bullwinkle, 12 oz		5 - 20
W2013 Dudley Do-Right, 12 oz		5 - 20
W2014 Mr. Peabody, 12 oz		5 - 20
W2015 Natasha, 12 oz		5 - 20

W2016   W2017   W2018   W2019   W2020

W1523   W1524   W1525

W1523 Cuddles/Oswald	20 - 40
W1524 Wally Walrus/Homer Pigeon	20 - 40
W1525 Woody Woodpecker/Splinter/Knothead	20 - 40

WARD
P.A.T. WARD COLLECTOR SERIES, Pepsi

W2000 Boris & Natasha, 16 oz, black & white letters	20 - 40
W2001 Bullwinkle, 16 oz, black & white letters	15 - 25
W2002 Dudley Do-Right, 16 oz, black & white letters	15 - 25
W2003 Mr. Peabody, 16 oz, black & white letters	15 - 40
W2004 Rocky, 16 oz, black & white letters	15 - 25

W2016 Rocky, 12 oz	5 - 20
W2017 Snidely Whiplash, 12 oz	5 - 20
W2018 Bullwinkle holding balloons, 12 oz	5 - 10
W2019 Dudley in a canoe, 12 oz	5 - 10
W2020 Rocky at the circus, 12 oz	5 - 10

Several of the Ward characters were featured on glasses in 1975 with a Holly Farms logo on the back.

W2025 Bullwinkle	20 - 40
W2026 Natasha	20 - 40

W2003   W2004   W2005   W2006   W2007   W2008   W2010   W2009

140

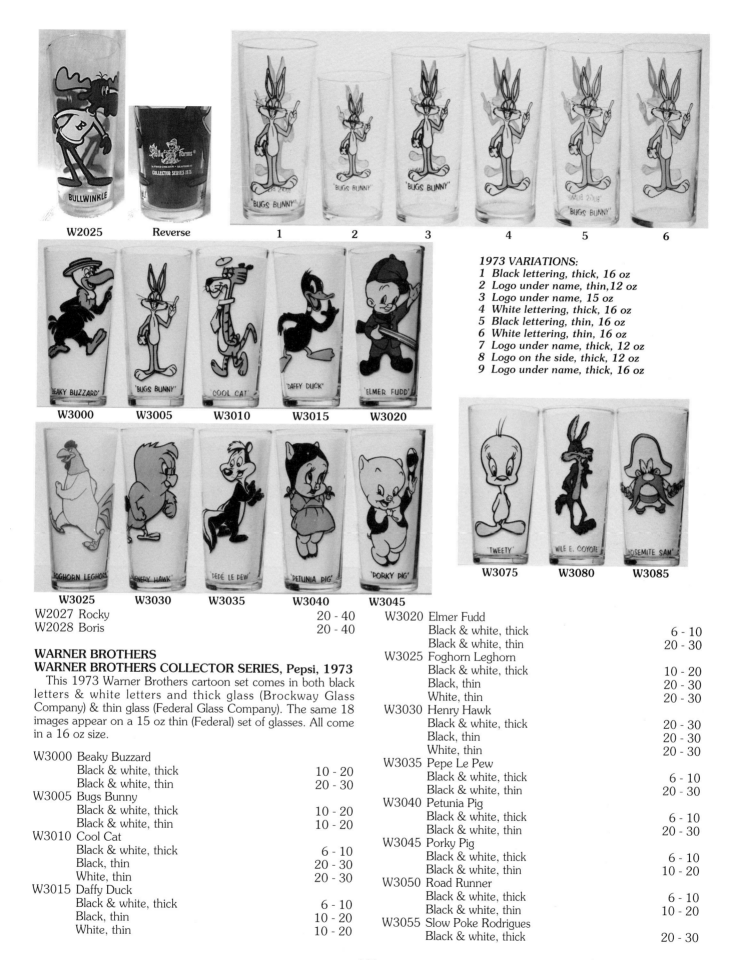

| W2025 | Reverse | 1 | 2 | 3 | 4 | 5 | 6 |

1973 VARIATIONS:
1 Black lettering, thick, 16 oz
2 Logo under name, thin, 12 oz
3 Logo under name, 15 oz
4 White lettering, thick, 16 oz
5 Black lettering, thin, 16 oz
6 White lettering, thin, 16 oz
7 Logo under name, thick, 12 oz
8 Logo on the side, thick, 12 oz
9 Logo under name, thick, 16 oz

| W3000 | W3005 | W3010 | W3015 | W3020 |

| W3075 | W3080 | W3085 |

| W3025 | W3030 | W3035 | W3040 | W3045 |

W2027 Rocky	20 - 40	
W2028 Boris	20 - 40	

WARNER BROTHERS
WARNER BROTHERS COLLECTOR SERIES, Pepsi, 1973

This 1973 Warner Brothers cartoon set comes in both black letters & white letters and thick glass (Brockway Glass Company) & thin glass (Federal Glass Company). The same 18 images appear on a 15 oz thin (Federal) set of glasses. All come in a 16 oz size.

W3000 Beaky Buzzard		
Black & white, thick	10 - 20	
Black & white, thin	20 - 30	
W3005 Bugs Bunny		
Black & white, thick	10 - 20	
Black & white, thin	10 - 20	
W3010 Cool Cat		
Black & white, thick	6 - 10	
Black, thin	20 - 30	
White, thin	20 - 30	
W3015 Daffy Duck		
Black & white, thick	6 - 10	
Black, thin	10 - 20	
White, thin	10 - 20	

W3020 Elmer Fudd		
Black & white, thick	6 - 10	
Black & white, thin	20 - 30	
W3025 Foghorn Leghorn		
Black & white, thick	10 - 20	
Black, thin	20 - 30	
White, thin	20 - 30	
W3030 Henry Hawk		
Black & white, thick	20 - 30	
Black, thin	20 - 30	
White, thin	20 - 30	
W3035 Pepe Le Pew		
Black & white, thick	6 - 10	
Black & white, thin	20 - 30	
W3040 Petunia Pig		
Black & white, thick	6 - 10	
Black & white, thin	20 - 30	
W3045 Porky Pig		
Black & white, thick	6 - 10	
Black & white, thin	10 - 20	
W3050 Road Runner		
Black & white, thick	6 - 10	
Black & white, thin	10 - 20	
W3055 Slow Poke Rodrigues		
Black & white, thick	20 - 30	

W3050	**W3055**

W3060	**W3065**	**W3070**

W3100	**W3101**	**W3102**

W3103	**W3104**	**W3105**

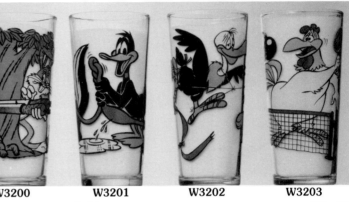

W3200	**W3201**	**W3202**	**W3203**

Black, thin	
White, thin	
W3060 Speedy Gonzales	
Black & white, thick	9 - 12
Black & white, thin	6 - 10
W3065 Sylvester	
Black & white, thick	6 - 10
Black & white, thin	6 - 10
W3070 Tasmanian Devil	
Black & white, thick	20 - 30
Black & white, thin	30 - 40
W3075 Tweety	
Black & white, thick	10 - 20
Black & white, thin	10 - 20
W3080 Wile E. Coyote	
Black & white, thick	6 - 10
Black & white, thin	10 - 20
W3085 Yosemite Sam	
Black & white, thick	6 - 10
Black & white, thin	10 - 20

Six of the above images appear on a 16 oz Brockway glass with the Pepsi logo under the name of the character.

W3100 Bugs, 16 oz, Pepsi logo under name	20 - 30
W3101 Daffy, 16 oz, Pepsi logo under name	20 - 30
W3102 Porky, 16 oz, Pepsi logo under nam)	20 - 30
W3103 Road Runner, 16 oz, Pepsi logo under name	20 - 30
W3104 Sylvester, 16 oz, Pepsi logo under name	20 - 30
W3105 Tweety, 16 oz, Pepsi logo under name	20 - 30

These same six Looney Tunes/Warner Brothers characters appear on a 12 oz size glass in both thick & thin, with the Pepsi logo under the characters name. This set of six came with a metal tray.

W3106 Bugs, 12 oz, logo under name, thick & thin	20 - 30
W3108 Daffy, 12 oz, logo under name, thick & thin	20 - 30
W3110 Porky, 12 oz, logo under name, thick & thin	20 - 30
W3112 Road Runner, 12 oz, logo under name, thick	

& thin	20 - 30
W3114 Sylvester, 12 oz, logo under name, thick & thin	20 - 30
W3116 Tweety, 12 oz, logo under name, thick & thin	20 - 30
W3117 Litho Metal Tray	25 - 40

These same six glasses come with the logo on the side. Although they are more difficult to find they are valued the same as the above.

WARNER BROTHERS INTERACTION SERIES, Pepsi, 1976

Please note the 800 classification numbers used after the name of each glass. These were the original numbers used by the Brockway Glass Co. Inc. of Darien, CT. Brockway called them the "Pepsi Cola/ Looney Tunes Interaction Series." Characters 801 – 812 were stock items & were packed in three dozen of one character & were sold at $2.74 per dozen. Characters 813 – 824 were special run characters & a distributor or restaurant had to order a minimum of 600 cases. Areas of the country with a large population or a heavy tourist business would order 813 – 824.

W3200 Bugs-Elmer, tree, 801	10 - 20
W3201 Daffy-Pepe, hose, 802	6 - 10
W3202 Cool Cat-Beaky, kite, 803	6 - 10
W3203 Foghorn-Henry, tennis, 804	6 - 10
W3204 Tweety-Sylvester, Marc Anthony, 805	6 - 10
W3205 Wile E.-Road Runner, catapult, 806	6 - 10
W3206 Porky-Petunia, mower, 807	6 - 10
W3207 Daffy-Tasmanian, chef hat, 808	6 - 10
W3208 Tasmanian-Porky, fishing, 809	6 - 10
W3209 Yosemite-Speedy, panning gold, 810	11 - 20
W3210 Tweety-Sylvester, saw tree limb, 811	11 - 20
W3211 Yosemite-Bugs, cannon, 812	11 - 20

Characters 813 – 824 are special run characters	
W3212 Cool Cat, hunter, 813	30 - 40
W3213 Wile E.-Ralph, sheep, 814	30 - 40
W3214 Granny-Tweety, Sylvester, 815	30 - 40

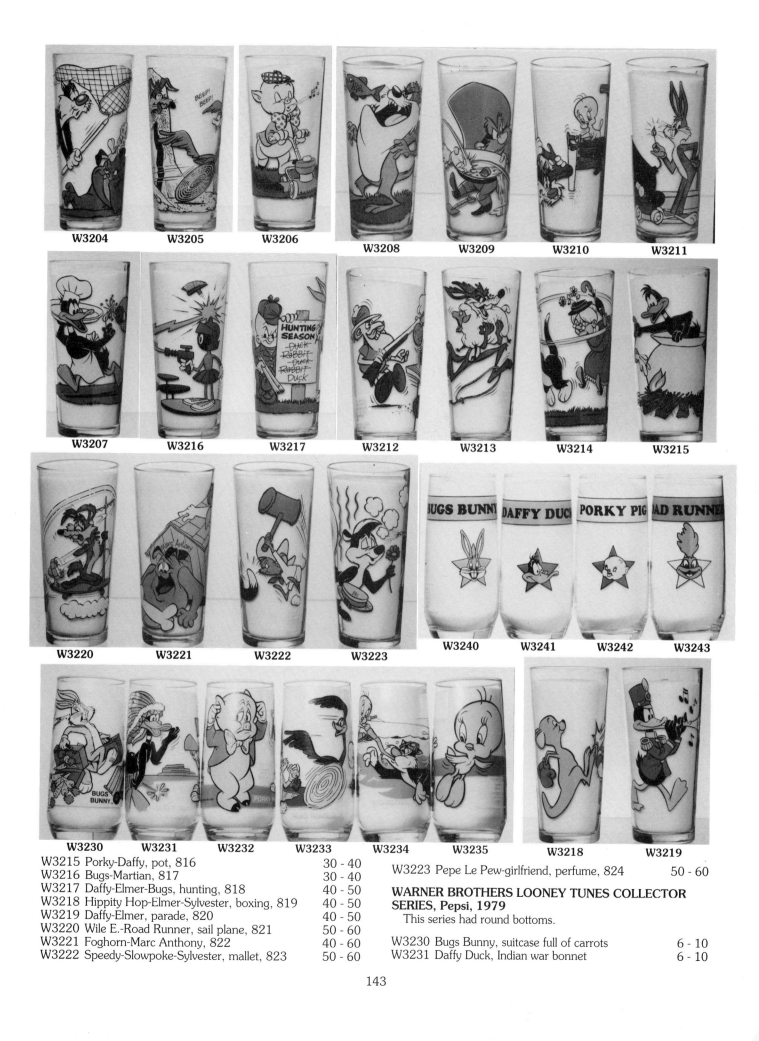

W3204	W3205	W3206
W3208	W3209	W3210
W3211		

W3207	W3216	W3217
W3212	W3213	W3214
W3215		

W3220	W3221	W3222	W3223
W3240	W3241	W3242	W3243

W3230	W3231	W3232	W3233
W3234	W3235	W3218	W3219

W3215 Porky-Daffy, pot, 816	30 - 40	
W3216 Bugs-Martian, 817	30 - 40	
W3217 Daffy-Elmer-Bugs, hunting, 818	40 - 50	
W3218 Hippity Hop-Elmer-Sylvester, boxing, 819	40 - 50	
W3219 Daffy-Elmer, parade, 820	40 - 50	
W3220 Wile E.-Road Runner, sail plane, 821	50 - 60	
W3221 Foghorn-Marc Anthony, 822	40 - 60	
W3222 Speedy-Slowpoke-Sylvester, mallet, 823	50 - 60	

W3223 Pepe Le Pew-girlfriend, perfume, 824   50 - 60

WARNER BROTHERS LOONEY TUNES COLLECTOR SERIES, Pepsi, 1979

This series had round bottoms.

W3230 Bugs Bunny, suitcase full of carrots   6 - 10
W3231 Daffy Duck, Indian war bonnet   6 - 10

143

| W3270 | W3271 | W3272 | W3273 | W3274 | W3275 | W3274 | W3275 |

| W3240 | W3241 | W3242 | W3243 | W3244 | W3245 | W3246 | W3420 |

| W3250 | W3251 | W3252 | W3253 |

| W3280 | W3281 | W3282 | W3283 |

W3232 Porky Pig, plugging his ears   6 - 10
W3233 Road Runner, being pursued by Wile E.   6 - 10
W3234 Sylvester, snorkeling   6 - 10
W3235 Tweety-Granny, hitting Sylvester   6 - 10

WARNER BROTHERS LOONEY TUNES COLLECTOR SERIES, Pepsi, 1980

Commonly called "Star in Head" series. Comes in both Pepsi & Arby's logos. The Arby's set omits the Road Runner. The Pepsi set is valued slightly higher.

W3240 Bugs Bunny   6 - 10
W3241 Daffy Duck   6 - 10
W3242 Porky Pig   6 - 10
W3243 Road Runner   6 - 10
W3244 Sylvester   6 - 10
W3245 Tweety   6 - 10
W3246 Yosemite   6 - 10

LOONEY TUNES GREAT AMERICA SERIES, Marriott, 1975

Marriott's "Great America" is an amusement park in California. From time to time glasses and/or milk glass mugs are issued as souvenirs to be sold in their gift shops. The following are 12 oz glasses.

W3250 Porky   20 - 30
W3251 Road Runner   20 - 30
W3252 Tweety   20 - 30

W3253 Wile E.   20 - 30
W3254 Sylvester   20 - 30
W3255 Bugs Bunny   20 - 30

LOONEY TUNES GREAT AMERICA SERIES, Marriott, 1982

The same images appear on glasses that say "ASTROWORLD" and "6 FLAGS".

W3270 Tweety   10 - 25
W3271 Tasmanian Devil   10 - 25
W3272 Daffy   10 - 25
W3273 Sylvester   10 - 25
W3274 Bugs   10 - 25
W3275 Honey Bunny   10 - 25

ADVENTURER SERIES, Arby's, 1988

This set was issued in the Louisville, KY area only.

W3280 Bugs Bunny "Diving for Carrots"   20 - 30
W3281 Daffy Duck "Jungle Jitters"   20 - 30
W3282 Porky Pig "Lunar Lunch"   20 - 30
W3283 Sylvester "Anchors Away"   20 - 30

WARNER BROTHERS, Welch's, 1974

W3300 "I Tawt I Taw a Puddy Tat"   4 - 6

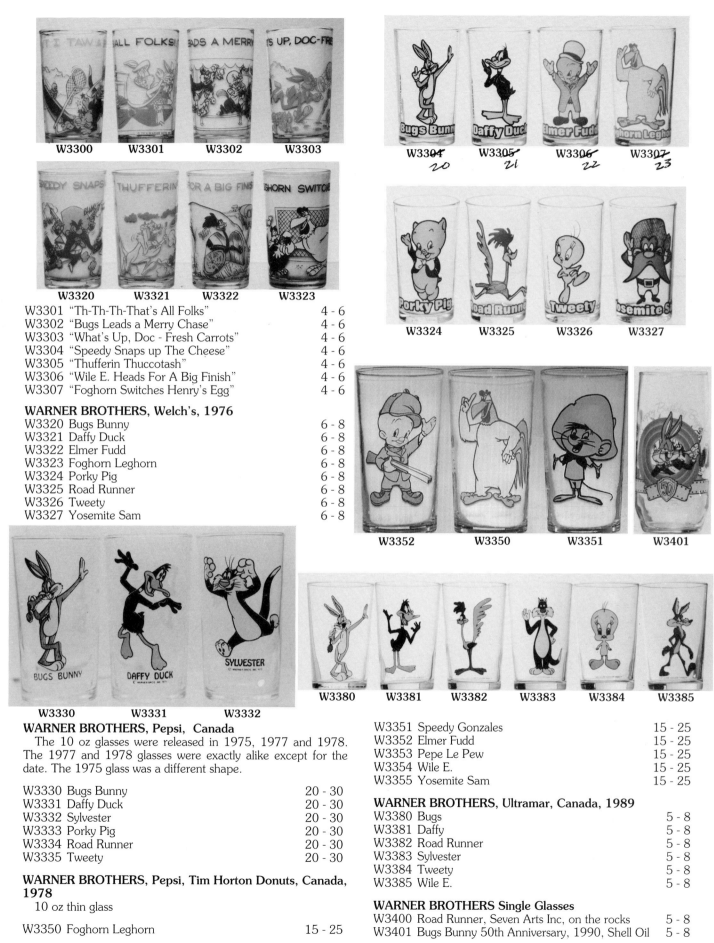

W3300	W3301	W3302	W3303

W3304	W3305	W3306	W3307
20	21	22	23

W3320	W3321	W3322	W3323

W3324	W3325	W3326	W3327

W3301	"Th-Th-Th-That's All Folks"	4 - 6
W3302	"Bugs Leads a Merry Chase"	4 - 6
W3303	"What's Up, Doc - Fresh Carrots"	4 - 6
W3304	"Speedy Snaps up The Cheese"	4 - 6
W3305	"Thufferin Thuccotash"	4 - 6
W3306	"Wile E. Heads For A Big Finish"	4 - 6
W3307	"Foghorn Switches Henry's Egg"	4 - 6

WARNER BROTHERS, Welch's, 1976

W3320	Bugs Bunny	6 - 8
W3321	Daffy Duck	6 - 8
W3322	Elmer Fudd	6 - 8
W3323	Foghorn Leghorn	6 - 8
W3324	Porky Pig	6 - 8
W3325	Road Runner	6 - 8
W3326	Tweety	6 - 8
W3327	Yosemite Sam	6 - 8

W3352	W3350	W3351	W3401

W3330	W3331	W3332

W3380	W3381	W3382	W3383	W3384	W3385

WARNER BROTHERS, Pepsi, Canada

The 10 oz glasses were released in 1975, 1977 and 1978. The 1977 and 1978 glasses were exactly alike except for the date. The 1975 glass was a different shape.

W3330	Bugs Bunny	20 - 30
W3331	Daffy Duck	20 - 30
W3332	Sylvester	20 - 30
W3333	Porky Pig	20 - 30
W3334	Road Runner	20 - 30
W3335	Tweety	20 - 30

WARNER BROTHERS, Pepsi, Tim Horton Donuts, Canada, 1978

10 oz thin glass

W3350	Foghorn Leghorn	15 - 25

W3351	Speedy Gonzales	15 - 25
W3352	Elmer Fudd	15 - 25
W3353	Pepe Le Pew	15 - 25
W3354	Wile E.	15 - 25
W3355	Yosemite Sam	15 - 25

WARNER BROTHERS, Ultramar, Canada, 1989

W3380	Bugs	5 - 8
W3381	Daffy	5 - 8
W3382	Road Runner	5 - 8
W3383	Sylvester	5 - 8
W3384	Tweety	5 - 8
W3385	Wile E.	5 - 8

WARNER BROTHERS Single Glasses

W3400	Road Runner, Seven Arts Inc, on the rocks	5 - 8
W3401	Bugs Bunny 50th Anniversary, 1990, Shell Oil	5 - 8

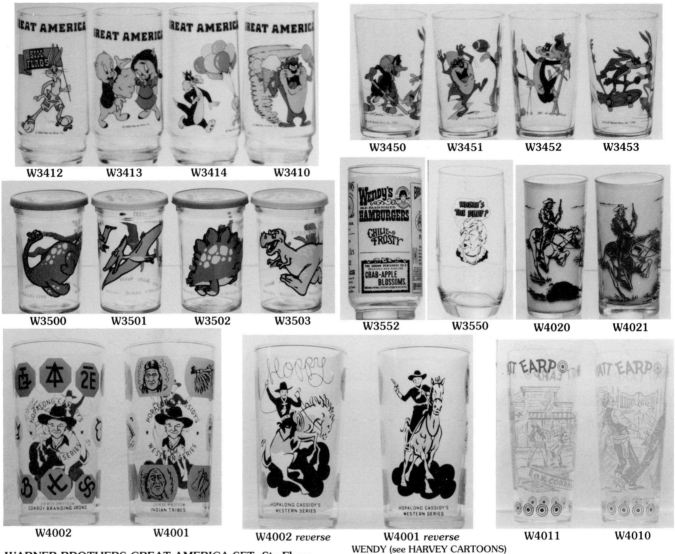

W3412   W3413   W3414   W3410

W3450   W3451   W3452   W3453

W3500   W3501   W3502   W3503

W3552   W3550   W4020   W4021

W4002   W4001   W4002 *reverse*   W4001 *reverse*   W4011   W4010

WARNER BROTHERS GREAT AMERICA SET, Six Flags, 1989

Came in 2 different sizes – 6" standard and large short pedestal style. There is also a set in both sizes which says "Great Adventure".

W3410 Bugs, skates	3 - 10
W3411 Porky	3 - 10
W3412 Sylvester	3 - 10
W3413 Tasmanian Devil	3 - 10

LOONEY TUNES GREAT AMERICA, 1987

| W3420 Looney Tunes characters on tropical island, multi-colored, in 5⁷/₈" and 7" | 8 - 15 |

BUGS BUNNY SPORTS ACTION SET, Pioneer Gas, 1991

These glasses show bugs on one side and another Looney Tune character in a sport activity on the other.

W3450 Daffy/Hockey	3 - 8
W3451 Tasmanian Devil/Football	3 - 8
W3452 Sylvester/Skiing	3 - 8
W3453 Road Runner/Skateboarding	3 - 8

WELCH'S, DINOSAURS SERIES, 1989

W3500 Brontosaurus	1 - 2
W3501 Pterodactyl	1 - 2
W3502 Stegosaurus	1 - 2
W3503 Tyranosaurus Rex	1 - 2

WENDY (see HARVEY CARTOONS)

WENDY'S RESTAURANT

W3550 Wendy's Clara Pella "Where's the Beef?"	4 - 6
W3551 Wendy's Clara Pella	4 - 6
W3552 Wendy's Newspaper Ad	2 - 4

WESTERN HEROES (for Frontier heroes, see DAVY CROCKETT, DANIEL BOONE)

HOPALONG CASSIDY

W4000 Hopalong Cassidy w/western wagons	20 - 30
W4001 Hopalong Cassidy w/Indian tribes	20 - 30
W4002 Hopalong Cassidy w/branding irons	20 - 30

WYATT EARP

| W4010 Wyatt Earp fighting villain | 20 - 30 |
| W4011 Wyatt Earp Gunfight at OK Corral | 20 - 30 |

WESTERN HEROES

W4020 Wild Bill Hickock, Expert Marksmen	8 - 12
W4021 Buffalo Bill, Chief of Scouts	8 - 12
W4022 Wyatt Earp, Marshall	8 - 12
W4023 Annie Oakley, Sharp Shooter	8 - 12
W4024 The Lone Ranger	10 - 15

BUFFALO BILL

| W4028 Chief of Scouts, different from above | 8 - 12 |

ROY ROGERS

| W4050 Roy Rogers Degree of Milk glass | 10 - 20 |

W4058   W4055   W4100   W4101   W5000   W5001   W5002

W4024   W5525   W5526   W5527   W5528   W5529   W5530   W5556

6 DIFFERENT OZ DESIGNS

W5003   W5004   W5005

W5500   W5501   W5502   W5504   W5505   W5506   W5543   W5544   W5545

W4055 Museum glass (current)	10 - 15
W4058 Roy Rogers' Restaurant	8 - 12

WILD WEST SERIES, Coke

	Lid
W4100 Calamity Jane	10 - 15
W4101 Buffalo Bill	10 - 15
W4102 Annie Oakley	10 - 15
W4103 Title unknown	10 - 15
W4104 Title unknown	10 - 15
W4105 Title unknown	10 - 15

WHITE ROCK

W4200 White Rock, frosted	6 - 10

WILE E. COYOTE (see WARNER BROTHERS)

WINNIE THE POOH (see DISNEY)

WIZARD OF ID, Arby's, 1983

W5000 Bung	10 - 15
W5001 King	10 - 15
W5002 Larsen E. Pettifogger	10 - 15
W5003 Sir Rodney	10 - 15
W5004 Spook	10 - 15
W5005 Wizard	10 - 15

WIZARD OF OZ
WIZARD OF OZ, Loews & Metro-Goldwyn-Meyer, 1939
First was used to promote the sale of Sealtest cottage cheese. Manufactured by Corning Lowe's Inc.

W5500 Dorothy, blue	20 - 40
W5501 Scarecrow, red	20 - 40
W5502 Tin Woodsman, gray	20 - 40
W5503 Toto, black	20 - 40
W5504 Cowardly Lion, yellow	20 - 40
W5505 Good Witch, pink	20 - 40
W5506 Bad Witch, green	40 - 100
W5507 Wizard, said to exist	??

WIZARD OF OZ, Swift's Peanut Butter, 1955 – 1960
Plain base glass ©S & Co.

W5525 Dorothy, pink	15 - 25
W5526 Toto, blue	15 - 25
W5527 Scarecrow, white	15 - 25
W5528 Tin Woodsman, green	15 - 25

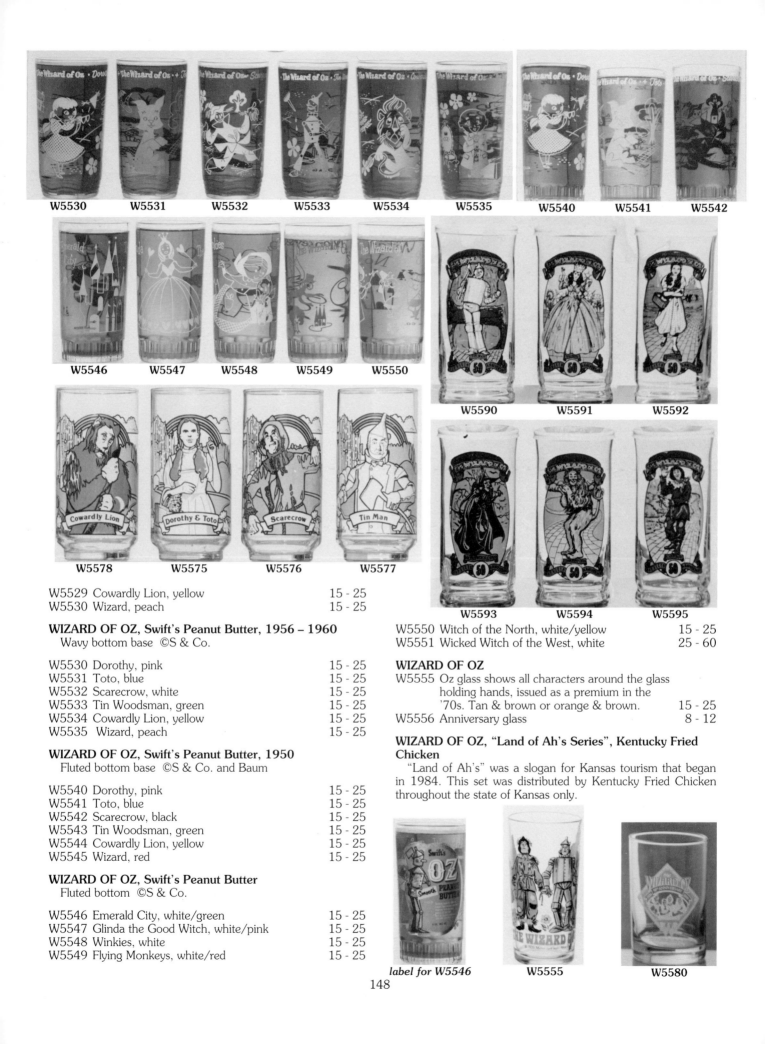

W5530	W5531	W5532	W5533	W5534	W5535	W5540	W5541	W5542

W5546	W5547	W5548	W5549	W5550

W5590	W5591	W5592

W5578	W5575	W5576	W5577

W5593	W5594	W5595

W5529 Cowardly Lion, yellow — 15 - 25
W5530 Wizard, peach — 15 - 25

WIZARD OF OZ, Swift's Peanut Butter, 1956 – 1960
Wavy bottom base ©S & Co.

W5530 Dorothy, pink — 15 - 25
W5531 Toto, blue — 15 - 25
W5532 Scarecrow, white — 15 - 25
W5533 Tin Woodsman, green — 15 - 25
W5534 Cowardly Lion, yellow — 15 - 25
W5535 Wizard, peach — 15 - 25

WIZARD OF OZ, Swift's Peanut Butter, 1950
Fluted bottom base ©S & Co. and Baum

W5540 Dorothy, pink — 15 - 25
W5541 Toto, blue — 15 - 25
W5542 Scarecrow, black — 15 - 25
W5543 Tin Woodsman, green — 15 - 25
W5544 Cowardly Lion, yellow — 15 - 25
W5545 Wizard, red — 15 - 25

WIZARD OF OZ, Swift's Peanut Butter
Fluted bottom ©S & Co.

W5546 Emerald City, white/green — 15 - 25
W5547 Glinda the Good Witch, white/pink — 15 - 25
W5548 Winkies, white — 15 - 25
W5549 Flying Monkeys, white/red — 15 - 25

W5550 Witch of the North, white/yellow — 15 - 25
W5551 Wicked Witch of the West, white — 25 - 60

WIZARD OF OZ
W5555 Oz glass shows all characters around the glass
holding hands, issued as a premium in the
'70s. Tan & brown or orange & brown. — 15 - 25
W5556 Anniversary glass — 8 - 12

WIZARD OF OZ, "Land of Ah's Series", Kentucky Fried Chicken
"Land of Ah's" was a slogan for Kansas tourism that began in 1984. This set was distributed by Kentucky Fried Chicken throughout the state of Kansas only.

label for W5546   W5555   W5580

148

| W5900 | W5901 | W5902 | W5904 | W5905 | W5906 | W5907 | W5903 |

W5908

| W5850 | W5851 | W5852 | W5853 | W5854 | W5855 |

Z3020   Z3021

| W5920 | W5923 | W5924 | W5925 | W5926 | W5927 |

Z3022   Z3023

W5575	Dorothy & Toto	30 - 40
W5576	Scarecrow	30 - 40
W5577	Tin Woodsman	30 - 40
W5578	Cowardly Lion	30 - 40

WIZARD OF OZ, Whataburger, 1989
The Turner Entertainment Co. & Whataburger released this glass in the summer of 1989 to celebrate the 50th anniversary of the movie.

| W5580 | Etched crystal Wizard of Oz characters, "50th Anniversary" | 10 - 20 |

WIZARD OF OZ, 50th Anniversary, Krystal, Coke
W5590	Tin Man	10 - 15
W5591	Good Witch	10 - 15
W5592	Dorothy	10 - 15
W5593	Bad Witch	10 - 15
W5594	Lion	10 - 15
W5595	Scarecrow	10 - 15

WOLFMAN (see UNIVERSAL MONSTERS)

WOODY WOODPECKER (see WALTER LANTZ)

WORLD'S FAIR CELEBRATION GLASSES
World's Fair, 1939
| W5850 | Theme Building & Court | 15 - 20 |
| W5851 | 20th Century Transportation | 15 - 20 |

W5852	Washington Statue/Constitution Mall	15 - 20
W5853	Parachute Jump/Amusement Area	15 - 20
W5854	Court of Ships/Marine Activities	15 - 20
W5855	Fountain & Lagoon	15 - 20

Seattle World's Fair, 1962
These glasses came in a short 12 oz black and white matte finish with gold trim and a tall 16 oz frosted.

W5900	Boulevards of the World	5 - 12
W5901	U.S. Science Pavilion	5 - 12
W5902	Monorail	5 - 12
W5903	World's Fair Panorama and Mt. Rainier	5 - 12
W5904	Gay Way	5 - 12
W5905	Space Needle	5 - 12
W5906	Coliseum 21	5 - 12
W5907	World of Art	5 - 12
W5908	Frosted	7 - 14

New York World's Fair, 1964
W5920	New York State Exhibit	5 - 12
W5921	Port Authority Building	5 - 12
W5922	Circus	5 - 12
W5923	Federal Pavilion	5 - 12
W5924	Shea Stadium	5 - 12
W5925	Unisphere	5 - 12
W5926	Pool of Industry	5 - 12
W5927	Hall of Science	5 - 12

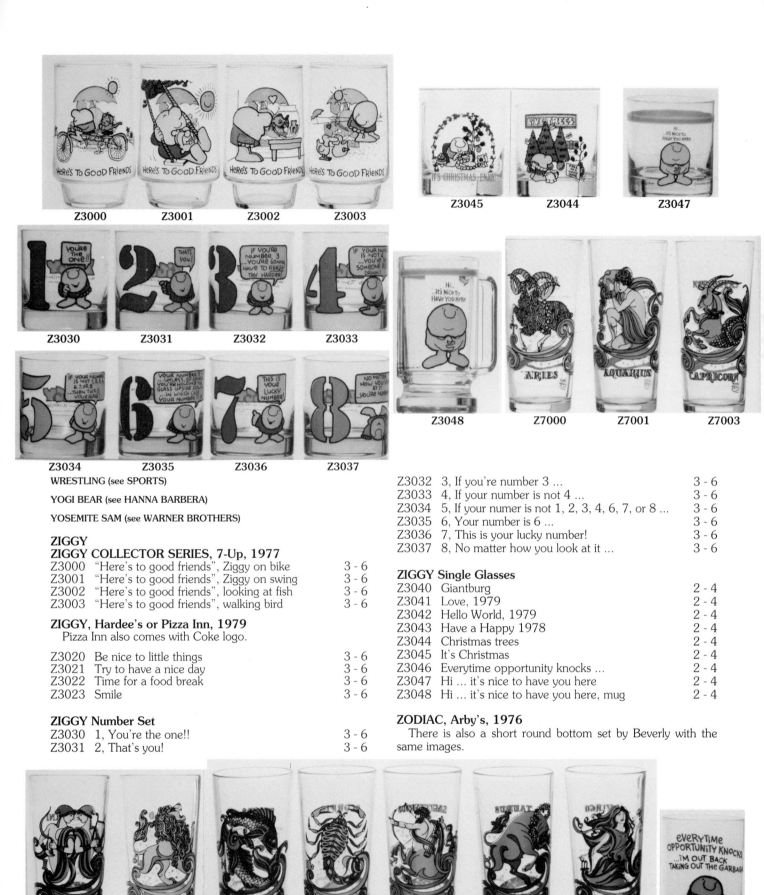

Z3000   Z3001   Z3002   Z3003

Z3045   Z3044   Z3047

Z3030   Z3031   Z3032   Z3033

Z3048   Z7000   Z7001   Z7003

Z3034   Z3035   Z3036   Z3037

WRESTLING (see SPORTS)

YOGI BEAR (see HANNA BARBERA)

YOSEMITE SAM (see WARNER BROTHERS)

ZIGGY
ZIGGY COLLECTOR SERIES, 7-Up, 1977
Z3000	"Here's to good friends", Ziggy on bike	3 - 6
Z3001	"Here's to good friends", Ziggy on swing	3 - 6
Z3002	"Here's to good friends", looking at fish	3 - 6
Z3003	"Here's to good friends", walking bird	3 - 6

ZIGGY, Hardee's or Pizza Inn, 1979
Pizza Inn also comes with Coke logo.

Z3020	Be nice to little things	3 - 6
Z3021	Try to have a nice day	3 - 6
Z3022	Time for a food break	3 - 6
Z3023	Smile	3 - 6

ZIGGY Number Set
Z3030	1, You're the one!!	3 - 6
Z3031	2, That's you!	3 - 6
Z3032	3, If you're number 3 ...	3 - 6
Z3033	4, If your number is not 4 ...	3 - 6
Z3034	5, If your numer is not 1, 2, 3, 4, 6, 7, or 8 ...	3 - 6
Z3035	6, Your number is 6 ...	3 - 6
Z3036	7, This is your lucky number!	3 - 6
Z3037	8, No matter how you look at it ...	3 - 6

ZIGGY Single Glasses
Z3040	Giantburg	2 - 4
Z3041	Love, 1979	2 - 4
Z3042	Hello World, 1979	2 - 4
Z3043	Have a Happy 1978	2 - 4
Z3044	Christmas trees	2 - 4
Z3045	It's Christmas	2 - 4
Z3046	Everytime opportunity knocks ...	2 - 4
Z3047	Hi ... it's nice to have you here	2 - 4
Z3048	Hi ... it's nice to have you here, mug	2 - 4

ZODIAC, Arby's, 1976
There is also a short round bottom set by Beverly with the same images.

Z7004   Z7005   Z7007   Z7009   Z7008   Z7010   Z7011   Z3046

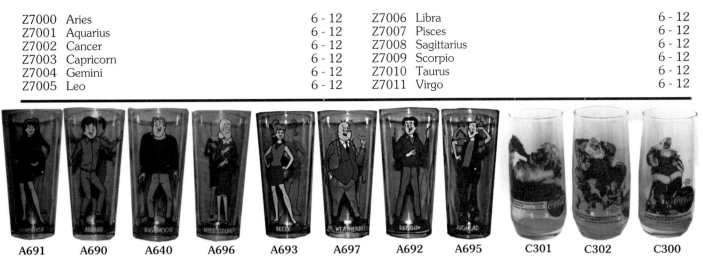

A691 A690 A640 A696 A693 A697 A692 A695 C301 C302 C300

APPENDIX A – Salesman Samples, Test Sets, Limited Edition

Prototype – the original or model on which something is formed. Many prototypes are crude and incomplete. Some will not have all the logos on them, only the space for them. Glass companies, using the designs provided them by the artists, will create a design prototype on several different style glasses to be submitted for approval. In most cases, they have no idea who the sponsors are.

Salesman Samples – when a prototype has been approved the company commissioning the production of the glasses will order anywhere from 25 to 100 glasses or sets of glasses to be made to distribute to their sales force. The salesmen will take the samples to their respective territories and try to sell the promotion on a pre-order basis. An agreement is usually made between the production company and the glass manufacturer to produce a certain amount at a given price. If the sales force cannot meet this pre-production amount, the promotion is cancelled.

Test Sets – after a prototype has been approved and an agreement has been made between the company commissioning the glasses and a sponsor, several test glasses or sets of glasses are made – at least three sets (in case of breakage). The glasses are sent to an advertising firm/photographer for a promotion layout.

Limited Edition – is when a pre-arranged amount of glasses are made of a given character or design and the mold, die and/or stencil is destroyed.

Case in point:

When the 7 Up Company decided to produce *Indiana Jones: Temple of Doom* glasses to promote the sale of their soft drink, they commissioned a set of glasses with only the 7 Up logo on it for *every* one of their salesmen. The sales force, in turn, sold the idea to co-sponsors such as Wendy's, In-and-Out Burger, Taco Villa and Broun's Chicken. Licensing and production costs were split. The fast-food restaurant advertised their establishment and made a profit off the soft drink. Seven Up sold more syrup to the fast-food restaurant and advertised their product. Everybody was happy and we got a glass.

When the Pepsi Cola Company launched the Warner Brothers cartoon characters promotion in 1973, they sent a sales force out to every corner of the U.S. Carol's restaurant chain in upstate New York to LuLu's in southern California bought the promotion. They were charged just slightly above cost for the glasses if ordered by the gross and if contracted to buy the appropriate amount of syrup it would take to fill the glasses with Pepsi. When fast-food restaurants could anticipate their volume, they ordered the glasses directly from the glass manufacturer itself. This was the case with the Warner Brothers

Interaction Series in 1976. Minimum order for the first 12 was 300 cases. There were 36 glasses of one character to a case. Don't forget this was the bicentennial year and tourism was high. It was not unreasonable for a highly populated area to sell 10,800 glasses during the summer. By the time the second 12 were released, it was the middle of the fall, tourism had died down and so did the popularity of the glasses. Brockway had also increased the minimum case requirement to 600. I image that's the reason why the second 12 are more difficult to find. It was not uncommon for the local bottling companies to buy the minimum case requirements from the manufacturer and distribute the glasses to smaller, lower volume restaurants. I remember visiting a local Coca-Cola bottling plant in 1989 and seeing cases of Norman Rockwell summer scenes stacked high. The glasses were promoted through Arby's in 1987. I asked the manager what he was going to do with all those glasses. He told me he was going to give them free to the 4 local Arby's restaurants for re-distribution to the public.

ARCHIE, Pepsi

A690	Archie
A691	Veronica
A692	Reggie
A693	Betty
A694	Big Moose
A695	Jughead
A696	Miss Grundy
A697	Mr. Weatherbee

BUCK ROGERS, Coke, 1979

Although I have only seen the Buck Rogers glass itself, I have seen an ad featuring all four glasses. How they could be obtained at the time of the ad or if they were ever produced is unknown.

B800	Buck Rogers
B801	Draco
B802	Wilma Deering
B803	Twiki

B800

CHRISTMAS, Haddon Sunblom Santa Set, Coke

This 3 glass set is similar in style to the other 2 sets (see C3100-3105), but was never released. Only 3 sets are known. Two different variations of this tester set exist.

C300	Santa w/toys, Coca-Cola in circle
C301	Santa drinking Coke, Coca-Cola in circle
C302	Santa & Elves, Coca-Cola in circle
C303	Santa w/toys, Coca-Cola on bag
C304	Santa drinking Coke/reindeers
C305	Santa & Elves

C303   C304   C305

C460   C461   C462   C463

C550   C551   C552

C553   C554   C555

CLASSIC CARS, Test Set, Coke

C460   1955 Thunderbird
C461   1956 Cadillac
C462   1957 Chevy
C463   1965 Corvette

COKE Single Test Glasses

C550   Sports Goofy, Disney, Coke
C551   Beach Scene, Coke
C552   I Love N.Y., Coke
C553   1920 Calendar Girl, Coke
C554   Lion In Jungle Scene, Coke
C555   Victorian Lady
C556   Balloon
C557   Man and Woman
C558   1920 girl holding Coke
C559   Lady w/umbrella holding Coke
C560   Sprite
C561   Duck, Coke

C562   Duck, Coca/Cola
C563   Rax Roast Beef, 2 colors
C564   Birds, Coke
C565   Indian motiff, Coke
C566   W.C. Fields, look alike, Coke
C567   Needlepoint design, Coke (same as Dr. Pepper)
C568   Flowers and Butterflies, Coke
C569   Flowers, Coke
C570   Gay '90s, Coke
C571   Advantage, Coke
C572   Enjoy Coke, tear back

COSBY KIDS, Pepsi

C650   Bill Cosby
C651   Rudy
C652   Bucky
C653   Mushmouth
C654   Russell
C655   Dumb Donald
C656   Weird Harold
C657   Fat Albert

DISNEY SINGLE CHARACTER SET, Pepsi

The set was released in round bottoms only; however, some tester glasses were made in the 16 oz Brockway shape. Only three are known so far.

C556   C557   C557   C559   C561   C561

C560

C563

C564

C572

C651

C652

C565

C567

C568

D341

D342

H195

D340   Mickey, similar to D2680
D341   Daisy, similar to D2683
D342   Goofy, similar to D2684

DISNEY, AMERICA ON PARADE, Test Glass, Coke
Different shape than the one produced for circulation

DISNEY CHRISTMAS CAROL, Test Glass, Coke
Different shape than the one produced for circulation. It might have been produced in the foreign market.

DISNEY RESCUERS SERIES, Pepsi, 1977
D350   Rufus, sitting on a pillow.
        Probably a prototype - the design was changed
        to what is shown as D2587.
   NOTE: A photo of this Rufus glass can been seen on the
cover of the *Collector's Glass News*, January 1992, No. 6.

HANNA BARBERA COLLECTOR'S SERIES, Pepsi, 1977
The folowing glasses were made as prototypes and never

C570

C571

C569

C656   C651   C655   C654   C653   C652   C657   C650

H050 **H051** **H052** **H050 - H052 REVERSE**

went into production. At least 3 of each can be accounted for. The set was also made in round bottoms. Exactly how many of the round bottoms were made is unknown. I have seen the Yogi and the Flintstone glass in round bottoms.

H050   Frankenstein Jr.
H051   Space Ghost
H052   Mutley

HELLO KITTY, Test Set, Coke
How many glasses in this set are unknown.

H195   Kitty Bunny
H196   Kitty w/horn in hand

HOWDY DOODY SERIES, Pepsi
The following glasses were made as prototypes and never went into production.

H196 **H575** **H577**

H575   Howdy
H576   Buffalo Bob
H577   Clarabell
H578   Flub-A-Dub
H579   Phineas T. Bluster
H580   Princess Sumer-Fall-Winter-Spring
NOTE: A photo of Mr. Bluster and Flub-A-Dub can been seen on the cover of the *Collector's Glass News*, January 1992, No. 6.

OLYMPICS
Olympics, Los Angeles, Test Set, Coke, 1982
Etched crystal style, similar to images put on the McDonald's mugs.

O450   #1
O451   #2
O452   #3
O453   #4

Olympic Test Glasses, Coke
O454   Fencing
O455   Archery
O456   Boxing
O457   Weight Lifting
O458   Wrestling

Olympic Test Set #2, Coke
Different style than #1

O459   Fencing
O460   Archery
O461   Boxing
O462   Weight Lifting
O463   Wrestling
O464   Baseball

O450 **O451** **O452** **O453**

O454 **O455** **O456** **O457** **O458**

PEPSI PROTOTYPES
P175   Big Bird
P176   1 Rover 1
P177   Pete's Dragon

PETER PAN, Set of 3, Coke
P190   Peter and Captain Hook
P191   Peter and Wendy
P192   Peter, Wendy, Michael, John

O460   O459   O460   O461   O463   O464   P175   P176   P177

P190   P191   P192

ROUGHHOUSE   SWEE'PEA   POPEYE   BRUTUS

P578   P577   P575   P576

S525   S526   S527   S531

White Lettering

Happy   Sleepy   Doc

Bashful   Grumpy   Snow White

S525 - S530 *Black Lettering*

POPEYE KOLLECT A SET, Coke, 1975

Similar in design to the regular set, only all the characters are dressed in pirate outfits. I have no knowledge as to how many of these sets were produced or if they were just tester sets or salesman samples.

P575   Popeye
P576   Brutus
P577   Swee' Pea
P578   Rough House
P579   Wimpy
P580   Olive Oyl
P581   Castor Oil
P582   Geezel

RAIDERS OF THE LOST ARK, Coke

Glass shows head of main character and film strip of scene from the movie in background.

R040   Indiana Jones in turban
R041   Marion
R042   Indiana Jones switching sand for statue

SNOW WHITE AND THE SEVEN DWARFS, Coke

These salesman samples come in both white and black letters. Two different sizes of this set exist.

S525   Grumpy
S526   Doc
S527   Bashful
S528   Dopey
S529   Sleepy
S530   Happy
S531   Sneezy
S532   Snow White

S770   S806   S805   REVERSE   T190   T191

T192   T193   T194   T196   T195   T886   T885

W042   W040   W041   W050   Z346   Z347

STAR TREK, Test Glass, Coke, 1980

This glass was the prototype of S8210 before it was decided to put McCoy and Spock on the same glass as Kirk and put the *Enterprise* on a separate glass.

S770   Kirk

SUPER HEROES COLLECTORS SERIES, Pepsi, 1978

S805   Supergirl, breaking chains. This is the 8th glass to the collection, but was never released.

S806   Wonder Woman, flying in a different pose. Never released.

Other variations of color and size of character exist in all the Super Hero glasses. In the Super Series, some of the tester glasses were made without the moon in the background.

TERRYTOONS, Pepsi

T190   Mighty Mouse
T191   Deputy Dwag

T192   Possible Possum
T193   Lariat Sam
T194   Sad Cat
T195   Little Roquefort
T196   Heckle and Jeckle

TWICE UPON A TIME, Test Set, Coke

How many glasses int his set are unknown.

T885   Ratotooie, Synonamess Batch, Murkian Minion
T886   Ralph Mumford, Flora, Fauna, & Rod Rescueman

WARNER BROTHERS LOONEY TUNES, Pepsi, 1980

More commonly known as "Star in Head"

W050   Road Runner, character is running toward the holder, looks awkward. This design was never released for mass distribution.

ZIGGY

Z346   I wonder why my fortune cookies are always
Z347   I ordered extra cheese, but this is ridiculous

Index

The Table of Contents on page 3 provides a page number index to all major categories in this book. Extensive cross-references are also found in the alphabetical text. Tomart ID numbers are used here to pinpoint the exact location of individual glasses. It's a simple system. The book is arranged A-Z with numbers up to 9999 following in each letter. The letter provides an idea of where to open the book. Once the correct letter is found locate the code number. It's no different than looking for page numbers, but look for the reference numbers in the text rather than the page number at the bottom. When you find the ID number, you have located the exact glass indexed...not just the page it is located on.

159

Rosie Tomato-P3801
Ross, Betsy-B2070
Rough House-P6015, P578
Round Table Pizza-R7050
Roy Rogers-H1610, W4050
Royal Standard of Spain-F6046
Royals-S5181, S5200, S5210
Rozema-S5160
Rudy-C651
Rufus-D2587, D350
Ruling His Sun-O3030
Running Horse-O3028
Russel-C654
Russell-S6009, S6033
Ryan, Jimmy-S7208
Ryan, Tom-C4700
Sabrina-A2305, A2311
Sad Cat-T194
Sad Sack-H1903
Saddle Bronc Riding-S7704, S7730, S7740
Sadie Hawkins-A1204, A1225, A1235
Sagittarius-Z7008
Saguaro Cactus-A2456
Saints-S6212
Sam the Eagle-M4067, O4000
Sam's-C6200
Samson-D2403
San Antonio de Valero-M6004
San Antonio Fiesta-D8020
San Antonio-C4249, C4274, T1302
San Carlos Borromeo-M6005
San Diego Chargers-S6700, S6730
San Diego-C4253, C4280, P2355
San Francisco-F0805
San Gabriel-M6002
San Jacinto Monument-T1305
San Jose-M6010
San Juan Bautista-M6003
San Xavier-M6001
Sanders-S5240
Sandy's Drive-In-S1000
Sandy-A1576
Santa Barbara-M6000
Sarajevo-O4150
Saturday Evening Post-N5500
Savage, Macho King Randy-S7634
Savannah, GA-C42088
Scarecrow-W5501
Schmidt, Mike-S6104
Schools of Mines, NM-C6079
Scifo-S7283
Scooby Doo-H1526, H1540, H1566, H1571, H1665
Scorpio-Z7009
Scottish Terrier-D7753
Scrappy Doo-H1573
Scrooge, Ebenezer-C3003, D2665
Scrooge-D1506
Sea Hag-P5981
Sea World-S1900
Seahawks-S6080, S6212
Sealtest-W5500
Search for Spock-S8215
Searles Dairy-D1386
Sears-D2445, S2000
Seattle Seahawks-S6080
Seattle Slew-S7844
Seattle Supersonics-S7030
Seaver, Tom-S5103, S5277
Secma Inc-A1350
Secretariat-S7840
Seessel's-C4318
Selma-C4209
Sequoyah-O3032
Serapis-F6056
Sesame Street-M9010
Seuss Navy-D8500
Seven Arts Inc-W3400
Seven Dwarfs-D2101, D2162, D2614, D2619, D4999, S525
Seven Wonders of the World-S2580
Seven-Eleven-S2100, S9450
Seven-Up-I5000, S2500, Z3000
Sevensen's-C4377
Shadow-P1003
Shakey's Pizza-C4310, D1403, D1411, P2392, S3001
Shamu-S1901
Share Bear-C2013
Shawnee-C4210, O3000
Shazam-S9410, S9424, S9433
Shea Stadium-W5924
Shelbyville-C4211
Shell Oil-S6018, S6031, S6250, W3401
Shelton-S7031
Shere Khan-D2557, D7083, D7265
Sheriff of Nottingham-R6507
Shirt Tails-S3400
Shmoos-A1206
Shock Wave-M1352
Shoney's-B2402
Short Round-I5001
Shut Out-S7805
Si & Am-D2355
Sigmund-T1037
Sikma-S7033
Silver City-B2306

Simmons, Ted-S5133
Simon Bar Sinister-L2002
Simon-C2402
Simpson, Bart-B1125
Sims-S6083
Sinclair Gas-S3420
Singapore-F0801
Sipe, Brian-S6050
Sir Brian-I8007
Sir Rodney-W5003
Sir Shake A Lot-B8063
Sirloin Stockade-S3450
Sirops Pam Pam-S3460
Six Eyes-G2004
Six Flags-M1352, W3270, W3410
Skeletor-M1501
Skiing-S5005, S5017
Skipper's Legend of the Sea-S3500
Skywalker, Luke-S8501
Sleeping Beauty-D2400
Sleepy-D2101, D2131, D2146, S529
Slimer-G2000
Sloth-G4000
Slow Poke Rodrigues-W3055
Smash of Demolition-S7630
Smedley-W1522
Smilin' Jack-S9106
Smith-S6083, S6110, S7032
SMU-C4254
Smurfette-S3807
Smurfs-S3800
Smythe Division-S7478
Snap! Crackle! Pop!-K3005
Snead, Sam-S7952
Sneak-G8009, G8019
Sneaky Pete's Hot Dogs-A1230
Sneezy-D2104, D2134, D2149, S531
Snepts, Harold-S7430
Snidely Whiplash-W2005
Snitch-G8008, G8018
Snoop-G8001, G8011
Snoopy-P1400
Snow White-D2100, D2130, D2145, D2162, D2221, D2614, D2619, D4999, D7070, S532
Snowflake-D1404, D1412
Soap Box Derby-C4235
Soccer-S7200, S7220, S7275
Solo, Han-S8523
Songs-S4300
Sonic-C4372, S4800
Sonny's Real Pit Bar BQ-C4374
Sopworth Camel-R2502
Sorcerer's Apprentice-D7191
Southland Corp.-C4185
Space Ghost-H051
Space Mouse-W1503
Space Needle-W5905
Space-S4875
Spacemen-F10030
Spain-C4607
Sparkie-S4900
Spartanburg-C4213
Spectacular Bid-S7846
Speed Buggy-H1541
Speed Queen-M5005, M5032
Speedy Gonzales-W3060
Speedy-P1002
Spenda Buck-S7852
Spider-woman-S9464
Spiderman-S9454, S9463
Spike-M1103
Splinter-W1525
Splittorff, Paul-S5201
Spock-S8201
Spook-W5004
Sports-S5000
Sprite-C5000, C560
Squirt-S8000
St Louis Zoo-S8100
St. Bernard-D7752
St. Mary's of Nazareth Hospital-M4045
Stage Coach-T5001
Staley-S8100
Stallworth-S6015, S6025, S6033
Star Spangled Banner-F6013, F6041, F6076
Star Trek-S8200, S770
Star Wars-S8500
Star, Brenda-S9100
Starbuck-B1153
Starr, Bart-S6095
Starr, Ringo-B1303
Stars & Stripes-F6006, F6040, F6073
State University, Canton, NM-C6080
Statue of Liberty-B2332, C4556, 0504
Statue of Zeus at Olympia-S2586
Staub, Rusty-S5241
Stautner, Ernie-S6800
Steak and Shake-C4314
Steamboat Willie-D2720, D2730, D6030
Steele, Larry-S7005
Steelers-S5901, S6000, S6015, S6025, S6030, S6202, S6800
Steer Wrestling-S7703, S7733, S7743
Stefan-S7423
Stegosaurus-W3502

Stoutner-S6033
Strawberry Shortcake-S9000
Strike the Gold-S7858
Stromboli-D2206
Stuffy's-C4375
Subway Ltd-C3000
Sunday Funnies-S9100
Sunday Silence-S7856
Sunkist-S9170
Sunny Halo-S7850
Sunoco-A1401, D2730, G2000
Sunshine Pizza Exchange-S7020
Super Heroes-S9200, S9420, S9440, S9450, S805
Super Mario 2 Brothers-N4000
Super Series-S9400
Superbowl -S6015, S6025
Supergirl-S9411, S805
Superman-S9206, S9300, S9320, S9330, S9412, S9425, S9434, S9440
Supersonics-S7030
Sups-C4329
Surrey-T5006
Sutton's General Store-C4376
Swale-S7851
Swan Resort-D5040
Swann-S6032
Swaps-S7821
Swee' Pea-
Swee' Pea-P5980, P577
Sweet Polly-L2001
Swensen's-A1576, C4383
Swenson-S6111
Swift's Peanut Butter-W5525
Sylvester-W3065
Synonamess Batch-T885
Taco Bell-S6700, S8215
Taco Mayo-T1005
Taco Time-C4378, T1025
Taco Villa-T1030
Taft, William H.-P8004
Tasmanian Devil-W3070
Tasty Freeze-T1100
Taunton-F6014, F6045
Taurus-Z7010
Taylor-S6111
TCU Frogs-C6201
Team Roping-S7700
Tecumseh-O2000, O3006
Teela-M1503
Temple of Artemis-S2581
Tenderheart Bear-C2005, C2065
Tennis-S5002, S5015
Terry & The Pirates-S9107
Terrytoons-T1200, T190
Tess Trueheart-D1402, D1410
Texaco-S3850
Texas A&M-C6042
Texas State-C6043
Texas Tech-C6044
Texas-T1300
TG&Y-T0090
The Prophet-O3005
Theodore-C2403
Thielemann-S6071
Thomas, Derrel-S5195
Thomas, Gorman-S5132
Thompson, Jason-S5243
Thompson-S6112, S7023, S7030
Thor-B1105, B1112, S9455, S9462
Thorton-S6028
Three Little Pigs-D2031, D2163, D3005, D7125, D7260
Three Musketeers-L3003
Thugee Guard-I5002
Thunderbird-R7051, C460
Thundercats-T3000
Tiant, Louis-S5250
Tico and Taco-B6205
Tierney, Paul-S7754
Tiger-E5004, V3005
Tigers-S5160, S5170, S5180, S5240
Tigger-D2452
Tim Horton Donuts-W3350
Tim Tam-S7824
Timothy Mouse-D2234
Tin Woodsman-W5502
Tinkerbell-D2334, D7269
Tiny Tim-C3001, D1507, D2667
Tippe-L3083
Toastmaster-M5007
Tolbert-S7031
Toledo Zoo-M4050
Tom Sawyer-L3005, M1201
Tom-M1104
Tommy Lee-S7826
Tomorrowland-D2348, D2740
Tony Jr.-K3002
Tony Scoleri-G2001
Tony the Tiger-K3001
Total Gas- S7430
Total-S5138
Totem Pole-A1303
Toto-W5503
Toucan Sam-K3003
Toughy-D2356

Tour de France-C4149
Towson State-C6045
Trailblazers-S7000, S7020, S7035
Trammell-S5160
Transportation-T5000
Treasure Island-L3000
Tresler Comet Auto-S5116
Trinity College-C6046
Tripucka-S6113
Trivial Pursuit-T6000
Troll-M1126
Troy State University-C6047
Trusty-D2351
Tubby Tompson-L3081
Tuffy-M1105
Tuiasosopo-S6081
Tuner, Roy-S7209
Turner Home Entertain.-M1110, W5580
Turner-S6110
Twardzik, Dave-S7006
Tweedle Dee & Dum-A1354, D2322
Tweety-W3075
Twice Upon a Time-T885
Twiki-B803
Twinkle Toes-G8007, G8017
Twins-S5185
Two ft 3 Eagle-U4005
Tyranosaurus Rex-W3503
U.C.L.A.-C6048
U.S. Capitol-B2330, L0501
U.S. Science Pavilion-W5901
U.S. War Bonds-P5000
U.S.A.-D2760
Ugly Duckling-D2165, D2222
Ultimate Warrior-S7613, S7635
Ultra Moo-U4000
Ultramar-S9210, U4000, W3380
Unbridled-S7857
Uncle Scrooge McDuck-D7100
Underdog-B2016, C1004, L2000
Unisphere-W5925
United-S5200, S5260
Universal Monsters-U4500
Universal Studios-B1150, E1000, E1004, U4500
University of Alabama-C6049
University of Arkansas Razorbacks-P2310
University of California-C6050
University of Colorado Buffaloes-C6203
University of Colorado-C6081
University of Delaware-C6051
University of Georgia-C6052
University of Hawaii-C6082
University of Illinois-C6083
University of Indiana-C6053
University of Nebraska-C6054, C6084
University of New Hampshire-C6085
University of New Haven, CT-C6086
University of New Mexico-C6055
University of New York-C6056
University of Notre Dame-C6057
University of Pittsburgh-C6058
University of South Florida-C6087
University of Southern California-C6059
University of Texas-C60602
University of Wisconsin-C6061
Unocal '76-S5117
Unwashable Jones-A1207
Upchurch-S6112
Urchins-U6000
Valaparaiso College-C6063
Valentine-S7024
Valentino's -C4317
Valentino, Rudolph-R6400
Valenzuela, Fernando-S5194
Valley Forge-B20726
Van Der Elst-S7280
Van Der Linden-S7277
Van Heusen-S6112
Van Note-S6070
Van Slyke, Andy-S5153
Vanderbilt College-C6064
Venetian Way-S7827
Veronica-A2302, A2307, A691
Versavel-S7281
Videopolis East-D2789
Vikings-F1004, S6210
Viola, CA-P2370
Virgo-Z7011
Visual Creations-V3000
Vitamin Flintheart-D1405, D1413
Volkenants Appliance Stores-M5033
Vranes-S7030
Vuckovich, Pete-S5130
Wagner-S6015, S6032
Wake Forest University-C6065
Walgreen's-C4302
Wallace Berrie & Co-S3800
Wally Walrus-W1504
Walt Disney Studio-D6036
Walt Disney World-D2506
Walter Lantz-W1500
Walters-S6062
Walton, Bill-S7007
Ward, P.A.T.-W2000
Warner Brothers-W050
Warner Brothers-W3000

Washington College-C6066
Washington Cruisers-F6015, F6053
Washington Monument-B2329
Washington Redskins-S6710
Washington Statute-W5852
Washington University-C6088
Washington, D.C.-F0808, L0501, P2350
Washington, Geo.-B2052, B2071, B2187
Waters, Charlie-S6154
Watson-S6113
WDW Village-D5045
Webby-D7101
Weber, Wolfgang-S7221
Webster-S6016, S6032
Weight Lifting-O457
Weird Harold-C656
Welch's-A2300, A2306, H1501, H6000, M1110, S6200, S6210, S6216, W3300, W3320, W3500
Wendy's-C4380, S6050, W3550
Wendy-D2333, H1906, P191
Werewolf-B8006
Werhoeven-S7023
West Point, NY-L0500
West Point–La Grange-C4214
West, Mae-A1123
Western Heroes-W4020, W4100
Western Stores-M5012
Wet-Rex Corp.-A1301
Whacko Wolf-B6206
Whataburger-C4312, C4319, W5580
Whitaker-S5163
White Eyes-O3007
White Rabbit-D2327
White Rock-W4200
White Sox-S5181
White Water Rampage-M1351
White, Dwight-S6010
White, Frank-S5203
White, Randy-S6155
White-S6030
Whitman Mission-B2314
Wichita Wings-S7200
Wicked Witch of the West-W5551
Widener College-C6067
Wilbur Van Snobbe-L3084
Wilbur-D2167
Wilcox-S5161
Wild Bill Hickock-W4020
Wild West-W4100
Wile E. Coyote-W3080
Wiley-B1106
Wilkens-S7033
Will Scarlett-R6505
William Paterson College, NJ-C6089
Williams, Buck-S7040
Williams-S6073, S7033
Williamson, Stan-S7755
Wilma Deering-B802
Wilma Flintstone-H1602, H1617
Wilson, Willie-S5200
Wimpy-P5976, P579
Winchester-M1003
Wings-S7200
Winkies-W5548
Winnie the Pooh-D2445, D3002
Winning Colors-S7855
Winston-S6025
Wisconsin Badgers-C6850
Wisconsin University-C6058
Witch of the North-W5550
Witchita State-C6069
Wizard of Fries-B8064
Wizard of Id-W5000
Wizard of Oz-L3007, W5500, W5507
Wizard-M1127, W5005
Wolf-O4150
Wolfman-U4503
Wometco-Beckly-C4215
Wonder Woman-S9413, S9426, S9435, S9442, S806
Woodstock-P1400
Woody Woodpecker-B2014, W1505
World Cup-S7222, S7275
World Wrestling Federation-S7630
World's Fair-C4278, S4850, S5903
Wrestling-S7600, O458
Wright Flyer-R2503
Wright-S6110
Wyandot-O3027
Wyatt Earp-W4010, W4022
Yankees-S5184
Yastrzemski, Carl-S5275
Yellow Submarine-B1341
YesterEars-D6050
Yogi Bear-H1525, H1563, H1670
Yosemite Sam-W3085
Yount, Robin-S5131
Yucca Cactus-A2457
Yzeman-S7422, S7432
Zalapski, Zarley-S7403
Zephyr-D2795
Ziggy-Z3000, Z346
Zodiac-Z7000
Zorn-S6082, S6725

160